MISSIONARY
MERCENARY
MISFIT

STORIES OF POLICING AND PEACEKEEPING

Dennis LaDucer

Copyright © 2012 Publisher Name
All rights reserved.
ISBN: 1479276731
ISBN 13: 9781479276738
Library of Congress Control Number: 2012916866
CreateSpace Independent Publishing Platform
North Charleston, South Carolina

PREFACE

✭ ✭ ✭

Each of us chooses the tone for telling his or her own story. I would like to choose the durable clarity of platinum print, but nothing in my destiny possesses the luminosity. I live among diffuse shadings, veiled mysteries, uncertainties. The tone of telling my life is closer to that of a portrait in sepia.

Isabel Allende, *Portrait in Sepia*

My father was a mystery to me, as were my grandparents. I have some general information about them all, but I was never curious enough in my younger days to ask questions about their lives. By the time I thought about their early lives, they were long gone. Even my mother, who lived into her eighties, wasn't forthcoming about her life. I didn't want my daughter and my two grandsons to wonder someday in the future about my life. I started writing little vignettes about my law enforcement experiences, expanded that to stories about funny or interesting things that had happened to me and eventually discovered a narrative covering my entire career.

Memoirs, over the last several years, have come under scrutiny, and some authors have been called out for fabrications and outright lies. My stories are simply the way I remember the various incidents. It may be that others remember these incidents differently. So be it. They can write their own book. In some cases, the narrative may not be chronologically accurate. I moved some things around so the stories flowed better. I've avoided names, except in a few cases, mostly to not embarrass anyone; although, I suspect the people who were involved might be able to figure it out.

When I was in trouble, there were some people who supported and helped me by remaining friends. Many more people, whom I thought were my friends, dumped me. I wish I had the words to say that last sentence in a more sophisticated way, but I think it accurately portrays what happened at a time of crisis in my life. It surprises me that both groups of people were equally inspirational in prompting me to write this book, not so much as a record of my life, but more so as a catharsis for my troubled thoughts.

So to Susan and Vince (may he rest in peace), Orville and Carolyn, Frank and Dawn, Ken and Linda, Doug, Linda, Bobby, Marilyn, John, you have my heartfelt appreciation for your continued friendship. There were others, too, outside the workplace who realized that allegations alone regardless of the sordid portrayal of me in the news media didn't tell the whole story; didn't define me. Kathy and Kip, John and Vonnie were two couples who always reached out to me, and like the friends from work, tended to be non-judgmental and supportive.

My non-supportive colleagues are owed a debt of gratitude as well. Although they were cowards in every definition of the word, they taught me the value of true friendship. Saying to someone that you'll always be their friend, then never speaking another word to them borders on the profane. To have worked with people for more than thirty years and to have shared so many experiences yet simply be immediately dismissed as a colleague and friend wasn't something I would have expected from brother officers. Truly, it was such a shame, for I loved the work and I loved most, but not all, my colleagues. Their behavior reminds me to always be a better friend.

My sheriff was a big star on a small stage and, while vainglorious, he was far from being a great man. But I'm sure he thought he was great. The following quote from Christoph Tiedemann, a minister without portfolio in nineteenth-century Germany about Otto von Bismark, seems to capture what happened to me and others: "There is something great to live one's life in and through a great man, to enter into and be absorbed by his thoughts, plans, decisions in a certain sense to disappear in his personality. One's own individuality runs the risk of being ground down." And, indeed, many of us lost a little of our sense of self.

I wanted my story to be recorded so my family would see a total picture of my work life and in a certain way how those work experiences shaped who I am today. Above all, there's been no one as encouraging as my family. My wife, whose life is recorded already in her vast academic body of work, was an uncomplaining and helpful reader of my many different permutations of this work. Her editorial skill and great insight was invaluable.

My daughter, a teacher, worked diligently in correcting my many errors, poor sentence structure, non-specific pronouns, and confusing and strange changes of tense. My son-in-law, already a published author with his novel, *Epiphany: The Untold Epic Journey of the Magi*, provided me with sage and cogent advice when it was most needed. My grandsons, the boys, always provided unconditional love and support even though they're not old enough to understand how important that is in my dotage.

My extended family never stopped encouraging me and always treated me as part of the family. Fred and Lilly, Ken and Jan, and my brother-in-law Alan made sure I was included in family events. Their sensitivity to me and my plight gave me solace.

Mike, Tim, Jamie, Jane, and Janet made my job easier and made me look better than I actually was when I was in Bosnia. Thanks too to Pascal, who had the tough job of herding a bunch of cops during my Bosnian mission.

I tried, but wasn't successful, in producing an objective story of portions of my life in police work and peacekeeping. Really, how could I? It's about me by me, so I'm not attempting to fool anyone into thinking that I always took the high moral ground. Usually I didn't; that's just the way I am. But I did try hard to restrain myself from always looking on the dark side of things and being too negative about some people with whom I didn't enjoy working. I suppose that's one of the reasons I used so few names. In the end it's not an autobiography; it's not even the complete story of my life. It's just some of the things I remember most about my work. There are only a few things about my personal life, and that was deliberate on my part. It's my work, I'm responsible for it, and anything wrong with it is on me.

Remember not my name
My crime or my fame
But every once and a while stop
And remember I loved being a cop

Dennis LaDucer
Southern California 2012

ONE

FROM THERE TO HERE IN ONE CHAPTER

✭ ✭ ✭

Good, better, best
Never let it rest
Until the good is better
And the better is best.

Favorite and frequently repeated saying of Sister Elizabeth Thomas, seventh grade teacher at St. Joseph's School, Newport, RI, 1956

Mr. Barth and His Three-Wheeled Police Motorcycle

Mr. Barth would sit on his three-wheeled police motorcycle on the corner of Hillside Avenue and Admiral Kalbfus Road. I lived at 61 Admiral Kalbfus, a few houses from the intersection where he would watch for speeding cars, and I would anxiously keep an eye out for his arrival during the days of my summer vacations. Whenever I spotted him, I would run to my closet, ferret out an old pair of World War I puttees (the provenance of which has long since been forgotten), put them on over my high-top sneakers, and sprint full speed to the corner.

There I would chat up Mr. Barth and ask if I could sit on his motorcycle. He always said yes, as he knew our family. My older brother Jack went to De La Sal academy, the local Catholic boy's high school with Mr. Barth's eldest son, Al. My older sister Janice attended the girl's high school, St. Catherine's, and was acquainted with his daughter, Connie. Both my mother and father grew up in Newport, as did Mr. Barth and his wife, so, as is normally the case in a small town, Mr. Barth not only knew who I was, he knew all about me and my family.

I would sit on the motorcycle as he monitored the traffic. Sometimes this was as long as thirty minutes or so. He was particularly watchful of cars coming down the slight decline on Admiral Kalbfus Road. There was no fancy police equipment like radar. His many years of experience served as the basis for his judgment about the speed of the vehicles. When he spotted a speeder, he didn't give chase; he simply stepped off the curb and blew his whistle. I never saw a car fail to stop. Mr. Barth would walk over to the car and speak with the driver. I don't remember him ever actually writing a speeding ticket.

Of course, it was the mid-1950s, and we lived in a small town. Newport, RI, was famous for its mansions along the Cliff Walk that the rich owners referred to as summer cottages. For a young boy, Newport was loaded with exploration opportunities. But the most exciting adventure was always the time spent playing on Mr. Barth's police motorcycle.

To a young boy, all police officers appear larger than life. Mr. Barth wasn't tall but, like most police of the day, he was overweight. Many years later, as an adult, I was visiting Newport and was pleased to run into him again. He had been promoted to sergeant and shortly thereafter retired. He had gained a bit more weight, looked older but didn't appear any the worse for wear. I'm not sure he knew who I was.

I don't think Mr. Barth was overly friendly to me when I would suddenly appear on the street corner to assist him (in my mind) with his traffic duties. But he was always nice and tolerated me the way adults in the 1950s usually did with children. There was something about him in his dark blue uniform, complete with jodhpurs, regular black street shoes set off with shinny puttees, just like mine. He didn't wear a helmet; perhaps the motorcycle didn't go that fast. He wore, at a jaunty angle, the same soft uniform police hat all the other officers wore and it made him seem more approachable. The best thing about him was his willingness to let me mess around on his motorcycle.

The days when Mr. Barth didn't show up at the corner were a disappointment. I would make my way over to my friend Eddy Barker's house on Hillside Avenue. I'd walk slowly past the intersection where Mr. Barth would normally take up his traffic duties in the hope he would suddenly appear at the last minute. When he didn't, on those days when traffic was left to run wild, I would have to contend myself with playing in Eddy's father's milk truck. Mr. Barker would park the truck in front of his house when he was finished with his milk route. The milk truck was a bit of a step down from the motorcycle but we still had fun times, especially when we would pretend the milk truck was a paddy wagon.

Mr. Barker was also a volunteer fireman and, as such, he had the authority to have a red light mounted on the front bumper of the family car, a 1954 cream-and-mint-green four-door Plymouth. We were never allowed to play inside the car, but if we had been it would have become a police car, not a volunteer fireman's car. And, probably, we would have worn out the red light. When there was no Mr. Barth, no milk truck (a.k.a. paddy wagon), the afternoons were spent playing guns. Sometimes we'd play cops and robbers, sometime cowboys and Indians but always a good-over-evil scenario of some sort.

Growing up in Newport was idyllic in my memory, even though my father died when I was seven years old. We lived in a nice new house near a beautiful park where winter snows provided some outstanding and dare devilish sledding. At eleven, I was given a small paper route for the *Newport Daily News*. It netted about four dollars a week. As a young businessman with cash in his pocket, I could take the local jitney all around town. Sometimes these rides were free, as Manny, a driver who had been a friend of my father, would allow me to ride free.

Camping

My mother went to work after my father died. I became a latchkey kid, which was a one-off phenomenon among my schoolmates and friends. By 1954, my mother was worn out. She was raising obstreperous nine-year-old me, my thirteen-year-old brother, and my trouble-prone sixteen-year-old sister for whom private school was a daily morality battle. Mom struck upon the idea of sending my brother and me to camp.

I didn't think my brother was so keen on the idea. I was only mildly excited myself and maybe a little nervous. Since my brother would be there, my anxiety was somewhat assuaged. My sister never said a word, probably because she was happy my mother hadn't packed her off to a convent.

The Fall River Boy's Club in Massachusetts operated the camp. The camp was located an hour outside the city in a rural part of the state. How or why she happened upon this particular camp was never made clear to me. Money was an issue, so I suppose the camp was either cheap or free.

It was a weeklong camp with campers returning home for the weekend. We were signed up for four long weeks. Each Monday we'd board a bus near our house for the hour-long ride to Fall River. The Boys Club was next door to the bus depot, so trudging along with our small travel bags was easy enough.

In front of the club, we were rounded up, piled onto one of two stake-bed trucks, and driven through the city out into the hinterlands of Massachusetts. As the trucks rumbled along, we would hang on to the sides of the trucks and spend an hour or so being jostled and jerked this way and that depending on the helter-skelter movements of the truck. Apparently there weren't any safety regulations, and a sudden deceleration of the truck would cause many of us to lose our grip and fall. We all thought it was great fun, as we sang camp songs and exaggerated our crashes to the bed of the truck.

Arrival at my first camp was, I have to admit, pretty damn exciting. There were lots of kids yelling and running around, something I had never experienced in Catholic school, but the counselors soon organized us into groups. Ally, our counselor, had been tipped off by my mother to keep an eye on us. We must have been considered charity kids or something.

Things were going swimmingly throughout the first day, but I noticed my brother wasn't talking much. Just before dinner, he dropped a bomb. He was going to run away. My God! I had never done anything so dangerous in my life. I didn't think the camp was so bad; in fact, it might have been fun. I was desperately trying to talk him out of running away because I didn't want to be there alone. Once he was discovered missing I would surely be interrogated and, if tortured, I would spill my guts. What could I do? I signed on to runaway with him.

As the other campers gathered for dinner, we snuck into the luggage room, took our travel bags, hopped a back fence (luckily no guard towers), and headed off through the Massachusetts wilderness to freedom. After an hour of scampering through the woods, we managed to find a road. Running away was dangerous enough, but then we did another dangerous thing, we hitchhiked. Within an hour, my life had become replete with danger as I trailed after my brother, whimpering the whole time. I thought my heart was going to burst out of my chest. I was scared. We hadn't thought the whole escape thing out well.

What was our mother going to say when and if we showed up on our doorstep in the middle of the night? I knew her reaction wouldn't be good for my mental or physical well-being. I pleaded with my co-conspirator to turn back. We were on a rural, not well-traveled road, and no cars had passed. We walked for quite a while and finally heard a car coming in our direction.

It turned out to be a delivery van and it was slowing before we stuck out our thumbs. The driver said he would give us a lift to the village down the road a couple of miles. While driving he questioned us about where we were headed. He asked if we were running away from the camp. Obviously we weren't the first boys to try to escape. No, we weren't running away; we were simply out hiking the backwoods all the way from Rhode Island. He stopped at the village, locked us in the truck, and called the camp. In a few minutes Ally, the counselor, who was already on the road looking for us, stopped behind the van, took us into custody, and returned the prisoners to the gulag.

On the ride back to camp, he explained that no one had successfully escaped, ever. Jack and I settled in for our first week, putting the whole sordid episode behind us and trying not to think about what would happen when Mom learned about our failed attempt at freedom. The weeks at camp passed quickly. I actually had a good time while my brother learned to accept his confinement. I think that for him it was a puberty thing. He had had big plans for the girls in town during the summer. So sad. After camp ended, we had only a few weeks remaining of our summer vacation. Finally, we were free to run around Newport unsupervised.

By the end of the next school year, I was ready for camp. My brother had spent most of his school year pressuring our mother not to send him to camp again. She caved. I was sent off alone for what would be my last year at camp and pretty much the last camping experience of my life. Our mother never learned about our short-lived escape until the last week of camp the year I was there on my own. She was surprised and laughed. I figured it was all for show, and I dreaded being alone with her, but she never mentioned it again.

Even though my school, St. Joseph's, was kind of scary, I generally enjoyed my youth in Newport, even the camping experience. The nuns at school ranged from kind and patient to scary and mean. Through the years, I managed to get an equal share of both. In 1956, I was in the seventh grade and my teacher, Sister Elizabeth Thomas, wasn't prone to fits of pique. While she did wield a mean ruler as punishment when someone would misbehave, I was spared during the entire school year, not because of good behavior, but rather a penchant for sneakiness and fortuitous timing.

Toward the end of the 1957 school year, my mother told me that we (she, my brother Jack, and me) were moving west. My sister Janice, who was nineteen, didn't want to move. The plan was for her to stay with our maternal grandparents who lived in a big old house in Newport. In late June, off we went to California in a brand new 1957 Chevy Bel Air with

Jack at the wheel and his six-month-old driver's license in his pocket. My job on the trip was to sit in the *backseat* and be quiet.

High School Records

As much fun as I used to have playing on Mr. Barth's motorcycle, I never thought about it once we headed west. I didn't think about police stuff at all. For the first time in my short life, I was going to attend public school where I would have several teachers each day, not one nun whose teaching style could vary with her moods. Catching a nun on a bad day meant the whole day was going to be bad.

At least in public school a teacher in a bad mood only meant fifty minutes of the day was crap. The whole day wouldn't be ruined. In California, we would have a new place to live and I'd have new friends and a whole new lifestyle. California was, for me, more socially advanced than the East Coast, and it was exciting, although I was extremely naïve and socially awkward. I was growing up, and the idea of playing on a police motorcycle waned.

One day near the end of my senior year in high school, we were asked to select a profession we might be interested in pursuing for an upcoming career day. There weren't many that interested me, even though I had set a number of high school records. I was graduating with the lowest possible grade-point average while attending the fewest number of days legally required. Rocket scientist, chemist, English professor, and the like were a stretch for me. Happily, I noticed that our local police chief would be hosting a talk for those interested in a law enforcement career. Since I had previous law enforcement experience with Mr. Barth, I figured that was the place for me.

The police chief did a great job. He showed us his handcuffs and his pistol. He seemed tough as nails but he also sounded as if he thoroughly enjoyed being a cop. The chief told us the monthly starting salary was almost five hundred dollars a month. I was seventeen years old and wondered how anyone could spend so much money in one month. I had no marketable skills, yet I could make more money than I ever thought possible. But I had to be twenty-one to be a cop, so I needed to do something to fill those four years. By then my sister had married and divorced, moved to California, and took up with a man who would become her second in a long series of husbands. Wayne was a rough carpenter, and it was decided, without any input from me, that I would be his laborer during the summer following my senior year of high school. Wayne was a pretty cool guy. He took me under his wing in a not so veiled effort to make a man out of me by introducing me to the world of construction. We would leave the house for the construction site at five in the morning and not return home until seven or later each night. He was paid for each house he framed, so the more houses he framed, the more money Wayne would earn each week.

He gave me a flat rate of fifty dollars each week regardless of how many houses we framed. He worked me hard, and it now occurs to me as I write this that I was getting screwed. It was hot, smoggy, and exhausting work. Wayne had a nineteen-inch right arm from swinging an eighteen-ounce hammer all day. On the weekends, all I wanted to do was sleep and rest up for the coming Monday. By the end of summer, I had put a quarter of an inch on my skinny right arm, had a great tan (the cumulative results of which keep my dermatologist in a Mercedes today), added a variable treasure trove of curse words to my daily vocabulary, and learned that construction work wasn't for me.

Police Science

In the fall, I enrolled in the local two-year college. When I told my mother I was going to college, she was surprised. While I always tried to keep my high school report cards from her by forging her name, I think she understood that my academic performance was poor. Of course, I had to take *dumbbell* English and *dumbbell* Math. Nevertheless, like many academic underachievers, I was accepted and became a college student. Naturally, I chose criminal justice as my major since five hundred a month still sounded good to me. I also remembered all the fun I had on Mr. Barth's motorcycle.

My first college class was "Introduction to Police Science." It was a survey course for first year criminal justice majors, which provided a broad spectrum of information about the varied forms of police work. A Los Angeles Police lieutenant from their vice detail taught the course. He had a shaved head when shaved heads weren't in style. Maybe he was just bald. But he was tall, carried himself well, and dressed in well-tailored suits. I remember him speaking the first day about his career, and I noted he had the same kind of enthusiasm about his work as the police chief from my high school's career day program.

When the class ended, I was hooked. I knew I wanted to be a cop. When I left the class, my whole outlook changed. I actually attended all my courses, made good grades, and graduated in two years.

I graduated high school when I was seventeen and community college when I was nineteen. I was still too young to become a police officer and had no money to enroll in a four-year college. I learned a large sheriff's office was creating a new position for non-sworn personnel whose duties would involve the supervision of minimum-security prisoners. The pay was nearly as much as a deputy sheriff's starting pay. The minimum age was only nineteen. I signed up right away. I spent an anxious summer waiting to see if the program would get off the ground and if I would be selected. On a Saturday morning, I received a telegram directing me to report to the sheriff's academy the following Monday to begin the five week training program.

Well, I wasn't a cop yet, but I was working in law enforcement and being paid a good salary, especially for a nineteen-year-old. By the time I was twenty and a half, many law enforcement agencies would allow job seekers to take the written examinations. Never a particularly critical thinker, I took tests for at least a dozen Southern California law enforcement agencies and a few federal ones.

My well-thought-out career plan was this: I would accept the first police position I was offered. I didn't think much about the size of the force, the pay or benefits, the training opportunities, or the reputation of the force. My work in a non-sworn position in a sheriff's office reinforced my desire to become a sworn officer. I was anxious to become a cop.

My luck held, however, and I was hired by another sheriff's office as a deputy sheriff. I had taken the test about six months before my twenty-first birthday, gone through an interview, and completed all the paperwork so they could conduct a background examination of my worthiness.

A few days after my twenty-first birthday, I called to see what was happening and where I was in the process. They asked me to come down to their headquarters. There, a detective spoke to me for about an hour. It was my impression he was trying to let me down gently. After a while, he handed me a copy of the penal code, then gave me a copy of the department's rules and regulations. Then, surprisingly, he handed me a baton and a box containing a service revolver. Since I had the service revolver, he told me he would have to swear me in before I could take the weapon out of the building. I stood, swore, and was handed a badge. We walked across the street, and I was issued an identification card. That afternoon I drove back to my non-sworn position in the other force and gave my two weeks notice.

A Uniformed Crime Fighter

Without any formalized training, I arrived in full uniform two weeks later for my new job. I was placed as a bailiff in the superior court until such time as I would be assigned to a twelve-week basic peace officers' course at the training academy. I was pretty proud of myself. After some trial and error, I had the uniform on properly with everything in the right place. My time in front of the mirror before leaving for work, practicing my quick draw, and admiring my handsome uniformed image wasn't more than fifteen or twenty minutes. I was ready.

The department didn't have any locker rooms for deputies to change into their uniforms. Deputies would wear their uniforms back and forth to work and cover their uniform shirt with a light jacket while driving their personal vehicles. I knew I was supposed to do that, but I wanted people to check me out and know I was a deputy sheriff. My 1958 Triumph TR3 with its loud exhaust, shredded rag top, and overall unusual looks generated its share of interest from passing motorists anyway, so how cool would it be when they saw a genuine deputy sheriff behind the wheel?

This little demonstration of bravado was short-lived. I reported to my sergeant in the Civil Division. He wasn't in. I waited about ten minutes before he arrived. His first comment was that I should wear a jacket to cover my uniform shirt while driving back and forth to work. He also suggested I purchase a different car, as the one I was driving didn't seem reliable, especially considering the speed I was driving. Apparently I had blasted past him at some point during my drive to work. I was busted the first day on the job.

Work as a bailiff was one long snooze. Bailiffs are basically the "hey boys" for the judges. All judges believe, to some extent, they were created full-born from the mind of Zeus and clad in a coat of mail ready to dispense perfect justice in an imperfect world. Some bailiffs were assigned to criminal courts and had duties much more exciting than befell me each day in a civil courtroom. In a criminal court, the bailiff had to watch the prisoner on trial and make sure no one interfered with the jury. The bailiffs in the criminal courts were usually older deputies who opted for the more routine schedule with weekends off as they neared the end of their careers.

The young, yet-to-be-trained deputies usually were assigned to a civil court where the most important function each day was filling the water pitchers. The chances of getting in trouble or performing anything remotely resembling police work were nil.

Working as a bailiff had a definite upside. It allowed me plenty of time to study for the upcoming training. The lunch break was at least an hour and a half, and sometimes it would run into two hours. This gave me time to check out a car, drive to the firing range, and practice shooting. Or I could go a gym around the corner from the courts and work on my physical conditioning. By the time the training academy started ten months later, I was in great shape and was an excellent shot; so good, in fact, that I was asked to join the department's pistol team.

There were thirty of us in my training class. The department trained the police officers from the various cities in the county as well as its deputy sheriffs. Our class had a scattering of city police recruits and two Marine military police officers as well. The state-of-the-art training style was patterned after military boot camp in a way. We went home each night, but the training officers still tried to emulate a Marine Corp drill instructor at boot camp.

I think there were only two of us in the training class who didn't have any military experience. At least for me I had the five weeks of previous training to become a corrections officer. My prior training had also been based on a military model. I had learned how to march, wear a uniform, spit shine shoes, and generally handle the tirades of training officers.

There was little in the academic portion of the training that I hadn't learned in college. The classroom sessions were more of a review for me. Through the weeks, I would fluctuate between first and second place academically. No one could touch me on the shooting range. Physically there was only one other person who came close to matching me on our daily agility tests. For me, the academy was an easy experience. The time flew by. I left the academy with trophies for shooting and physical prowess and second place for academic achievement.

The end of the academy was a letdown because I had to go back to the courts to await an opening in the patrol division. It seemed as if my time would never come. There were only five hundred employees for the whole sheriff's office. Promotions were slow. It didn't appear we were growing. I was waiting for a patrol officer to be promoted to detective so I could fill his slot in patrol.

There were only about a hundred thousand people living in the unincorporated area of the county where the sheriff provided law enforcement protection. I didn't see much chance for growth in my force and feared I would be a bailiff my whole career. In many counties in California, the law had been changed to add the duties of the coroner to the sheriff. This happened in my force, and the deputies said the legislators had decided to make the sheriff the coroner as well because he was already dead.

I was depressed. I didn't want to be a bailiff. I wanted to be in patrol. The prospect didn't look good. It was another six months of filling the water pitchers before, finally, there was an opening in patrol. At last I was going to do what I had wanted to do since my high school career day program.

What I didn't know during those anxiety-filled days in the courts was that my future felicity was secure. Our force would grow to more than 3,500 employees during my thirty-two-year career, and we would provide police services to three quarters of a million people in twelve contract cities. Today the force is over 4,000 people and even more cities receive their police protection from the sheriff. I wasn't paying attention to all of that, however; I was busy being a cop and buzzing around in my hulking Dodge 440 black-and-white patrol car with my patrol partner.

A police chief who spoke at our graduation ceremony said something to the effect that when an officer pins on his badge, he has a ticket for a ringside seat for the greatest show on earth. Patrol work makes that point. I was constantly amazed at the messes people would get into and the brazenness of criminals. Also, I was amazed at the varying levels of people skills my colleagues demonstrated.

Some were outstanding. They could speak to people without getting them upset and had the ability to calm a person down. Me, I was barely twenty-two and looked as if I were seventeen. If someone yelled at me, I'd yell back. That's not a good technique for calming things down. I was in a constant buzz. I was a uniformed crime fighter and was going to right wrongs. I was always ready for the next perceived battle, even when there was no one to fight. My lack of maturity and training during those early patrol years manifested itself in an inappropriately aggressive, cocky, and self-centered style of police work.

All young cops strut around at first. My first job out of community college with the other sheriff's office was a uniformed, but non-sworn position. It meant I had no peace officer authority; in other words, I couldn't arrest anyone or carry a gun. Since the job involved supervising (more like baby-sitting) minimum-security prisoners, it didn't require such authority. Only prisoners and colleagues would see me in uniform. The uniform was never worn outside the jail.

Working as a deputy sheriff, however, I was out in public each day in uniform. It never occurred to me so many people would look at me. If I walked into a restaurant, people turned to look, or if I was walking on a sidewalk, people would look to see what I was doing or where I was going. This made me self-aware. Although I've been walking pretty much all my life, it felt different. Now I was wearing a hat and seven pounds of equipment around my waist, and it seemed as if everyone was staring.

Whenever I moved my head, it felt different because I had a hat with a large metal cap badge on the front. There was a twenty-six-inch long plastic baton hanging down my left leg and a four-inch Colt Python revolver with cool hand-carved grips a guy in the district attorney's office made for me on my right hip, and all those people were focused on me.

Now the simple act of walking in a normal way was confounded. I was dressed in a way I hadn't been before. I was carrying heavy objects, wearing a hat, so my mental image of how I should act changed. I became aware of maybe not being in a ringside seat for the greatest show on earth, but rather being in the center ring.

Eventually, with time and experience, I grew out of my self-consciousness and into the job. To be a good crime fighter, I knew I had to develop good communication skills. Since most crime happens outside the purview of the police, law enforcement officers must rely on information from the general public. Successful crime fighters have the skills to garner critical information. Over time, with the help of training officers and a few mentors, I became a successful officer.

On Being a Boss

Some people want to be in charge of things. That's me. I soon wanted to be a boss. The sheriff's department was growing and that meant there would be new positions available. My first desire after seven years in patrol was to become a detective. It was surprising in some ways that I wanted to get out of the uniform I'd been so desperate to wear.

In many police forces, a detective position is the same rank as a patrolman, although the latter carries, in the mind of the public, more prestige. But in my force, detective (we called them investigators) was an actual rank.

The first time I took the test, I failed it miserably. I didn't think I needed to study as I had been a patrolman for a long time and thought I knew everything one needed to know about police work. I couldn't believe I didn't know everything. My first thought when I received the test results was that someone mixed up the test scores. But, indeed, I did fail to the extent that if it were a foot race around a track, I would have been lapped several times by the guy with the lowest passing score. The next time I studied for the test, passed it, and was duly promoted.

This experience caused me to think about my future in the force. If I wanted to be a boss, I needed to go back to school. There were only a few officers who had college degrees, and I noted they always did well on tests and were getting promoted quickly.

I enrolled in a four-year college that used a trimester system and was able to complete the entire set of requirements and receive a bachelor's degree in two years. I was on a roll and immediately entered graduate school, obtaining a master's degree eighteen months later. After a short hiatus, I enrolled in another graduate school's doctoral program, completed all my course work in three years, and was advanced to doctoral candidacy. It's been almost thirty years since I was advanced to candidacy. All I needed to do to get a PhD was to write the pesky dissertation.

I discovered another way. I left the university with the two things I wanted: a PhD and a Porsche. I married one of the university professors who drove a Porsche. We're still together five Porsches later, but I haven't written a line of my dissertation. I still think about it though.

Once I made detective, my promotions came quickly. Within ten years, I was a captain responsible for a whole patrol division. Three years after making captain, I was promoted to assistant sheriff, responsible for all law enforcement operations of the department. This required an incredible amount of "sucking up." I enjoyed every minute of my work from the day I started. There were almost no bad days.

I wasn't even forty, and I held a police executive rank. The pay was outstanding and the work, while demanding, was exciting. This left me with a sense of accomplishment at the end of the day. By then we had over 3,000 employees, and 1,000 of them fell under my aegis. Not only was I responsible for patrol and detectives, but also our harbor patrol, SWAT teams, security at our airport, helicopter patrols, and the bomb squad, all exciting stuff.

Then good fortune turned its head away and I was left to fight mutinous crews and treachery. I lost the fight. After almost thirty-two years with the same sheriff's department, I was forced to retire in lieu of termination following allegations of sexual harassment. The day I left police work, I felt like a gyro spinning out of control. Events became surreal, and everything moved in slow motion.

Slowly I gained equilibrium, and even more slowly, I began taking stock of where I was in life and what I needed to do. Allegations turned into lawsuits, then I gave up hope former colleagues would call and offer support; I relied on my attorneys, my family, and the few courageous friends who provided solace.

After two and a half years, the lawsuits settled out of court. This was exactly what the attorneys told me would happen when the suits were first filed. We all held each other harmless in the settlements. The issue wasn't my behavior, but rather how much money the allegations about my behavior would bring to the table. Of course, I'm putting myself in the best possible light as a complete saint. My accusers would probably say I was a hound from hell. The reality is probably somewhere in between.

The damage to me wasn't only monetary; it was also physical and emotional. I had lost a job I loved, my blood pressure climbed to dangerous levels, and my self-image was shattered. For over a year, I was eviscerated in the news media. I was embarrassed and ashamed and didn't know what the future would hold for me.

The media attention was so aggressive, I was told, because of my high-ranking position. I was beginning to believe I was more significant than I had ever dreamed. The irony was if I hadn't been so diligent in seeking quick promotions, and if I had been a low-ranking officer, the news coverage, if any, would have been far less dramatic.

In those dark days, I never thought redemption would be found in a land of warring factions and landmines, but it was.

TWO

BETWEEN THE SLIME IN THE GUTTER AND THE BABY IN THE CRIB

✭ ✭ ✭

We sleep soundly in our beds because rough men stand ready in the night to visit violence on those who would harm us.

– Winston Churchill

Watching the Pros

Part of any good police science program in the mid 1960s included a course on patrol procedures. The course would cover the basic essentials of how to stop cars, how to arrest dangerous felons, and how to handle various types of calls. The best part of the course was the ride-along. Students were allowed to ride with a police officer during one of his patrol shifts and observe the theories learned in the classroom applied to real-life situations. For the students, of course, it was considered a fun weekend night riding around in a police car. I was assigned to the police force in my hometown. Now how much fun was that? Not only would I be seeing police work from the inside for the first time, but also there was a chance some of my friends might see me.

The officer to whom I was assigned was gigantic. He became the police chief many years later. He didn't say much. I wasn't sure he was excited about having a young kid in the police car with him. The whole concept of the ride-along program was new. Like many new innovations, law enforcement officers weren't quick to accept it.

For most of the shift, we drove around town and, at one point, drove past my house. I wanted to ask the officer to stop or at least honk, but good sense prevailed—an unusual demonstration of self-restraint for me at nineteen. At around eight o'clock, we went to dinner at a small café. The officer called over his police radio to say we would be Code 7, police talk for "out to eat," then gave the telephone number of the restaurant to the police radio dispatcher. This was before the days of the small personal radios officers carry on their gun belts today. When we finished dinner, I was amazed to learn we only had to pay half the listed price: what a good deal. As a cop, I would earn five hundred dollars a month and pay only half price for my meals. It just kept getting better.

In the patrol car, the officer informed the dispatcher we were back in service. The dispatcher advised a rape report was being taken in our area. Another officer was already on the scene. Since this was my officer's patrol area, he was dispatched to the location to assist the other officer. Off we shot at about sixty miles an hour through residential streets, a few alleys, and finally out onto a busy street where the officer turned on his red lights as he burst through a congested intersection against the red stoplight. *More! More!* I thought, but after one or two quick turns, we arrived at the scene.

"Wait here," he said, as he gathered his notebook and headed for the house where the rape had taken place. Well, how the hell was I going to learn anything sitting in the patrol car? So far, all I had seen was my hometown from the passenger seat of a police car, learned the police only had to pay half price for meals, and that they could drive fast and go through red lights. All in all, this was useful but limited information. When the officer returned to the patrol car, I anticipated getting the lowdown on what had happened, a description of the suspect, and any other pertinent information. The officer said nothing to me about the incident at all. We continued patrolling.

Nearing the end of the shift, I was silently hoping for something exciting to happen or at least some excuse for him to drive fast again. Finally I heard him say, "Let's head for the barn." The shift was over, and I only had one incident to write on the patrol log our instructor had given us to complete.

The next time the class met, those of us who had participated in the program read our patrol logs. A class discussion followed. Two other students had participated on the same weekend as me. One was involved in a high-speed chase of a burglary suspect. The other was with an officer who responded to a bar fight with several other officers and, later in the evening, captured a prowler. When it was my turn, I stood and said we had taken a rape report.

When the instructor asked what happened, I sadly said, "Don't know; the officer told me to wait in the car." Apparently, my lack of action was extremely funny to the rest of the class.

Three weeks later I was assigned to another ride-along. Perhaps the instructor felt sorry for me. This time I was with a small city police force in another county. The officer was about the same age as the previous one in my hometown, but he was shorter, lighter, talkative, and enthusiastic. I had the impression he enjoyed having someone in the patrol car with him. Again there wasn't much in the way of action during most of the Friday evening shift. The downtime gave the officer time to explain police work. He explained why he was doing things in a particular way. It helped the somewhat boring evening go by quickly.

Then something happened demonstrating how police work was often boring and routine, but also unexpectedly punctuated by high adventure. As we neared the end of the shift, we received a call of a major traffic accident. We were there in under a minute as it was close by our location. As first on the scene, the officer jumped out of the car to check on the injured. I assumed he was going to tell me to stay in the car, but he told me to get the flares out of the trunk and put them out along the roadway. Fortunately, I had taken an accident investigation class and knew how to do this. As another police car rolled up to the scene, my officer yelled at me to tell the arriving officer an ambulance was needed. One officer collected the driver's licenses of people involved in the accident and handed them to me to hold.

The time at the accident scene went by quickly. I would have guessed we spent a half hour there and was surprised to learn we had actually spent over an hour and a half. When we arrived back at the police station, the officer still had reports to do. There were some serious injuries in this four-car pileup, but no one died. The drivers and passengers all fared better than my officer. Sadly, I learned, three years after I became a deputy sheriff, the officer was shot and killed by a man he was trying to arrest on a fugitive warrant.

This didn't dissuade me from wanting to be a cop. All I saw was romance and glory, adventure and intrigue, red lights and sirens, busting doors, and shooting people. I wanted to stand tall, as tall as I could at five foot ten and one half inches, on the thin blue line between the slime in the gutter and the baby in the crib.

Code Three

Most people know Code 3 means operating an emergency vehicle with lights and siren. An emergency vehicle, police car, fire engine, or ambulance is allowed to violate most of the rules of the road when their emergency lights are flashing and sounding a siren. Some cops will say they signed up for red lights and sirens.

All new officers want to experience the thrill of driving Code 3. I know I did. During recruit academy training, I was sent to a three-day school during which time I practiced driving skills under extreme conditions. It was especially enlightening to me and the other recruits to learn people driving directly in front of a patrol car whose siren is blasting away may not be able to hear it. The speed of the vehicles, the noise of an air conditioner, or sound level of the radio will affect the ability of a driver to attend to the noise being made by a siren coming at them in their rearview mirror. This information was filed away by all of us to recall on our first Code 3 run.

Although officers entering patrol have academy training, they are assigned to an experienced Field Training Officer (FTO). Today, FTOs are selected carefully and most attend a special school to learn the craft of training a new officer. Many states have specific requirements about how the training should be conducted, what experience and training a FTO should possess, and require a detailed progress report reviewed by supervisors. FTO programs emerged from what was no more than On-The-Job-Training (OJT) conducted by senior officers. The senior officer would be left to his own devices and judgment about when and if a new officer could handle a radio car by himself.

I remember the story told by an academy instructor about his first Code 3 experience. He'd been riding with his training officer for several weeks but wasn't allowed to drive the car.

"Observe and learn," his training officer told him. He did, but in the back of his mind was a growing desire to drive the patrol car.

After stopping for coffee one day, the senior officer asked if he wanted to drive. "Okay, no problem, if you want me to," was the reply. He didn't want to sound too excited, but he was.

Within a few minutes, they received a call of an armed robbery in progress. *What luck*, he thought. He responded to the dispatcher with a calm voice, turned on the red lights and siren, and floored it. Within seconds they were flying down a busy street weaving in and out of traffic with, to his way of thinking, great dexterity. The siren grew louder and louder as his speed increased.

He was surprised when the left arm of the senior officer came across his chest and pinned him to the back of the seat. He looked at the senior officer, who said something but he couldn't hear him, as the siren was too loud.

He saw the senior officer turn off the siren and heard him yell, "You're going the wrong way!"

One quick turn and he was headed in the right direction. It was their call, and they were within blocks of it, but they were the last car to arrive. The suspects had fled and the suspects' descriptions were already being broadcast over the police radio. The other officers on the scene wanted to know why they had arrived so late, as they had been close to the scene when the call came out. He heard the senior officer mumble something about idiot trainees.

The next day at briefing, the sergeant asked the officer to explain why they were so late to a hot call. The officer's hair was buzzed, and he looked as if he were fresh out of the crate. The room was filled with officers who had seniority hash marks on their sleeves, who had been in shootings and had experienced many hot calls. He had to explain how his excitement about driving Code 3 overrode his common sense.

A trainee doesn't want to stand up in front of a bunch of experienced officers and tell them about something stupid he may have done. I remembered this story, as told by the academy instructor, and remembered the siren wasn't as loud as it sounded inside a patrol unit. Other drivers could easily fail to hear it. But none of this knowledge prevented me from doing something stupid on my first Code 3 call.

In Service

When I was notified of my transfer to patrol from the courts, I was beside myself with anticipation. I rushed to the local police store and purchased a doublewide briefcase exactly the same as the patrol officers carried. I stocked it with all the necessary report forms, binoculars, evidence tags, plastic bags, an extra pair of handcuffs, a box of bullets, spare batteries for my Sportsman flashlight, pens, pencils, steno pads, a ruler, and a traffic accident template. There was sufficient room left for small copies of the

Penal Code and the Vehicle and for the citation book I'd be issued when I arrived in patrol.

Like most of my fellow officers, I would buy nearly any cop-related item if it met one of three criteria: Any object with my force's name on it or the words "sheriff" or "police" was always a big seller. Anything painted black and white would catch my eye, and frequently the eye of any discriminating cop wandering around a police store looking to spend money. If it were made of black basket weave, it would make its way to my must-have list.

Since I would be issued a citation book, I wanted to have a nice, professional cover for it. I bought the most expensive one, in black basket-weave leather with my initials carved into it. It would house the citation book, a cheat sheet with quick references to the most frequent vehicle code violations, the addresses of the various courts into which I would cite violators, and a small calendar to determine the court appearance dates.

My first day in patrol arrived. Excited couldn't describe my feelings. I was assigned to the swing shift from four o'clock until midnight. My training officer had been with the sheriff's department for ten years. He had worked in a small city police force for several years before becoming a deputy sheriff. He was about fifteen years older than I. He looked young, however, and his youthful vigor belied his forty-plus years.

My new partner was six foot two, slim, and had a rangy quality to him. He took long strides when he walked and was quick to smile at people, usually catching them off guard. Our assigned patrol area was in the near center of the county. We were responsible for patrolling a large swath of unincorporated land bordering four different cities.

Before we started patrolling, we attended the shift briefing with all the other deputies scheduled on the same shift. Briefings normally lasted about fifteen minutes during which the patrol sergeant would read the latest crime bulletins, pass along any administrative information, and hand out the most recent hot sheet which contained a long list of stolen vehicle license plates.

The sergeant ended the briefing by asking if any of the deputies had anything to add. Seldom would any of them add anything. But on my first day, obviously because I was anxious to start, some deputy had an inane procedural question. This sparked a debate among several deputies and the sergeant about the correct way a case number should be issued when there was a single criminal act with multiple victims. I knew the answer, and I hadn't been in patrol more than fifteen minutes. I didn't say what I was thinking although I wanted them to know the answer was simple. They were wasting my time.

When the briefing finally ended, I went to the patrol secretary to sign for a new citation book. She was out of citation books! "What!" I exclaimed, "I'm going out on patrol right now; how I can do that without a citation book?" I was trying not to sound agitated, but I was.

"If you need to write a ticket, use your partner's book," she said in a calm and professional way. The new books were on order and were expected next week. I was devastated. My great new citation book cover sitting in my briefcase was going to waste.

I caught up with my training officer in the parking garage. He instructed me on the standard pre-patrol inspection procedures. They would become a routine every time I was issued a patrol car. The inspection included making sure the shotgun was working properly. It involved unloading the weapon, checking to see if the cartridges (only five of them) weren't crimped, working the slide back and forth, and then reloading. Two things occurred to me. First, the shotgun made me nervous even though I was an excellent pistol shot. Second, I made a mental note to buy some extra shotgun shells for my briefcase. Five didn't seem nearly enough.

Finally, after having waited for this day since the end of high school, we headed out to our patrol area about fifteen minutes from the sheriff's headquarters. My partner told me to advise the radio dispatcher that we were "10-8," in service. I'd been practicing. I completed my first assignment from my training officer flawlessly.

I picked up my steno pad after reporting we were in service and was ready to write down all the pertinent information for our first call. I had my map book already opened to our patrol area. I waited, but the dispatcher simply acknowledged we were in service. Any minute now I thought the dispatcher would assign us our first call, but nothing happened. We spent an hour driving around our area in what my partner called an "orientation tour."

I liked driving fast. My training officer not only drove fast, he was a maniac behind the wheel. Either we were at a complete stop after heavy rapid braking, or we were balls to the wall heading nowhere in particular. Apparently, quick reflexes came with his heavy foot, and after a few weeks, I was eventually able to relax. The look of astonishment slowly diminished from my face and the hair on my head no longer stood straight up. We spent our first night going nowhere fast.

The orientation tour/thrill ride was finished, and we jetted over to the county airport in our area. Maybe someone would need us there. The airport in those days was a busy, cramped, small, and unsophisticated operation. Airport security was left to a force of county airport security officers. Mostly old military retirees staffed security. They had limited peace officer powers. Serious crime, oh how I was hoping we would have some, was handled by the area patrol car staffed by my training officer and me.

We spent a few minutes at the airport terminal where I was introduced to the three security officers on duty. We left and drove to the private plane section of the airport where there was an outdoor air museum. We were able to drive between all the old vintage planes. After one tour around the museum, my partner parked, got out, and started talking to one of the local private guards. I waited in the car listening to the radio in case some emergency developed requiring our immediate attention. My partner spent what seemed to me to be a long time wandering around the old planes.

When he got back into the car, he was animated, and as we raced from point to point, he would tell me interesting facts about some of the planes. I wanted to know where the hot spots were in our patrol area, what were the major crime problems we needed to target, how was the workload in the patrol car divvied up? The last question became clear in a few short days. He would drive and I would do everything else. But on my first day, there was no "everything else." He drove around our patrol area at a high rate of speed, and I sat in the passenger seat closely monitoring the radio for the hot call that never came.

The next day as he drove us to our patrol area, he told me he had something I would enjoy doing. Perhaps he sensed my lack of interest in old airplanes. We drove to a rural part of our area dominated by large tracts of orange groves. Eventually, after following a dirt road along a windbreak in the groves, we came to a closed private shooting range. It was nothing more than a few benches and a couple of targets with wrought-iron frames against a dirt and sand hillside backstop.

A shooting contest, I thought. *Is this guy crazy?* Was he not aware that I had a shooting trophy from the academy and recently medaled at the monthly countywide police pistol match? Maybe this was my chance to make some money from a friendly wager. He walked me around to the trunk of the patrol car. He opened the trunk. There was a large sand shifter and two shovels. He said we were going to mine the backstop for lead. He reloaded bullets as a hobby, he said. *How is that a hobby?* I wondered.

Now, to my way of thinking, how an officer wears his uniform is important. A neat, clean, well-tailored, and properly worn uniform enhances the officer's command presence. Even if that were not the case, I was always fastidious about my clothes and the way I looked. I never liked being dirty. Maybe I'm a bit foppish, somewhat of a sissy when it comes to appearances, and even a little anal retentive, to use a Freudian term, in my compulsion for orderliness.

When I arrived at work, I was immaculate. My uniform was pressed each day, my shoes spit shined each night, and my leather gear polished. I cleaned my revolver thoroughly every time I shot at the range. And this fool wanted me to dig in the dirt with him for used lead. Surprisingly, he took my rejection of this fun activity in stride. I sat in the car waiting, now hoping a call would come our way.

Sweating, and with dirt all over his Wellington boots and bottom half of his trouser legs, my training officer climbed back into the car. He proudly showed me a coffee can full of the lead he had recovered. He was beaming.

"Is lead expensive?" I asked.

"Well, it adds up," he replied.

In other words, no, the lead wasn't expensive, but this lead was free for the taking. I would learn the word free had a magical quality to it for my training officer and other deputy sheriffs. The owners of the range encouraged deputies to come by and take the lead. It saved the owners the cost of hiring a company to mine the backstop each month.

During the next few weeks, we received a couple of report calls, but nothing exciting. This slow period afforded me an opportunity to familiarize myself with all the different report forms, practice my report writing, learn the patrol area, and calm down a little.

Dispatched to take a car burglary report in the airport parking lot, we met the victim standing next to his brand new VW. The interior of the car had been equipped with special racing front bucket seats. The seats had been stolen. The crook, however, was nice enough to have left two old and tattered VW seats. Obviously the crook was a VW owner who was out looking to upgrade the interior of his older car. I took the report without any need of assistance from my partner. It was a straightforward theft report. When the victim asked to take the old seats so he could drive his car home, I turned to my partner for advice. He told the victim to take the seats, as we had no use for them.

I wrote a complete report on the incident and turned it in at the end of the shift. Arriving at work the next day, I was summoned to the watch commander's office. I didn't know what I had done, but being in patrol for only a few weeks and having to see the watch commander couldn't be a good thing. Was I getting fired, suspended, reprimanded, or spanked? When I walked into the lieutenant's office, he asked me how long I'd been a deputy. He confirmed I graduated from the recruit academy. He said he'd heard I even had an associate's degree in criminal justice.

"Yes, yes," I said. Maybe he'd heard good things about me and I was going to receive a special assignment.

"Then I suppose you know," he said, looking at me sternly, "those two seats left by the car burglar in the airport parking lot were evidence."

"Yes, but—" I stammered.

"And there's nothing in any of our procedures or the law," he interjected, "which allows you, with your vast two weeks of experience, to give the evidence to the victim."

If the lieutenant had been holding a sword, I would have thrown myself on it. I offered to go to the victim's house and recover the evidence. The lieutenant relented, saying something about this being a learning experience and directed me to get out of his office.

I couldn't wait to find my training officer to learn from him why he allowed the victim to take the seats. When I told him the story, he looked at me in disbelief. He couldn't understand why I included the fact that we gave the seats to the victim in the report. I had a lot to learn about the finer points of police work.

Along about my third week in patrol, I was adjusting to the slow pace of police work in our not-so-crime-ridden patrol area. Cars all around us were getting calls; some were hot calls, requiring a back up unit. It always seemed we were in the wrong location and weren't called to assist the other cars. The dispatcher would send closer cars to assist the unit handling the hot call.

Blood Runs

Since sheriff's cars were deployed throughout the county, my agency accepted the responsibility of transporting blood from one hospital to another when the blood was needed in emergency situations and time was critical. A blood run was a dream call. It meant racing Code 3 to one hospital or the county blood bank, running into the location where the life-saving liquid was waiting, confirming it was the right cargo, racing carefully back to the patrol car, and driving to the hospital in need of the blood.

Sometimes the receiving hospital would be at the other end of the county. This meant there would be a twenty- to thirty-mile Code 3 run. The driver would rush toward the hospital while the passenger officer held the packaged blood between his feet on the floorboard of the car. Upon arrival, the passenger officer would jog into the hospital and hand the blood to a waiting nurse. Blood runs were exciting and there was little report-writing effort required when they were over. In most hot call situations, the incident may be over quickly, but the report-writing requirements lingered on long into the night.

My training officer and I had fallen into a comfortable partner relationship. He was an easygoing guy. He would sincerely try to answer my many questions about patrol work. He was definitely not a young pup. I'm sure the bosses put us together so my exuberance was tempered by his maturity and more studied approach to policing.

One night he asked if I wanted to drive. You betcha I did. In reality, I think he was tired driving all the time. From then on, we split the driving each night fifty-fifty. Usually the passenger officer was responsible for writing the reports. But since this was a training car, I would still handle most of the reports even if I were driving.

This arrangement was fine with me because, one, I had no choice, two, I wanted to drive because I knew it would increase my chances of catching a Code 3 call, and three, I enjoyed checking myself out in the storefront windows as we drove past.

The deputies who worked the area to the north of us received many hot calls. Because they had several hospitals in their area and the county blood bank, they handled many of the blood runs. They were twice blessed. I was so near yet so far from the stream of exciting calls.

On one particular busy weekend night, busy for everyone except us, I was driving aimlessly around our patrol area. Two patrols north of us were busy on a domestic disturbance call where shots reportedly had been fired. The disturbance call left two patrol districts without any patrols, so my partner directed me to the north end of our beat in case something else happened in their areas. My hopes were elevated a little and I thought maybe this would be the time for us to get a hot call.

The radio blared, "Any unit in the area of the blood bank, identify and respond." I had the red lights on, the siren going, and was heading to the blood bank before my partner could pick up the microphone to tell the dispatcher we were responding.

On the way, the dispatcher gave us all the information about the blood run. We were taking the blood to a hospital in the south part of the county. Not only was I driving Code 3 for the first time, I'd be driving Code 3 for a long time. Our route to the hospital would take us through surface streets mostly and along the coast through a popular beach resort. This was going to be great.

We arrived at the blood bank without incident. My partner went in and picked up the blood. While he was gone, I took a quick look at the map so as not to embarrass myself by going in the wrong direction. I had our route down and when my partner was back in the car, we were off.

In the late sixties, there wasn't much to a police car. It had a distinctive paint job and a high-powered engine sans some smog control devices. The inside was pretty plain. There was a leatherette bench seat, a couple of toggle switches to operate the red lights, a shotgun locked along the front of the seat, and a tube radio.

There was also a toggle switch and a brake button for the mechanical siren. The siren was powered by a compressor in the engine and completely unlike the electronic sirens you hear on emergency vehicles today. The siren was operated by flipping the toggle switch and then by pressing down on the horn ring. The siren would get louder the longer you held the horn ring down. When the horn ring was released, the siren would wind down to a lower pitch and eventually stop. It took a while for the siren to stop so there was a siren brake button.

Out of the blood bank parking lot, I was pressing down hard on the horn ring. The siren was whining up to a high pitch. I was taught to release the horn ring periodically to allow the siren to whine down, which lowered the pitch, and then press on it again. This procedure allows the siren sound to fluctuate, enabling more drivers to hear it. The faster I drove, the harder I pressed the horn ring until the siren reached a high-pitched squeal. My partner reached over, tapped my arm, and motioned for me to let off on the horn ring. Now I remembered the horn ring and the gas pedal weren't connected.

Within the first mile, I had the whole speed-driving thing fairly well under control. Nevertheless, I did continue to sneak a few peaks at myself in the storefront windows as we sped though business districts. After all, I had never seen myself driving Code 3 and I wanted to see how I looked. Check me out I thought seeing my reflection driving that powerful Dodge with red lights flashing. In the gloaming, the red lights cast a warm diffused light on objects around the patrol car. I was looking good.

Perhaps my problem was emulating my partner's driving habits. We were going fast and I was nose-diving cars in front of us, jamming on the brakes at the last minute if they failed to get out of our way in time. My partner was working the right spotlight, waving it up and down, helping to get the attention of the cars in front of us. His screaming and yelling at the cars was apparently more cathartic than helpful in getting drivers to yield. We wanted them to get the hell out of the way. We were uniformed crime fighters on a life-saving mission.

All things considered, we were doing pretty well. The driver my partner flipped off didn't see him do it, so we didn't get in trouble for that misadventure. I was powering into the curves, modulating the pitch of the siren. I hadn't rammed anyone, yet I had this little annoying sense the brakes weren't working well. Then I thought I felt a little hiccup in the engine when I floored it powering out of a curve.

We were near the end of a two-lane canyon road approaching a main highway along the coast in a beach town when I felt the hiccup again. We turned left along the coast road. In the middle of the town with the gas pedal floored, the engine blew. We coasted to the curb, and noticed we no longer had brakes either. The patrol car rolled to a stop at the curb. The hundreds of tourists who had been taking a stroll in the twilight of this warm summer evening looked at us and wondered why the patrol car, with lights flashing and siren growling down, had stopped.

Across the street was a large storefront window so I could clearly see myself in all my ignominy. We were still about five minutes from the hospital. We turned off the red lights. The siren finally ground to a stop. There we sat, unhorsed. We advised the dispatcher of our plight. Within minutes, we heard a siren and saw a city police car approaching us. The officer stopped, got out, and said he'd been assigned to take the blood on to the hospital.

Well, crap. For a split second, I wanted to say, "No it's all right, we want to borrow your car. You wait here and watch ours." We gave him the blood and watched him drive off Code 3, steadily getting smaller in the fading light.

We sat in our broken patrol car as people walked past us wondering, I'm sure, what we were doing parked at the curb in the middle of town. We were waiting for the county tow truck to come and get us. It was a long wait, and it was dark when the tow truck arrived. We rode in the truck back to the county garage where we would check out another patrol unit. The ride back to the county garage was a long, slow one, with me, as the junior officer, sitting in the middle bouncing along in the tow truck on the same route we had used on our glory run.

I made a mental note to remember that, while patrol cars were powerful machines, they weren't indestructible. They were much like my powerful but fragile ego. It could be crushed by my own exuberance and poor driving skills.

The Pretty Deputy

Near the end of my training, we received an "Unknown Trouble" call. Our response time was quick, and a back-up unit with two other deputies arrived minutes after us. The dispatcher told us a man was alone in his house and was threatening suicide. His method was unusual. He was going to drink acid. Not a good choice if one wants *to go gentle into that long goodnight*. The four of us huddled near our patrol cars devising a plan of action when the dispatcher warned us the man was now threatening to throw acid in the face of anyone who came into the house.

It was time for more serious planning. The back-up officers were both seasoned patrol deputies. There was no training relationship between them. They knew how to handle calls and what their responsibilities were when assigned to assist another crew. Both, however, saw humor even in the dark side of police work.

Since it was our call, the back-up unit deferred to my training officer. My partner suggested he and I could distract the man, engage him in sympathetic conversation while they would sneak through the back door, and rush the man.

"Hey," one responded, "we're here to back you up, not handle the call for you." Good point, but I kind of liked my partner's suggestion. It would have surprised me if they had fallen for it. None of us wanted acid thrown in our face.

My training officer turned to me and said, "You'll have to go in first."

"What about you? You're bigger," I reasoned. He explained that as the training officer, it was his job to observe me and see how I handled the call. I looked at the back-up officers for some support, but they reiterated their role in assisting us. One said he would stand by with a garden house in case any acid was thrown on me. Great.

Clearly, I didn't want to be the first through the door either. Looking for some reason not to go in first, I blurted out, "But I'm too pretty."

This cracked them up, and we were having a good laugh when the front door opened. Standing in the doorway with a large glass filled with a clear liquid was the man threatening suicide. He wanted to know what was going on. We told him, from a distance, we were there because we heard he was going to hurt himself. My partner said we would have knocked, but we were afraid he would throw acid on us.

"It's water," he said. "I don't have any acid." He told us he was a frequent patient at the county mental health ward and he wanted us to drive him to the hospital.

"Done," we all said. He poured the liquid out on the lawn and we searched him, handcuffed him for safety reasons, and put him in the back of our car. Everyone at the mental health ward knew him. The hospital processing went quickly. I wrote a short report and the shift was over.

Briefing the next day was routine until near the end. Instead of asking if anyone had anything to add, the sergeant asked me to come to the front. He informed the entire shift that it was his pleasure to make a special presentation to the new kid, as he put it.

I was the only trainee on the swing shift and would be the new kid until another trainee would come along. The presentation, the sergeant said, was called for by my "great clarity of thought and originality in avoiding danger."

He handed me a small box. It contained a black basket-weave (my favorite) key case. Carved on the key case with each letter painted in a different bright primary color was the word "Pretty." I was required to put it on my gun belt before leaving the briefing room.

I liked it. I still have it.

Raining Dope

It was my training officer's responsibility to make sure I was capable of handling the wide range of police calls I would likely encounter as a patrol officer. In cases where a particular type of call didn't present itself during the training period, we would talk about what I would do on such calls. Murder cases didn't happen often, but we discussed the high points of being the first car at the scene of a possible murder. Surprisingly, later in my training, we were the first unit at the scene of an attempted murder. But there were many types of calls I wasn't exposed to during my six months of training. Nevertheless, I felt confident I'd be able to respond to any type of call appropriately.

Patrol officers fell into two broad categories. There were those who subscribed to the theory that they're out there to respond to calls for service. They opined that stopping a lot of cars for minor traffic infractions as a pretext for searching the occupants of the car wasted time. They thought of themselves as fireman on patrol, ready to respond to any emergency. This category of officer was usually older and had a great deal of experience.

Another category of officer, often younger, liked to beat the bushes for crime. Suspicious people riding around in a car with an equipment violation demanded their attention, these officers argued. They'd leave no stone unturned during their shift in the pursuit of criminals. I wanted to be in the latter category but my partner belonged to the former.

My training officer didn't think it was fruitful for me to stop cars for traffic violations. I had five months of training under my belt when I suggested we stop a few cars so I could learn how to write a traffic citation. He felt writing a citation was easy and I was smart enough to do it when the time came. We talked about stopping cars frequently. My constant ranting on this subject finally wore him down one night, and he pointed to a car we had seen make an illegal left turn. "Go stop him if you want," he said unenthusiastically.

The violator was driving a car that screamed "stop me." It was a 1958 Chevy Impala four-door. It was probably a fine car at one time. Unfortunately, time had taken its toll on this car. It had been lowered (probably not professionally) and sported three chrome rims. The fourth rim was painted white with white paint on part of the tire itself, and there was no hubcap. It looked as if the car had had a custom metal flake-green paint job. It was now faded, rusted, and a darker green pin striping tape had been added to the car in an effort to spruce it up. The trunk lid was held shut with rope. There were an inordinate number of bumper stickers plastered on the back of it. The bumper stickers all expressed, in witty but not subtle ways, the benefits of smoking dope.

I fell in behind the car. I turned on the red lights, and we immediately saw the driver throw something out the window. We watched the object as it made a long, loping arch and land on our windshield, catching on the passenger's side wiper blade. The driver now had our full attention. He started to speed up and, as I kept pace with him, the object, which we could plainly see was a large baggy of marijuana, slid off onto the roadway.

We stopped the patrol car, retrieved the dope, and caught the driver about a half-mile down the road.

In the 1960s, possessing marijuana was a felony crime. Even though it wasn't unusual to catch people with marijuana, it was still considered a good arrest. Unlike today where possession often results in a citation, a suspect back then would be taken to jail and booked. It's unusual, though, for a dope suspect to throw the dope onto a police car.

When I approached the driver, he asked why I stopped him. I told him about the illegal left turn. He apologized for it. Next I told him about the dope he threw on our car. He denied any knowledge of dope and was willing to let us search his car. We did and found the floorboard was loaded with marijuana seeds. There was a roach clip in the ashtray and cigarette papers on the seat. He used to smoke dope, but he recently quit, he explained. We asked if he decided to quit when we turned on the red lights and that's why he threw the marijuana away. He became quiet and sullen. My big grin and obvious pleasure from stumbling onto my first felony arrest pissed him off. He wouldn't talk to us the rest of night.

He was handcuffed, and we asked him for identification. He wasn't carrying any and he wouldn't tell us who he was. We explained how failure to properly identify himself would only result in him staying in jail longer. His car was towed away and he was booked in jail. As I was leaving the jail, I saw the suspect speaking to one of the jailers. The jailer later told us the suspect had several previous arrests for possession and sale of dope. He also had an outstanding arrest warrant for failure to appear in court for sentencing on an old dope case.

My first car stop for a traffic violation turned into my first felony arrest. I didn't get a chance to write my first traffic ticket, but I was able to practice making out a crime report, arrest report, and vehicle impound report. We never went to court on the case. I never learned what happened. The suspect probably pled guilty. Maybe the prosecutor dropped the case since the suspect was heading back to prison for the outstanding arrest warrant that had been issued.

My First Aid Patch

Our uniforms were crappy looking. They were an ugly dark green and only looked passable when they were properly maintained. The uniform had to be pressed daily to look presentable. Most officers didn't bother. They would wear the same uniform for four or five days at a stretch. Gun belts needed to be polished frequently, but few officers ever did this. Many preferred to have the dye wear off the gun belt, giving it a well-worn look engendering a sense of crustiness. Owing to my marginal obsessive-compulsiveness and belief that a well-maintained uniform would add to my command appearance and maybe add some age to my youthful looks, I was always well turned out in uniform.

During my early years in patrol, I noted many colleagues had service stars on their left sleeves. Every five years of service would earn a deputy an embroidered gold star worn above the cuff. Some deputies in patrol had two or three. I thought this dressed up the uniform. I was a few years away from earning a service star. How I longed for one of those stars. The slick left sleeve on my uniform told the world I was new in this game. Forget the fact I looked as if I were a police cadet rather than an actual deputy sheriff. To me, the lack of a service star set me apart from the other patrol deputies and told the world I was a rookie.

If nothing else, I was diligent about learning my job. On a day off, I decided to re-read the department's rules and regulations. Of course, I read them when I was going through the training academy, but I thought it would be helpful to read them again in light of my recently acquired patrol experience. There, in the section dealing with uniforms, I found a piece of information I had forgotten. The rules allowed anyone with an advanced first aid card to wear a small round first aid patch on the left sleeve. I had an advanced first aid card; I could wear the first aid patch. While it wasn't a service star, it was placed in the same general location on the uniform.

I didn't give it much thought. I rushed to the local police store to buy the patches. It took the owner a while to look around in the back room. Eventually, he came to the counter with a small dusty box filled with the patches. I bought two and handed him two of my uniform shirts so the patches could be sewed on right away. He seemed a bit confused about where they were to be placed, but I knew the exact location on the sleeve. He said okay and told me they didn't have much call for these patches. That should have been a clue, but I was too excited about adding a new dimension to my uniform. I wouldn't be just a rookie cop anymore. I'd be a rookie cop with an advanced first aid patch.

After two days off, I returned to work wearing my uniform replete with the new patch. Sitting in briefing, I tried to use my left hand for everything to show off the patch. No one seemed to notice. I looked around and was pleased to see that I was the only person with a first aid patch on the entire shift. In the patrol car my training officer asked me what I was doing wearing a religious patch on my uniform noting the large red cross in the center of the patch.

"No, this is a first aid patch. The rules and regulations allow me to wear it if I have an advanced first aid card," I hurriedly told him. Here I took my advanced first aid card from my pocket and waived it in front of him. It was my proof of my right to wear the patch on my uniform.

He told me I might want to rethink my decision to wear the patch. Nearly all the patrol deputies had advanced first aid cards. According to my training officer, there was only one other person in patrol who wore the patch. My partner said the guy was a jerk. I told him I'd think about it, but I liked having the patch on my sleeve. I was never in the Boy Scouts, so maybe it filled the void for all those merit badges I never had.

I wore the patch for a week despite the sergeant and several deputies calling me chaplain. When I returned to work after my days off, the patch was no longer part of my uniform. A close look at my left sleeve would reveal some small holes left from where I had ripped the patches off the sleeve.

Years later, when I wore six service stars, I was still looking forward to getting my seventh star. But that never happened.

Partners

Except for the day shift, all of our patrol cars were two-man units. There were no women working in patrol and it would remain woman-less until 1979. Some officers believed two-man patrol cars were safer. Others said it was better to deploy one person in a patrol car. For my force, it boiled down to a simple matter of economics when we changed to one-man units. We were able to deploy twice as many patrol cars with the same number of officers. The only cost was the purchase and equipping of the extra patrol cars. Many forces throughout the US today still deploy with two officers in each patrol car.

Two officers in a car, regardless of any other factor, bring a number of social issues into play. We recognized police officers aren't all equal in their knowledge of the law, their ability to exercise discretion, their problem solving skills, or the general practice of their craft. The teaming of officers in a patrol car is done in different ways. Generally, it involves the needs of the department, sometimes seniority, training, and a supervisor's assessment of these things. In some cases certain officers wanted to work together because they enjoyed each other's company or style of policing.

I worked a few day shifts in a car by myself, but most of my patrol work was done on the evening or midnight shifts with a partner. These partners were a mixed bag, to be sure. Some were great and others not so much. Most, though, turned out to be good partners after working out an initial period of give and take. One partner liked traffic work and had a penchant for stopping motorcycles. Another always wanted to get coffee as soon as he went in-service. It bothered him if we received a call before he could drink his coffee. One partner had a girlfriend who lived in a city quite a distance from our patrol area. He frequently wanted to drive into the city and have dinner with her.

These were all issues to be resolved. Since the partner who liked to stop motorcycles was enthusiastic and didn't mind working hard, it provided me an opportunity to learn about motorcycle violations. I wasn't much of a coffee drinker then, but my partner who liked starting his shift with coffee never took long and often took his coffee to go.

The partner with the girlfriend, however, endangered my career. If we were caught far outside of our area, we would have been reprimanded. After a couple of weeks riding together, I told him how I felt. He was receptive and arranged to meet his girlfriend a couple of times a week at a restaurant in our patrol area. All in all, I would have preferred not to stop a lot of motorcycles, stop for coffee, or have dinner with my partner and his girlfriend. I'm sure they found some bothersome things about me as well. Working a two-man car involved compromises, but in nearly every case, I learned from my partners.

Only once did I ask to have a partner transferred out of the car. He was hard to work with, and I didn't like him. I was slightly senior in patrol to him, but several years younger. From the start he acted as if he were the car commander who would guide us through each patrol shift safely. This wouldn't have been so bad if he'd been a good patrol officer. He wasn't. He liked to confront juveniles and because he was marginally tall (a little over six feet), he must have thought of himself as a big man despite his skinny frame. He would stand in front of an offending juvenile suspect, stick his hands in his pockets, and rock back and forth on the balls of his feet berating the young offender.

We worked an area of upper middle class housing and there were lots of juveniles. My partner had many opportunities to play out his tough cop fantasy. I told the sergeant there was a new officer coming to patrol. Since I had been in patrol for a number of years, I wanted to have an opportunity to be a training officer. The sergeant looked at me and asked the real reason. I told him I couldn't stand my partner. The sergeant said fine. The following week I was working with a new trainee.

Every once in a while, a patrol partner and I would click. This doesn't happen often, but when it does, it makes a great job better. Working a midnight shift was never fun for me until I teamed up with a partner who seemed to like police work as much I did. We worked in the southern part of the county and were deployed from our headquarters building.

We had no patrol stations in outlying areas, everyone deployed from headquarters. We took the freeway for our twenty- minute drive to our patrol beat (at about 80 mph). The minute we left headquarters, we were looking for crime. Many times we didn't make it to our area because we would catch a drunk driver, doper, burglar, or some other crook on our drive south.

My partner was a big man, standing at over six feet three inches tall. He was heavy, but not grossly overweight. We had been in patrol about the same length of time, but he was five years older and more experienced in life. He'd serviced in the military before becoming a deputy sheriff. He was a handsome man with a glib tongue. He could talk a suspect into letting us search his car even when the suspect knew full well there was dope in the car.

Prowling around in a patrol car in the middle of the night was the epitome of police work. Darkness and the lateness of the hour on the midnight shift gave us more probable cause to stop suspicious people. We liked to say more probable cause to screw around. A man walking down a residential street wearing dark clothes at eight o'clock in the evening isn't necessarily suspicious. Seeing the same man under the same circumstances at three o'clock in the morning gives the officer a duty to inquire why the man is out and about.

We took full advantage of our duty and responsibility to make those judicious inquiries whenever circumstances presented themselves. For six months we led our shift in the number of arrests. Some months we were the leading car for all three shifts. We were having big fun.

Early one morning we observed a car parked in the middle of a church parking lot. There were no other cars in the lot. We had never seen one there before at that time. Suspicious, we decided to check it out. We pulled behind the vehicle, turned on our high beams and spotlights. I approached first on the passenger's side, stopped at the edge of the back door. I could see a man in a sleeping bag lying with his head toward the right side of the car. I couldn't see the front seat. I let my partner know there was at least one person in the car. He approached on the driver's side, stepped forward of the front door, and faced the front seat. He let me know there was another person lying in the front. I heard my partner say, "Wake up and say good morning to the sheriff." This was a standard line.

The front passenger sat up. The rear passenger didn't move. His hands were inside the sleeping bag. Not being able to see his hands was worrisome. I could see his eyes were open. My partner engaged the driver in a relatively friendly way, asking who he was, where he was going, and why he was sleeping in the car. At no point was he aggressive with the driver. My partner behaved like a cop who was simply doing his job and upon answering his questions, the driver would be sent on his way.

Needless to say, my partner was wary of the guy in the *backseat*. He asked the driver to step out of the vehicle. The minute the driver's feet hit the ground, he threw his hands up saying he didn't have any guns on him. Now, no one had mentioned guns to the driver, although my partner and I were concerned about weapons in the car.

When the driver's hands went up, without any communication between us, we both drew our weapons. I opened the back door and pointed my revolver at the man in the *backseat*, telling him to slowly take his hands out of the sleeping bag. He complied, and I removed him from the car. Both men were handcuffed, and we searched the vehicle, first looking in the sleeping bag. I found a fully loaded M-1 carbine inside the sleeping bag. The men turned out to be escapees from a maximum-security juvenile facility. They were both nineteen and serving what we used to call hard juvenile time.

My partner and I were on the same wavelength all the time. We would see a particular car or a suspect and we both knew what the other was thinking and what we were going to do about it. I would know instinctively when he was going to stop a car, as he would know when I was going to pull someone over. We enjoyed working together. We made the most of our time during the six months we were together in a patrol car.

Regardless of how hard we tried, some shifts were slow. On a night when nothing much was happening, we decided to take the patrol car off road through a large tract of undeveloped area. Taking a patrol car off the road wasn't a violation of any rules, but it required a certain amount of caution. We were on a trail and interested to see where it would lead. We didn't notice the lights from our patrol district had all but disappeared. After a while, we came to a cliff, and to our surprise, we were looking at the Pacific Ocean. We estimated we were ten miles from our patrol area and five miles from any paved road. It wasn't a good time to get a call.

Our explorer instincts failed us, and we decided to head back before daylight. We figured we had forty-five minutes or so to get back to our patrol area. But there were lots of trails, and while we were heading in the right direction, we weren't going back on the same trail. We drove down a sharp decline and I floored it to make it up the other side. There was nothing worse than the sound of spinning tires. We couldn't make it to the top as the hill turned out to be quite a bit steeper than the downhill side. We were stuck at the bottom. We tried everything to get up the hill, but we were stuck.

If we called for a tow truck, we'd have to explain why and we'd have to give our location. We couldn't give our location because we weren't sure where we were. I don't remember what concerned us most, becoming the brunt of our fellow deputies' jokes for the next week, or bearing the brunt of the patrol sergeant's anger.

The hill we came down wasn't as steep as the one we were trying to get up, but there was no place to turn around. Finally, I drove as fast and as far as I could up the hill and, when we lost traction, I put the car in reverse, floored it again and with dirt flying everywhere we made it back to the top of the hill. The car was covered with dirt. Even the red lights on the roof were splattered with dirt, but the car seemed to be okay.

We headed off in a different direction where we could see the lights of houses, although it wasn't in the direction of our patrol area. At least getting to a paved road would allow us to get our bearings, and we could scoot back to our area with no one the wiser. It was one of the few times in my patrol career I prayed we didn't get a call.

The lights of the residential area grew closer. We were following an undulating trail. As we reached a rise close to the paved road, we saw two people sitting in a car on the trail in front of us, blocking our exit to the road. They appeared to be watching the sunrise. It was a beautiful sunrise. The man and woman seemed to be enhancing their sunrise experience by smoking dope. We looked at each other and couldn't believe what we were seeing.

I turned on the emergency lights. We saw the couple look at each other, and I'm sure they wondered why their car was suddenly filled with this soft red aura. *Wow, this is some good shit*, I'm sure was what they thought. The driver looked in his rearview mirror, looked away, and then looked again. To this day I swear I saw his eyes pop out like a cartoon character as he realized he was getting busted.

Now we had to call for a tow truck to impound the suspect vehicle and request a case number. It required us to give our location. We could either let them go or inform the radio dispatcher of our location, which meant the sergeant would know we were way out of our area. We chose the latter and were surprised not to hear from our sergeant. We learned later he had stopped for breakfast and didn't hear us requesting the tow truck and case number.

The man we arrested said he thought we never patrolled out in the hills, "You guys really patrol these remote areas?"

That we do, my friend, I thought.

THREE

THE DETECTIVES: PROS FROM DOVER

✼ ✼ ✼

Live as brave men and if fortune is adverse, front its blows with brave hearts.

– Cicero, 50 BC

Eighth Place

I really wanted to be a detective so I studied diligently for the test. I thought I had done well on the written examination and was confident I answered the questions in my oral board with great acumen. I knew I would receive a few extra points because of my education so, all and all, I was ready to become a detective except for buying some suits.

Two of my former patrol colleagues had been promoted earlier and were working in the Personnel Division of the sheriff's department. This was one of the "not real police work" assignments new detectives could be stuck in. I knew they would let me know the minute the new promotional list was published. There was even some hope, only on my part apparently, that they might slip me some inside information before the list was published. All of this didn't stop me, however, from going to their offices each day to see if the list was out, coming out, or if they had heard any rumors about the list and possible assignments for the deputies who would be promoted.

The longer I waited for the list, the more impatient I became. I started going to their offices twice a day, before and after my patrol shift. They were good-natured about it and appeared to find it endearing that I wanted to grow up and be a detective like them. It was taking, in my view, much too long for the list to appear. I was told all the data were at the county's Personnel Department, whose job it was to add the scores from the written and oral exams along with the automatic points awarded for seniority, education, and level of state certification. County Personnel would process the data and establish a numerical ranking for the first fifteen candidates with the highest cumulative scores. In this way, the theory went, the list would be free from any departmental or political manipulation.

One day, when I entered Personnel, one of the detectives signaled me to quietly come back to his office. He was in the office with the other former patrol colleague. His office was only a cubicle, so it was kind of crowded. In hushed tones they pledged me to secrecy. Slowly they lifted a notebook on the desk under which was the long-awaited promotional list. I looked at the first three places, but didn't find my name. Disappointment. I looked farther down the list and located my name in the number eight spot.

I wasn't completely discouraged. Perhaps I hadn't done as well on the written test as I thought. It was a tough test, and I remembered I had to make some best guesses on several questions. All the guys who took the test had been having long discussions about how many openings there would be and where the "drop dead" line would fall. The consensus was six people would be promoted to investigator off of the new list and if certain events happened, maybe seven. Being right below the "drop dead" line wasn't good, but often there were more promotions than anticipated.

I must have looked dejected when I left the office, but I thought I had put on a good face. I was scheduled to give a talk to a bunch of second graders at a school in my patrol area. I had been invited to stay for lunch. Since the teacher was a childhood friend, I had readily accepted. All of this helped fill my day and kept my mind off the promotion list and my mediocre showing.

On the long ride back to headquarters, I began to fixate on my poor promotional performance. It was disappointing I hadn't done better, especially since I had spent a lot of time studying for the test. I was either an idiot who couldn't take a written test, or I was an idiot whom the oral board couldn't see as having sufficient police skills to be a detective. Either way, whatever the circumstances for my poor showing involved the word idiot.

As I neared the headquarters, I received a message over the police radio to call one of the detectives in Personnel. I was a short distance from headquarters, so I didn't stop to call. When I arrived at the parking garage, both detectives were waiting for me. They had worried looks and asked if I was okay. They said I looked so sad when I left the office in the morning, they thought I was going "to do something stupid," as they phrased it.

Quickly they told me it was a ruse. The list they had shown me wasn't real. It was all a joke. The list was scheduled to come out the next day. They did this to get me off their backs. Obviously I was relieved, but I looked at them with a hurt expression and told them what a difficult time I had gone through. Actually, I thought it was funny, and it was a good joke on me.

When the list was published, my name was in the number two slot. Eventually I out-ranked them both. But, of course, I never let this long-ago cruel joke affect how I treated them—maybe a little.

Teaching the Little Bastards

When I was promoted to detective, I was assigned to the Juvenile Division. My job was to teach a high school course about law enforcement. The promotion made me happy. I was moving up in the organization. I saw it as recognition of my hard work. I would have been happier if I had been assigned to robbery-homicide, but I was given the high-profile teaching assignment, which was a plus. It also meant I would have weekends off, a first for me in a long time. I was never shy about standing in front of a group of people and speaking. I was sure it would be no different teaching high school kids.

It was unusual for police to be in a school classroom teaching a regular high school course. School anti-drug programs taught by police officers were starting, but many police administrators and school officials were dubious about the efficacy of these programs. We patterned our program for the schools after one developed by the Los Angeles County sheriff. Another deputy and I wrote the program for the department and personally presented it to the sheriff. He in turn directed the Juvenile Bureau commander to implement it. I was to be one of the first deputies in my force to teach the course at a local high school.

Although school officials were supportive of the program, especially since they were getting an additional teacher without any cost to them, there were concerns. While it was recognized that the major benefit of the program was having a cop on campus, school officials didn't want me to look like a cop or carry a gun. So each day I wore a suit to the classes. I never wore my uniform.

The gun issue presented some logistical problems. I started classes first thing in the morning and, of course, I would have my gun with me, since later in the afternoon I reported to the Juvenile Bureau. It wasn't safe to keep the gun in the trunk of my personal vehicle, which I drove to the school and from there to the sheriff's department. I kept the gun in the locked briefcase I carried into the classroom each day. I was told not to wear the gun, and I didn't consider having one locked in the briefcase the same as wearing it. I went through the whole school year this way without incident.

When I completed my bachelor's degree a few months into my teaching assignment I received a provisional secondary teaching credential. In the back of my mind I thought maybe, in my retirement, I could teach. This yearlong experience taught me many things. Among them was a respect for teachers. This was the hardest job I ever had. By the end of each day, I'd have a raging headache. I thought I had a brain tumor, but noted I didn't have these headaches on weekends and school holidays. When I arrived home at night, I would start thinking about my lesson plan for the next day. I found it difficult to sleep, and I'd start the next day tired.

While well intentioned, the school officials thought they should place every junior and senior student with a behavior problem in my class. Every day was like wrestling them to the ground to get their attention, teach them a little something, and keep them entertained. After the first couple of months, I knew I didn't want to be a teacher. But since this was my fledgling program, people were expecting me to make it successful. I felt my future in the department depended on me doing a good job.

The idea of the course was to teach students about the criminal justice system. What happens to someone who commits a crime? What are the powers and duties of the police? What can the police do and not do? Who are the police? What are the students' rights as juveniles? Their heads were filled with crap from television. It was difficult to convince them that just because they saw something on television didn't mean it was true, right, or smart. Some were amazed when I told them many things said on television weren't true.

Once, I had the students list all the make-believe crime fighters they could recall. They would shout out names quickly, and the list grew, although there'd be some arguments about whether a person from television was real or not. When asked to list any real crime fighters of national repute, the list started and often ended with the alleged closet cross dresser of the FBI, J. Edgar Hoover.

As an assignment, I gave the students a questionnaire. During the following week, they were to contact a police officer and ask the officer the questions I had given them. The questions were simple and involved the officer's name, department, assignment, what he or she liked about police work, and their educational level. Most of the students had never spoken to a police officer and had no concept of what a police officer was like. There were guidelines about where and when they could approach an officer and about how they were to conduct themselves. I thought my fellow officers would enjoy speaking with the students for the five minutes the exercise would take.

Most of the police officers were good-natured about the students and tolerated the inane questions. I was surprised, however, that some of the deputies were perceived negatively by many of the students. I was trying to enhance the image of the police in the eyes of the students and thereby maybe make the officers' jobs easier. Some deputies were working at cross-purposes to my efforts and for no good reason.

One day, one of the deputies who had been interviewed by a few of the students, confronted me in the locker room. All the students described the deputy as negative. The deputy asked me what I thought I was doing sending kids to ask him questions. I explained why we were doing the exercise. Surprisingly, he told me he thought it was a good idea. I told him the students who spoke to him didn't think he was friendly or helpful. He seemed surprised to hear this, but quickly recovered and told me he didn't give a shit. Truly, he didn't give a shit and left the department a few years later to pursue other interests. Good for him.

Fugitive Guy

There were two classifications of detectives in my force. We used the title investigator rather than detective. A grade-one investigator worked the more routine job assignments, such as arrest warrants, thefts, vandalism, minor assaults, bad checks, and other misdemeanors or non-violent felonies. The seasoned grade-two investigators who handled robberies, homicides, sexual assaults, frauds, and fugitive matters did the more interesting detective work.

By the time the school term finished, I had been promoted to a grade-two investigator without having worked a starting level detective job. I was assigned to the fugitive detail. This was a small detail and comprised three detectives. Never having worked any cases as a detective since I had spent my time teaching high school and, in some ways, missing the adventure of patrol, this couldn't have been a better assignment. The job was pure police work. Each of us had small caseloads of ten to fifteen suspects who had fled to California from other states to avoid prosecution. There were warrants for their arrest. Most of the time they were considered dangerous and often were suspected of being armed.

Arriving in the detail for the first time, the sergeant called me in for his routine briefing. The conversation was stilted because the sergeant was not a talkative person. I think the conversation was strained, too, because the sergeant didn't know what to tell me. Usually he would give this talk to the newly minted grade-one investigators who worked in the arrest warrant section, which was also under his command.

After five minutes of dancing around some awkward moments, he told me, "Handle your cases with as little fuss as possible. Get in and get out without causing a scene. Personally, I never found it difficult to handcuff an unconscious person."

"Okay," I said, "got it."

My two partners were like Mutt and Jeff. One was over six feet four inches tall and weighed more than two hundred and fifty pounds. He was an excellent athlete in college and had played pro baseball. He moved fast, belying his great bulk, and I was amazed such a big man with feet the size of a woman's didn't tip over when he stood. So very tall, and yet he wore size seven shoes. He was hard working, diligent, and easy-going. He had a manner about him most people found appealing.

My other partner was short and, although he purported to be five feet eight inches tall, the minimum height requirement for men to join a law enforcement agency in those days, he was hunch-shouldered, and this made him appear smaller. He had a dumpy appearance and an off-putting officiousness to him when he spoke to people. While my other partner was a free spirit and willing to try nearly anything, this partner was overly cautious. I would work with one partner for two days, then the other for the next two. During my two days off, they worked together.

My little partner considered himself glib and charming. This was especially so when women were involved. Working in the field, we often ate at various restaurants, but he liked Chinese restaurants. I liked Chinese food, but preferred more traditional foods. We happened to come across a Chinese/American restaurant. He suggested this was a great compromise for our disparate tastes in food, so we frequented the restaurant off and on for a month.

One night there was a new young, blonde waitress. Naturally we both gave her our business cards, in case she ever needed any help. This was what good police officers do. We were there to help. He was taken by this twenty-something tall blonde and regaled her with stories whenever she came by our table. While he was off to the rest room, I took a more direct approach since I was single and asked for her phone number.

A few days later, I called and made a date to pick her up after her shift, which finished about the same time as mine. We had a fun night during which she asked why my partner kept calling her at the restaurant. Maybe he's lonely, I mused. I met her brother with whom she was living. I thought he was a hard-looking case and had what appeared to me to be a jailhouse haircut.

He gave me only his first name, and since the girl was still using a married name, as she was recently divorced, I didn't have enough information to see if he had a criminal record. The whole situation didn't look good to me. A recently divorced woman living with her scruffy, down-on-his-luck brother in a cheap two-bedroom apartment should have given me pause. All men know a hard-on will drive you five hundred miles, but you always have to get up and drive yourself home. I wasn't going to pursue the relationship and forgot about her. We didn't go back to the restaurant, and I heard nothing from her.

Coming into the detail one day, my little partner told me the girl had called him. He was a little miffed I hadn't told him I was dating her. He told me she was going to call me back and I should wait by the phone. Something was wrong. When she called, she said needed my help. She had been arrested. This wasn't good, but throughout their careers, it wasn't unusual for cops to have friends and family get in a little trouble. They call for advice, and the smart cop will tell them to get a lawyer and otherwise stay out of it. Probably bad checks, I thought. I was shocked when she told me she had been arrested for armed robbery. She asked if I could help her get out of jail!

"You're in jail now?" I said, asking the obvious question.

"Yes, I was just booked along with my brother. This is one of the phone calls I get."

I told her I'd see what I could do and quickly hung up the phone. I called an attorney friend, gave him the circumstances, and asked if he would contact the woman and maybe represent her. He agreed to help her. I went to my sergeant and told him a woman I dated once, only once, was arrested for armed robbery. He wasn't too concerned and told me to put it all in a memo for file.

When I arrived back at my desk, there was a message from a deputy in the jail to call. Now what? The deputy told me she was placing the woman's property into inventory during the booking process and found my business card and my partner's business card in the woman's wallet. I told the deputy it was probably someone we contacted looking for a fugitive. I asked her to throw both cards away. I never heard from the woman again, but for years, I watched *America's Most Wanted* and wondered if she'd ever appear on the show.

The Demotion Test

Working in plain clothes gave me a window on the world without people knowing I was a cop. I saw weird and often funny things happen right in front of me. But when I think about the short amount of time I spent working as a detective, the strangest thing I remember was the manner in which my force dealt with the issue of women in police work.

The first year I worked for the sheriff, there was only one woman in detectives. She worked in the Juvenile Bureau. She'd been on the force for many years and was well respected for her expertise in handling juvenile matters. All the other women on the force held civilian positions or were matrons. A matron was basically a woman jail guard.

By the time I had finished my academy training, the matrons had been reclassified as deputy sheriffs, and though they hadn't gone through the same training as the male deputy sheriffs, they had the same authority and legal status. Future women, however, would go through the same training as the men. The supervising matrons were reclassified as sergeants, and the head matron became a lieutenant. The lieutenant would compete on promotional exams and become a captain. She was my first captain when I made lieutenant and was one of the best bosses I had in my police career.

There wasn't much opportunity for these women outside of the jail. The common wisdom of the time was that patrol wasn't a place for women. By the time I made detective, the matrons had been deputy sheriffs for seven or eight years. One of the sergeants was tired of working in the jail and wanted to expand into other areas of police work. She had always wanted to be a detective, and the Juvenile Bureau was scheduled to expand. She applied for one of the new positions. Since sergeant was a higher rank than investigator, she believed it was only a matter of taking a demotion and being transferred to the bureau.

Things aren't always as easy as they seem. Since she had been recruited as a matron, trained as a matron, and became a sergeant through a reclassification, it was decided she would have to take the investigator's written and oral examinations first. If she passed and was selected, then she could demote to the position for which she had to compete. There was some logic in there somewhere, I suppose. She did compete and was demoted.

When someone was promoted, everyone went out for drinks following the person's last shift at their old assignment. The newly promoted person was feted, given congratulatory cards, slapped on the back, and wished luck. Here, however, we were breaking new social ground and had an opportunity to start a new tradition of the demotion party. I attended the party, and it looked pretty much like a promotion party but to my knowledge, it was the only demotion party we ever had.

She settled in quickly to the Juvenile Bureau and competently handled her caseload. She was a studious-looking woman who wore thick glasses and had an English teacher quality to her demeanor. She found some solace in the mentoring by the only other female investigator who had been in the bureau for nearly twenty years. The men in the bureau were less empathic and became apoplectic when it was discovered she couldn't qualify at the shooting range. She simply was a poor shot. The issue was settled when she was told not to carry a gun. There was one detective who worked in robbery-homicide who had the odd habit of carrying his gun in a lunch bag, but this was the first time we had a detective who was unarmed as a matter of policy.

When looked at with less emotion than was swirling around at the time, she was working juvenile matters and most of the work involved interviewing juveniles and their parents in the sheriff's headquarters. There wasn't much chance she would be in a big shootout. She was a smart woman who learned detective work quickly but like all of us, would make mistakes.

One of her cases involved child abuse by a stepfather who had a violent history of criminal behavior. She obtained a warrant for his arrest and scouted out the suspect's house. Knowing her limitations and the suspect's violence-prone history, she called on her fellow detectives for help in making the arrest. She found herself briefing the others about the residence, its location, and the suspect's description as she passed around copies of his mug shot from a previous arrest. She drew a map on the chalkboard and marked the targeted house as the third one on the left.

She was in the lead car with two other cars, loaded with detectives, following her. Everyone was ready for a confrontation since the suspect had resisted arrest in the past. There were at least eight officers, and they all knew what they were going to do when they arrived at the house. Three would go to the back door, one would knock on the front door and kick it in if necessary, and the rest would enter the house with some of them deploying to the upstairs and others would handle the search for the suspect downstairs. They were like a well-oiled machine and were ready for action.

Field operations of this nature involving lots of planning and a crew of seasoned officers should go smoothly. There was no need to rush and certainly no need to drive fast. There was something about going to serve a warrant on a bad guy, or maybe it was getting a bunch of cars following each other that does weird things to the drivers. They started out at normal speeds but as they neared the target, the lead car picked up speed. With the newly demoted investigator in the lead vehicle, they hit the suspect's street doing about fifty mph. She screeched to a stop, the second car screeched to a stop tapping the first car's back bumper, and the third car had to go up on the sidewalk to keep from smashing into the back of the second car.

Everyone jumped out and headed for the house. The investigator held up her hands and said, "No, wait!" She put her index finger to lips, looked around at the house, looked up and down the block, and quietly said, "This doesn't look like it."

She had turned on the wrong street. They were one street away from the suspect's house. By the time they arrived at the right house, he was long gone. Later in the day, he turned himself in at a local police station. The *Keystone Cops* action of this group of detectives probably prompted his surrender.

The department slowly provided more opportunities for women, but this investigator enjoyed her work in the juvenile bureau. She spent the rest of her career in the investigation division working many different assignments. Unlike some detectives who lose their work ethic after many years, she was always considered a hard-working and knowledgeable investigator. But she never learned to shoot straight.

What the Dope Cops Taught Me

Before I made detective, I had the opportunity to have a couple of previews about working in plain clothes. One of my patrol partners had a friend who was a narcotics officer. My partner and I patrolled a large canyon area on our midnight shift, and there were many caves in the hills on both sides of the canyon. We had heard rumors about those caves being used by people to smoke dope. Some of the caves required quite a hike from the road to reach them. Others were a long way up from the roadway, but we found a way to drive to the top of the various hills and walk down to some of the higher caves.

Occasionally we could hear people talking loudly in the caves from the roadway. This was always a tip-off to get out of the car and head toward the caves. The watch commander didn't like us spending too much time checking out the caves because it would require us to be away from our radio for thirty minutes or longer. Remember, this was before each officer had a personal radio on his or her gun belt. When we walked away from the patrol car and followed the wooded trails to the caves, we were on our own.

We never had much luck in capturing anyone. Most of the time, they would either hear us or see us coming. So my partner talked to his friend in narcotics, hoping to generate some interest by them. They didn't seem interested when he told them, but before he left their offices, they invited both of us along on our night off to check out the caves with them. Maybe being in plain clothes in an undercover car would be more helpful in catching the people. During our patrol checks of the caves, we had found many indications of drug use, and in some cases, people had dragged furniture up to the caves and made them rather comfortable.

I was going to work with the narcotics officers and I was excited. For many officers, being assigned to narcotics was the high point of their careers. Here I was with only a few years in patrol, and I was going to spend a night working with them. Visions of major narcotic arrests danced in my head. I picked up my partner at his house and headed into work. I was surprised he had a mixed drink in his hand when he got in the car. I was then and am today a teetotaler, and while I don't object to people drinking, I thought it unwise to drink before you go off to do police work. I didn't have the courage to say anything to my partner though.

In the narcotics office, there was a lot of joking around among the detectives. They pitched pennies to see who would pay for coffee. There was a lot of general grab-assing between the officers from various teams. My partner and I hung around trying to look seasoned and interested in what was happening. He did a much better job of looking as if he belonged in narcotics than I did. My partner even joked around with his friend. I didn't think I had a good lay of the land and said nothing. I wanted to make a good impression and didn't want any of them to think I wasn't a good cop. After nearly two hours of doing virtually nothing, my partner, his friend and his partner, and I headed to the parking garage to get our undercover car.

It wasn't much of an undercover car. It looked like all other detective cars except it had white sidewall tires. The police radio was mounted inside the glove box. Our first order of business was dinner. During dinner, they each had a mixed drink. That was two for my partner, but I wasn't counting (out loud anyway). The rules of the department allowed undercover officers to drink on duty. Actually, the rule stated that undercover officers could drink if such drinking was required in the furtherance of their duties. Undercover narcotics officers trying to purchase narcotics in a bar, for example, were allowed to consume alcohol. But we weren't trying to buy narcotics in this restaurant; we were having dinner. Who was I to point out the discrepancy?

By the end of the meal, we were over three hours into the shift and finally headed toward the caves. Halfway there they stopped off at a liquor store and bought a six-pack of beer.

We all had a beer in our hands, and one of the officers said, "Listen, if you want to be good dope cops, there's a little trick you'll have to remember."

He then opened his beer, took the pull-tab, and put it into the beer. "We don't want to overlook a pull tab in the car and have someone bitch to the sergeant," he said in what appeared to be all seriousness.

Wow, this was my first lesson in how to be a dope cop. Almost forty years later, I still remember, but it was made obsolete by the invention of pop-tops on cans.

The talk in the car was inane and covered a wide range of topics except anything to do with police work in general or narcotics specifically. I was hoping to learn about narcotic suspects who lived or worked in our patrol area or any information about narcotics that would be helpful in my job as a patrol officer. There was nothing. My partner and I starting talking about some of our dope arrests and it seemed we were giving the narcotics officers much more information than they were giving us.

Our partners for the night wanted to know where the closest cave to the road was located. We directed them to a trail located on fairly level ground. It was five hundred yards from the main road, but the cave was concealed by heavy brush. By the time we reached the cave, one of the officers was breathing heavily despite the fact it was an easy walk up a slight incline. A couple of vagrants had apparently fled the cave upon hearing us coming up the trail. We discovered the vagrants had been using the cave as a campsite. There were some cigarette papers but no evidence of any narcotics. We headed back to the car and I asked them if they wanted to check out some of the other caves farther up the trail. They looked at each other and said they didn't see the point. We went back to the car, and they told us it was time to call it a night. It wasn't even ten o'clock.

At their office they told us they had paperwork to do and we were dismissed to go home.

I wondered what the paperwork would say; we drank coffee, went to dinner, bought some beer, taught two patrolmen not to leave their pull-tabs in the undercover car, looked at a cave, and came back to headquarters. They had to rest up from all the work. As I drove my partner home, I railed against the waste of a good night off. My partner was more sanguine about the whole affair, saying the officers were good solid cops who knew their stuff. I doubted it.

Two different narcotics officers approached me a couple of weeks later. They asked if I wanted to work a case with them. I wasn't so sure, but I said yes. This involved me working undercover purchasing a large quantity of LSD, one of the most popular drugs at the time. They said they would speak to their boss who would speak to my boss about me being loaned to narcotics for a month. When I saw them again, I learned my boss had said no. The patrol division couldn't afford the overtime to fill my vacant position for a month. They did get permission, however, for me to work with them during my time off. Since I worked midnights, this meant I could spend evening shifts and my days off with them. But, sadly, there was no money to pay me, and I would have to volunteer. I wanted to get ahead in my force, so I did whatever was required and didn't expect to get paid for it. I volunteered.

I don't know if they asked me to work this case because I looked young or because I was driving a '58 Triumph TR 3, a type of car no cop would ever own. I came in early on my first day dressed in my best undercover clothes. I wore old Levi's and a blue button-down shirt (starched and pressed) with the shirttail hanging out. They told me I looked like a cop on his day off. They suggested I wear chinos with the same shirt but tucked in. They wanted me to look like a college student. I asked how I would hide my gun if I tucked my shirt in. They said I wouldn't be wearing a gun when I was making buys.

"Oh," I said. I drove home and changed. When I returned, they were pitching pennies to see who would buy coffee. I lost and had to buy ten cups of coffee. Not only was I not earning any money for this work, I was losing money.

The first night was spent watching the suspect's house and monitoring the traffic going in and out. There were lots of people approaching the door, staying a few minutes, and walking away. The next night was spent doing the same thing, but I didn't have to buy the coffee.

On the third night, I was introduced to an informant who knew a friend of the suspect. The informant was to introduce me to the friend who would take me to the suspect. The friend wasn't home, so we rescheduled for the fourth night. The friend was home the next night, but he was busy and couldn't take me to meet the suspect. The narcotics officers had the next two nights off, so the case had to wait until they came back. I went about my regular patrol duties waiting for a call from them.

By the middle of week, I was back with the narcotics officers, and we had made arrangements with the informant to meet the friend who would vouch for me with the suspect. The friend climbed into my TR-3, and we drove the short distance to the suspect's house. The suspect invited us in, and I told them I wanted to buy a hundred tabs of LSD. The suspect told me to wait in the living room. In a short time, he came back with a small package containing the dope. I paid him with the marked money the officers had given me. I left with the drugs and drove to a nearby gas station where I met the narcotics officers who had been following me. They took the LSD, said thanks, and sent me on my way.

That was it. Several days later, armed with a search warrant based on my purchase of the drugs, they kicked in the door and arrested the suspect and his friend. I didn't get to participate in the fun part. I did eventually have to go to court to testify in the case. It was a fairly routine trial and both young men were convicted. While waiting to testify, during one of the breaks, the suspects, who were out on bail, walked by me in the corridor and in a threatening manner called me a snitch. They didn't have a clue I was a cop until I was in the witness box. I could see their expressions change and some color drain from their faces when they heard me say I was a deputy sheriff.

I was never asked to work another narcotics case, but from time to time, I would see other young-looking deputies heading toward the narcotics bureau carrying coffee. I wondered if they would learn to put the pull-tabs in the beer can, too.

Sitting on a Toilet and Other Fun Things

The next time I worked undercover, I was working for the vice detail. The vice officers had asked me to work, again on a volunteer basis, with them on a vice problem in a public toilet located near a beach. The vice officers had received complaints about illegal sexual activity taking place. Men were soliciting other men for sex in and around the toilets. They wanted me to be a decoy. I said yes without thinking about what this meant.

The following Saturday afternoon I found myself with two detectives heading for the beach. When we arrived at the restrooms, they told me to go into the restroom and sit on the toilet to see if anyone would bother me or solicit a lewd act. They would be standing by in their car. If anything happened, I was to leave the restroom, signal them, and point out the culprit. This didn't sound like a good idea to me, but who was I to question the wisdom of a detective?

I sat on the toilet for over two hours listening to people come and go in the restroom. No one approached me or spoke to me, and in some cases, I doubt anyone even knew I was there. I didn't know I would be sitting on the toilet for so long, and I didn't have anything to read. It was a long, boring two hours and nothing was accomplished, not even a bowel movement. We ended the operation and headed back to headquarters.

On the way back, they asked if I'd be interested in working with them again. I was direct with them and said I thought this was a waste of time. I told them I wasn't interested in hanging around toilets. They told me they had a more serious case involving a bar where a sexual predator had been picking up young men and sexually attacking them. The bar was also in a beach community, and they wanted me to work the following Friday night. They assured me that I would have plenty of backup officers watching me throughout the operation.

The next Friday night the vice detail sergeant briefed me. Then we drove to the bar with a total of four vice officers. The bar was popular with the gay community. It had a dance permit, the drinks were cheap, and the music was loud. I had never been in a gay bar before, so I tried to act nonchalant and not too prissy, but I was amazed to see men dancing together. It was a whole new world and I had never been in such a world before that night. At twenty-five years old with four years in law enforcement, I was surprised at my own naiveté.

I was in the bar as bait hoping that the sexual predator suspect would be attracted to me. But, of course, we didn't know who he was, although we had a vague description from a few of the victims. I ordered a soft drink, stood against the wall, and watched what was going on and who was coming in and out of the bar. There were many young men, but also a fair share of older and middle-aged men in the bar. I could see a few women, real women, not transvestites. That was a positive statement, but in truth, I guess I didn't know if they were real women. Occasionally one of the vice officers would drift in, have a drink, look around, and leave. I was surprised, but they didn't stand out as cops. They blended right in with the mixed crowd of patrons.

Several men asked me to dance. When the first one asked me, a slow tune was playing. I used a line that women had said to me, "I don't dance slow."

Eventually I did get out on the dance floor with a couple of guys and danced to some fast numbers, but my heart wasn't in it. I kept thinking, *Is this really what I signed up for? Is this the romance and glory of police work?*

As time passed, I felt more at ease until a man about my age walked up to me carrying a pair of handcuffs. *Is this a cop who's going to arrest me?* I wondered. Sometimes, different law enforcement agencies will get their signals crossed and two different agencies will end up working the same location without knowing of the other's presence. I shot a quick glance at one of the cover officers standing at the bar, but he wasn't looking in my direction. The man with the handcuffs told me he wanted to take me home and hooked one of the cuffs through a belt loop on my trousers and the other cuff to his wrist.

I decided my best course of action was to act tough. Using lots of bad language, I told him to take the handcuffs off me or I was going to beat the crap out of him. What I didn't realize was that he had four friends with him who, upon hearing my challenge, stepped up next to him. They pointed out that there wasn't much of chance I was going to beat the crap out of anyone and that I'd best calm down. Standing behind his four friends, I saw two of the cover officers and felt this was a fight we could win, but I figured it would be best to talk my way out.

The two of us talked for a while and eventually he lost interest in me, took the cuffs off my belt loop, and all five of them walked out of the bar. Was this the sexual predator? Maybe, but we never saw the guy again.

I was briefed that if anyone solicited a lewd act, I was to go outside with them, get in my car, and drive them to a nearby hamburger stand where the cover officers would swoop in and make the arrest. The guy with the handcuffs never made any type of solicitation and, in fact, sex never entered our conversation. There was nothing to be done in that case.

I hung around the bar another hour, danced a few dances with my new friends. One of the cover officers actually asked me to dance, but I turned him down, telling him he wasn't my type. I danced with one man who, after the dance, asked if I wanted to go back to his apartment for a drink. The apartment was nearby. I said no. He then told me that he would give me $25 if he could have oral sex with me. I said I wasn't sure, but that we could go and have some coffee. He and I got into my car and drove to the hamburger stand.

When we arrived, I thought the cover officers would jump out of their cars and arrest this guy. Before anything happened, he got out of my car and told me he was going to buy us coffee. In a short time he came back to the car with two coffees, and he began pressuring me about oral sex and boosting his offer to $50. The conversation dragged on for another ten minutes. I was running out of things to say. It dawned on me that the cover officers were messing with me. They wanted to see how long I'd sit in the car with this guy.

I told the suspect to hang on a minute, and I got out of the car, walked around to the passenger side of the car, and told him to get out. When he asked why, I told him I was a cop and he was under arrest. I wasn't carrying a gun, and I didn't have any police identification. Nevertheless, he got out of the car and put his hands up. I was searching him when cover officers finally drove up. It was obvious they were having a good time. I could see they were still smiling.

The cover officers asked why I didn't wait for them. I told them they must have had their heads up their collective asses, so I decided to take the necessary action. Later they told me how dangerous it was for me to arrest the man without them being there. I pointed out that the dangerous thing was not following the plan and making a joke out of the situation. I was never asked to work vice again.

When the Crooks Win

Cops don't win sometimes. One of my friends who was working in patrol was asked by detectives if he'd be willing to work a few evening shifts with them. Like me, he was excited at the opportunity to work in plain clothes, make his bones, and impress the detectives with his police abilities.

There was an auto-theft ring creating havoc in several coastal communities in our county. The detectives told my friend that two Porsches had been taken from a restaurant parking lot while the owners were inside having dinner. Since my friend owned a nice-looking Porsche, they asked to use his car as a decoy.

He agreed and spent five nights hiding in the bushes around the restaurant parking lot watching his precious car and waiting for the thieves to strike. Nothing happened. No one went near the car. The stakeout was called off. It was too expensive to maintain a stakeout when the rate of Porsche thefts had abated and, apparently, the thieves had moved on to greener Porsche pastures. Maybe they didn't like the color of his car.

My friend returned to patrol work with nothing but memories of his glory time on a stakeout with real-life detectives. The restaurant, however, played on my friend's mind. It was a nice restaurant overlooking the ocean and was popular for its cozy, romantic dinners. He'd never been inside the restaurant and wanted to give it a try.

He and his wife arrived one night for their romantic dinner a few weeks after the stakeouts. The view from the restaurant was great, the dinner was excellent, and the entire ambiance truly super. My friend had had a few drinks and, as he walked to the parking lot, he thought perhaps the booze had affected his memory. He couldn't see his Porsche in the spot across the parking lot away from other vehicles where he'd left it. Many Porsche owners have the habit of parking away from other cars in parking lots to avoid door dings. He thought he'd done this, but in his alcohol-induced, mildly addled state of mind, he wasn't sure.

There was no panic as he walked the entire parking lot looking for his vehicle. The realization that the Porsche thieves had struck entered his consciousness only slowly. The irony of the crooks taking the car of a cop who had spent several cold nights trying to catch them wasn't lost on my friend.

There wasn't much left of his Porsche when parts of it were located in a chop shop the following month. This car was not only his first Porsche, but it would also turn out to be his last. While left "Porsche-less" for the rest of his life (a sad state of affairs), he was left with a great story about his nascent experience working undercover.

Some say time will heal emotional wounds. For my friend, after a while, he was able to tell the story with great aplomb. The story became better and funnier as the years passed even though the crooks won this time.

FOUR

SERGEANTING

✵ ✵ ✵

Success didn't spoil me, I've always been insufferable.

– Fran Lebowitz

There Are Only Two Good Jobs

I was told early on in my career to take every promotional examination for which I was eligible. By taking these exams whenever possible, it helped me hone my test-taking skills and, if nothing else, gave me a shot at getting promoted. As soon as I met the minimum qualifications to take a test for a higher rank, I would take it. I did this despite the fact that maybe in the eyes of others I didn't have enough experience to move up to the next rank. One day I read a notice on the bulletin board in the fugitive detail that there would be a sergeant's test in a few months.

I signed up, studied, took the test, and passed. A few weeks after passing the written exam, I bought a new sincere suit with a testifying tie and tried to dazzle an oral board panel with my brilliance. The panel consisted of a captain, a lieutenant, and a senior, experienced sergeant. I must have sounded better than I actually was, and I was surprised when the list came out. I was ranked number two, which meant I would be promoted in one to six months, depending on when an opening occurred.

Most of the promotional vacancies were the result of retirements or terminations from the force. The department was growing slowly, so people on a promotional list hoped for rapid attrition within any higher rank. My work in the fugitive detail was enjoyable, but becoming a sergeant would make me a boss. I thought I would enjoy supervising even more. Many people told me there were only two good jobs; the one you used to have, and the one you're going to get. I would frequently repeat that adage throughout my career as advice to younger officers.

When I reported to work one day, the sergeant called me into his office as I was passing his opened door. He handed me a sealed envelope and said, "Congratulations."

I tore open the envelope and read the memo that stated I was promoted to the rank of temporary sergeant. Temporary? What the hell did temporary mean? Apparently I said this out loud, and my sergeant looked at the memo, chuckled, and said he had never heard of such a thing. I was the first temporary sergeant he'd ever met. "Perhaps," he joked, "they don't think you're going to be a sergeant long. How's your health?"

I trudged upstairs to see the brainpower in the Personnel Office. No one was in except some secretaries and two officers whom I knew from patrol. They had jobs doing the background investigations of new applicants. The two of them decided to chime in and set my hair on fire with sage advice such as, "Don't let them do this to you. I'd turn the promotion down if I were you. This is a slap in the face; file a grievance."

None of this sounded wise since I still didn't know why temporary was attached to my promotion. When the captain of Personnel came through the door, I followed him into his office. Halfway through his office door he changed direction and was startled to see me walking toward him. We nearly collided. "I take it you want to see me," he said.

I wanted to scream and shout since I thought there was a conspiracy afoot to screw me over and he, the personnel captain, was part of some cabal bent on my humiliation.

Instead, I simply asked what temporary sergeant meant. He explained that a lieutenant was taking a leave of absence, so one of the sergeants was being promoted to temporary lieutenant, and I was to fill in for the sergeant who was filling in for the lieutenant. Okay, it was relatively clear in a bureaucratic kind of way, but when would I become a permanent sergeant? I already knew the answer; it would depend on when a sergeant or someone of higher rank retired or otherwise left the force.

The captain explained the intricacies of temporary promotions. The personnel rules required that anyone working a higher-ranking position for more than thirty days was entitled to the full benefits of the higher position. I was pleased to learn I would actually wear sergeant's stripes and be paid as a sergeant. The captain told me I would be a temporary sergeant for at least six months. He thought an opening for permanent sergeant would be available by then. As I was leaving his office, I remembered to ask where I was going to be assigned. I'd be working in the main jail.

To say I was apprehensive about working in the jail was an understatement. I had never worked there, and I didn't have a clue about how it operated. This jail housed the full spectrum of criminal types, from murderers to petty thieves and unfortunate types who failed to take care of a traffic ticket. Yet, I was going to be supervising the deputies who babysat about a thousand of these prisoners. I walked into the afternoon briefing two weeks later in my new uniform complete with sergeant stripes and wearing my "Pretty" key case on my trouser belt. It was strange to be in uniform without wearing a gun.

Another sergeant showed me around for the first half of my shift, then left me on my own. It wasn't rocket science. It was fairly easy as long as everything was going according to plan. If the prisoners decided not to beat each other or to eat their meals in the mess hall without attacking the prisoners who were serving the food or if the prisoners didn't try to escape, then the job appeared to be routine. The sergeant told me if I had any questions I could call him or ask one of the deputies. Nothing untoward happened the first night, and I left feeling more confident. I knew then, however, that the adage was true. The really good job was the one I used to have working fugitives, and my next job had to be better than working in a jail.

The next afternoon I arrived for briefing and another sergeant handed me the briefing book. "You're acting lieutenant tonight," he informed me.

Boy, I was moving up. One day as a jail sergeant (albeit temporary) and the next day I'm the acting lieutenant. I must have done an outstanding job the night before. There was only one lieutenant scheduled on each shift and he was the jail watch commander responsible for the women's jail and two branch jails located in other parts of the county. My head was spinning. I would even have my own office on the first floor. The distinction between temporary and acting was clear. As an acting lieutenant, I would earn my sergeant's salary and I wouldn't be in the position for longer than thirty days. In fact, I was only a "pretend" lieutenant, as I liked to call it, for one shift, but I liked the subtle differences between supervising and managing.

About one hour into my first shift as the watch commander, it dawned on me that the lieutenant was responsible for the count. One of the most important responsibilities of the jail was to make sure the prisoners didn't get out. If we didn't count them periodically, we wouldn't know if a prisoner had escaped. I knew enough about jails to know an escape is a bad thing. The count was important. Math wasn't my strong suit, and I wasn't exactly sure how the count was done. We counted the prisoners twice during my shift. I was relieved to learn the watch commander didn't do much with the count. An administrative deputy prepared everything, handed me some papers, and I signed them.

The first count went fine with all prisoners accounted for in all the jails. The later count was more problematic since the count from one of the housing units didn't match the number of prisoners who were supposed to be housed there. Several extra deputies scrambled to the questionable housing unit and all the prisoners were held in place until the deputies resolved the difference. After ten minutes, I was sweating profusely sitting at my desk praying there hadn't been an escape on my watch. Finally, the deputies located the missing prisoner who had been transferred to a medical ward right after the first count. Someone forgot to remove the prisoner's name from the housing unit's personnel list.

After a month of working various shifts and supervisory assignments in the main jail, I began to relax and think about what I wanted to do when my permanent promotion came through. I didn't want to work in the jail for the next two or three years which was the customary and usual assignment for a new sergeant. But this seemed to be what the immediate future held for me. I was resigned to it.

Occasionally there would be some excitement. Sometimes an arresting officer and the suspect he was booking in the jail didn't hit it off. A suspect once released from his handcuffs in the booking cell, often wanted to take out his frustrations on the jail deputies who had nothing to do with the suspect's arrest. Then, too, some prisoners liked asserting their power over other prisoners. This frequently happened in the mess hall and from time to time, other prisoners would join in the fray. Maybe these events, I thought, would keep me sane for the next couple of years. But I kept thinking about my next assignment, whatever, whenever, and wherever it might be.

My permanent promotion arrived in a short ten weeks. On my last night in the jail, I was assigned to the first floor. I was responsible for making sure the booking process went smoothly. I was also responsible for the jail records section staffed by ten female civilian employees.

They processed the various booking forms into a simple computerized system, ran record checks to see if the people being booked were wanted elsewhere, filed property receipts for prisoners' money, jewelry, and other property, and answered inquires from the public about bails.

The records section was housed in a secure location away from prisoners. It required a long walk outside of jail security, down a corridor, and through several locked doors. Near the end of my shift, I was told I was needed in jail records. When I arrived, the supervisor of the section told me the water cooler bottle was empty and asked me to replace it. These were large, heavy glass bottles. They were unwieldy to lift from the floor where the bottles were stored.

Here was a chance to demonstrate what a gentleman I was and to show the women my physical prowess. I removed the empty bottle, set it on the floor, and grabbed a full bottle with one hand. As I lifted it from the floor by its neck, it slipped slightly, and I reached for it with my other hand. I tapped, merely tapped, the bottle against one of the other full bottles on the floor and both of them broke. There was an eighth of an inch of water everywhere covering the wiring for the Teletype machines and phone lines. Some of the water was seeping into the back of one of the computer's processing unit.

My first jail emergency happened on my last night and, much to my chagrin, it was of my own making. Two of the three Teletype machines stopped functioning. Every prisoner was booked into the jail with those machines. They were critical to the booking process. Without them, the entire booking process would come to a screeching halt. Fortunately, it was a Thursday night and the jail wasn't busy. One dry, functioning machine kept things running.

Two inmate workers (trustees) came to clean up the mess and various emergency repair people were called in to fix the Teletype machines. The watch commander ordered me to stay in jail records until everything was back to normal. I spent most of the three overtime hours writing a property damage report trying to make myself not look too stupid or clumsy. Ten weeks in the jail and it was my first and last jail report.

Keeping the Records Straight

During the school year when I was teaching the Students and the Law program, I would return to the Juvenile Bureau in the afternoons. At the end of the first semester, the number of classes I was teaching dropped from five to three. So I would arrive at the Bureau around noontime. The detective captain had been bending my ear about computers since he discovered I had enrolled in a graduate program studying communications.

I'm sure he thought the program was about computers, but it was related to interpersonal communication and more in line with management classes. At first, I couldn't understand why he would come to my cubicle often and talk about the pros and cons of various computer programs for the detective bureau. Maybe the vice cops, who worked under his command, told him I was a good dancer. Perhaps he was lonely or none of the other detectives was interested. I finally realized he thought I was studying computers. Naturally, I rushed to the library and tried to garner some knowledge of computers in the criminal justice system.

The detective captain was a larger-than-life character. Not only was he physically large, but also he had a quirky, almost hippy-like quality about him. He shaved his head and was known to wear an earring. He had worked narcotics for many years and was an expert in some type of martial arts. He had piercing, crazy eyes that made me think he was out on a weekend pass from a mental health ward. He was married to an artist and he, too, was an artist of sorts. He took great photographs and, along with his plans for computerizing the records in the detective division, he would share his photographs with me.

He wasn't the kind of guy I felt comfortable around, but he treated me nicely and I figured it couldn't hurt to have the detective captain as my rabbi. Rabbi, in police work, is someone of a higher rank who helps and mentors a younger officer interested in promotion.

When my school schedule changed, I started arriving at the Juvenile Bureau before noon. The captain invited me to lunch once or twice a week. He would also invite the captain of the Records and Identification Division. The Records captain, too, was an odd duck. Now I say this not from the standpoint of a young detective at the time, but as a person who's had many years to reflect.

He was as different physically and emotionally from the detective captain as night from day. The Records captain started in the force as an identification technician (ID tech). He moved up through the ranks, always in the ID Bureau, and he never did any other type of police work. He was so short he sat on a pillow when he drove. He was gray and balding (more balding than gray), though probably only in his mid-fifties. He wore wire-rimmed glasses, which accented the dark circles under his eyes. I saw pictures of him in earlier years, and he looked old even then. But his looks were deceiving. He was a firecracker of energy. He spoke rapid-fire, used big words that he usually mispronounced, and tended to be a tangential speaker. His favorite topic was automation of departmental records.

Why these two captains invited me along on their luncheons is still a mystery. They never told me any secrets, even though I was mindful they might let something slip, so I listened closely when they spoke. They would, on occasion, grouse about some of their employees or the undersheriff or sheriff, who were their two bosses. I never received any inside scoop from these two, and I made sure I never repeated anything they told me regardless of how harmless or even how well known the information might have been. Perhaps, I thought, this was all a test to see if I could keep confidences. Today I would have told them that I can keep a secret; it's those other people I tell who can't keep a secret.

I shouldn't have been surprised when my permanent sergeant's promotion wasn't in the jail as I had anticipated but in the Records Bureau. True, I wouldn't be working the jail for the next two to three years but I'd be working in records. I wouldn't supervise any law enforcement personnel, but rather about forty female civilian employees. Here was another chance to demonstrate my dexterity in changing water bottles.

Unlike jail records, the Departmental Records Bureau was located in the heart of the headquarters building. Patrol deputies, detectives, and many supervisors and managers were in and out of the Bureau each day to run records checks, get mug shots of suspects, obtain police reports, and check on the status of evidence that had been booked into the property room.

On the weekends, I would be the Bureau commander responsible for the day shift records operation as well as the operation of the ID Bureau. My days off were Monday and Tuesday. There were many fun things to do with these two days off, I mused. The girl I was dating was a woman who supervised the statistical section of records, and of course, she had weekends off. Don't complain, I kept telling myself. There was only one records sergeant, and it was an important assignment even if it wasn't my idea of what I wanted to do. I told myself to make the best of it.

I had a nice office with a big glass window that looked out over my domain so I could see the strange collection of women I supervised. Actually, there was a clerical supervisor who watched over the daily operation of records. She had three other women who managed the three different sections of records, one of whom was my girlfriend. The clerical supervisor was a knowledgeable and sophisticated person. She knew what was happening throughout the department.

On the first day, I told her I was dating one of her supervisors. She already knew. She told me she would handle all issues that involved my girlfriend. She told my girlfriend to avoid my office when possible. With a clerical supervisor like that, I figured the job was going to be much easier.

During the afternoon of my first day, the clerical supervisor came into my office carrying a Kotex dispenser. She put it on my desk and told me my first priority was to fix it. Well, she had come to the wrong guy. I explained that I was repair challenged. In my whole life to that point, and unfortunately even today, I never have been able to repair much of anything. Invariably any repair attempts by me made matters worse. But the former sergeant had done minor repairs around the Bureau, she told me.

"Not me," I said. I suggested she speak with my girlfriend, who had first-hand knowledge of my lack of repair skills. She went off to speak to my girlfriend and a few minutes later, she came back laughing after hearing some of the horror stories of repairs gone wrong. She took the Kotex dispenser to a sergeant in the ID Bureau for repair.

The Records Bureau was staffed by women who ranged in age from eighteen-year-olds fresh out of high school dealing with their first job to older women who had worked for the sheriff's department for many, many years. The former were smiley and enthusiastic, and the latter, more often than not, were dried up trolls who would look at me as if I were the enemy come to do them harm. They were a varied group. I couldn't think of two more unlikely people to manage them. They were being led by the perfectly strange Records captain and inexperienced me.

The captain had managed them for years with few outward signs of problems. My predecessor, who had retired, had been in his position as the Records' supervisor for twenty years. I never heard a bad word spoken about him, and people consistently described him as a nice man. No one described me like that, nor would they ever. Clearly, I had my job cut out for me.

There was a week of orientation to the new job. At the end of the week, I took stock of things. I had a nice office, wore a suit to work each day; I was learning an important, but often overlooked, aspect of police work, and working eight to five like normal people. Mondays and Tuesdays off weren't so great for my social life, but the benefits of the job outweighed any downside, even the downside of working directly for a peculiar individual.

I enrolled in a fingerprint classification course. A large part of the work in Records involved this skill. After many months of study, I was able to classify a set of prints. This was not easy to learn, but the more I practiced the more efficient and accurate I became. This bit of knowledge, however, was short lived. It didn't have much shelf life because within ten years, fingerprints became automated throughout the state, and eventually the system I learned was no longer used. I filed it away with the other piece of useless knowledge like what to do with pull-tabs.

Most people in the force believed the Records captain was the department expert in computers and, though he had some off-putting idiosyncrasies and foibles, he was extremely knowledgeable about our record keeping system. I eventually learned that, while he knew a lot of things, he didn't understand the basics of automation. There were major gaps in his understanding of computers and their capabilities.

Strangely, he would eschew other new technologies. Cassettes (he pronounced the word CAS set) were, in his opinion, unreliable and uncontrollable. The department had a state-of-the art voice reporting system whereby a patrol deputy or detective could simply make notes and call the report into a special number. Typists in Records would transcribe the report, process, and distribute it. Handwritten reports weren't allowed, even in cases where it was cheaper and easier to write short reports. When a deputy had his notes ready, he would find a pay phone and advise the dispatcher he wanted to call in his report. The dispatcher would tell the deputy what phone line was available (there were five), and the deputy would call in his report. He would also be reimbursed for the dime it cost to make the call from a pay phone. This, in itself, was a time-consuming bookkeeping operation. I think it cost more to keep track of the ten-cent reimbursements than the reimbursements themselves.

The reports were stored on an endless loop-type recorder. The idea of a deputy carrying his own cassette recorder was abhorrent to the captain. He had designed the system and defended it against any instrument or procedure that would lessen its importance. The fact that the machines were frequently in disrepair, reports were lost, the quality of the reports suffered, and it was inefficient, time-consuming, and unreliable didn't sway him.

I knew all of this and it should have given me pause before I drafted a memo suggesting deputies be allowed to write rather than record one page reports. I suppose it didn't help that I railed against the old system and at one point even referred to it as "a stupid waste of time." I wasn't on my way to becoming his favorite sergeant.

I'm not sure if it was my memo about recorded reports in and of itself that gave him grief or the fact that I sent copies to both the patrol and detective captains. My captain didn't like to confront people face to face. Instead, he would call three or four people together and "lay down the law," as he liked to say, to the whole group when his tirade was obviously meant for a particular person. So he never yelled at me about my memo, but he did yell at a group of us a few days later explaining why my proposal would never work.

He mentioned something about people needing to fully understand how the Records Bureau worked before trying to implement change and some people (me is what he meant but wouldn't say) shouldn't distribute memos to other divisions. Well, of course, he was right. I had no business sending copies of the memo to the other captains. The whole affair was worthwhile as it opened my eyes to the fact that the captain had no administrative courage and his frequent rages, during which he would throw things and shout, were simply empty bravado.

We were the largest law enforcement agency in our area and automating our records system was a major undertaking, so many different vendors would seek us out to see what we were doing. We didn't have any money to do anything. The vendors, however, assumed the county would fund a major computer program in the future. The vendors wanted to hear what we had in mind, explain what they could do to help, and, in so doing, place themselves in a good position should a request for a proposal be put out to bid.

The captain usually invited me along to these meetings, and I looked forward to them for one reason. I enjoyed watching the reaction of these men, who had years of experience with large prestigious companies, to the comments the captain would make. The men would have pens ready to take notes when the captain began to speak. Then I could feel and almost hear a change take place in the room.

At first, the men would shift their eyes from colleague to colleague, and occasionally they would glance over at me. I would be nodding as the captain extolled his crazy vision of what was needed. Eventually the pens were abandoned, and you would see a glazed look in their eyes. The claptrap the captain was espousing was mostly gibberish infrequently punctuated with a comment that made some sense, but not necessarily related to what he had said previously. I once tried to keep track of how many words he mispronounced during one of these meetings and noted a rate of about one every few minutes. Sometimes, when the vendors would ask him a question, they would mispronounce the word back to him.

As time went on, I began to feel sorry for the captain. He was a widower, he was nervous about a newly elected administration that would take office in six months, and he was well past the time he could retire. We became friends in the limited way colleagues do when thrown together by happenstance in the workplace. I was glad for the opportunity to work with someone whom I look back on now as maybe unique rather than odd.

Having worked with this difficult personality, I knew I could work with any of our captains.

Get Off Your High Horse

In the late sixties and early seventies, it was fashionable for law enforcement agencies to form riot squads. Often they were euphemistically called by a variety of names none of which contained the word "riot." The Watts riots in 1965 alerted many California police forces that they were ill prepared to deal with major public disturbances. A less destructive but equally troubling phenomenon for the police was the nascent tradition of rock festivals sweeping the country following Woodstock.

In 1969, my force decided our officers needed training in civil disobedience and the handling of large crowds. The department formed a sixty-man group specially trained and equipped for those purposes. The squad consisted of volunteers from throughout the department. As a young patrol deputy anxious to gain experience, I joined the squad for the potential excitement and the specialized training. The neat riot gear the members received was also an inducement. Assignment to the new group was an ancillary duty. No one was assigned on a full-time basis, as we didn't have a riot or a rock festival scheduled routinely.

The department administration also, finally, saw a need for a special weapons team to handle situations involving armed, barricaded felons in a more professional manner. The members of the special weapons teams had regular patrol and investigative duties in addition to their part-time work training for those infrequent, but often volatile situations where an armed suspect would refuse to surrender. A bomb squad was formed as well. These members were highly trained to handle explosive devices. They, too, had other regular police duties to perform, but were called when explosive material was found.

An unusual set of circumstances came together on a jail bus transporting about twenty-five deputies for special duty in a county park on an Easter Sunday. The park had historically been the scene of unruly crowds. One of the sergeants on the bus asked if anyone had horse riding experience. Two of us said we did and the sergeant came over to speak with us.

There were horse stables next to the park where horses could be rented. A plan was devised whereby the sergeant would get permission to rent a couple of horses for us to use throughout the day for crowd control. This would be an added dimension to the abilities of our special group.

Though the two of us were in our regular patrol uniforms, not dressed for riding a horse, we made do. The owner of the rental string of horses gave us two of his best horses (as best as we could get considering the sorrowful repertoire of behaviors these animals learned from so many encounters with poor riders) and off we went into the park to the amazement of many.

The scene in the park was surreal. It was a large park and on Easter, and several other holidays throughout the year it was packed to capacity. People were picnicking on every blade of grass available. Most days the park was under-utilized, and it was a peaceful, bucolic, and enjoyable place to bring a family. There was a small lake, trails for hiking, many large old oak trees for shade, and it was beautifully landscaped in a naturalistic style.

On holidays, it would fill mostly with people who would drive many miles from other counties to enjoy the park. The heat, the booze, and the mere frenzy of bravado combined to make the overcrowded park a place where groups of picnickers often antagonized each other, and fights would break out. Any enforcement action, regardless of how minor, would cause a tense and frequently hostile reaction from onlookers. Teenagers would steal bikes from younger children, people would drink to excess even though alcohol wasn't permitted, and drivers would speed along the narrow one-way roads winding through the park.

We spent the day on horseback watching over the deputies on foot as they asked people to pour out their beer in lieu of being cited, broke up fights, or tried to get people to turn down the volume on loud radios. The day was a success for the reemergence of deputy sheriffs on horseback, even if under such humble circumstances—rental horses, improper uniforms, and no training in crowd control from horseback. On horseback, we had made a significant difference in the ability of our force to maintain peace and security in the park.

A few months later, the Mounted Squad was official, and it became part of my ancillary duties for many years. When I made sergeant, I eventually became one of the supervisors for the Squad. Over time, more deputies were added to the Squad. Some would bring their own horses for mounted patrol work. We received more training and the department, through donations, acquired horses. The donated horses were stabled at an honor farm, one of our branch jails.

In the past, the Squad had looked a little worn, but as it grew the tack for the horses and the special uniforms for the deputies improved. As a deputy in patrol, a detective in the Juvenile Bureau and fugitive detail, as a sergeant in Records, and eventually as a sergeant at the training academy, I was part of the Mounted Squad. I was always surprised to see how effective police officers can be on a horse, yet how willingly the general public accepted them. Except, of course, when they crapped near their picnic—the horses, not the officers.

For the first two years, most of the deputies rode rental string horses. They had to be good riders to deal competently with these often-stubborn animals. One day as several of us were waiting by the stables, I overheard one of the workers telling another to get "Crazy Charlie" for the string of six horses we were renting. Hmmm, not the horse I want to ride, I thought. As they brought the horses, I took Palio, a horse I had ridden previously. Palio was a big, well-behaved horse, and he was easy to ride. The others selected their horses, and we walked them over to the park office a short distance away. I noticed the deputy leading Charlie was an experienced rider; at least he purported himself to be an experienced rider. He was from Oklahoma, so I figured he probably was.

The sergeant conducted a short briefing in the office. Following the briefing, we went out to mount up. The deputy tightened Charlie's cinch, and I watched as the horse danced around. The deputy climbed aboard and, as his butt hit the saddle, Charlie took off at a full gallop with his rider barely hanging onto the saddle horn. I saw Charlie and his now nearly dismounted rider fly across a large grassy knoll. Picnickers scattered in all directions some carrying small children out of harm's way. So that's why they call him Crazy Charlie. I guess I should have said something, I mused.

The deputy was unseated quickly. He hit the ground hard. Charlie headed back to the stables at a more leisurely trot, having calmed the demons that possessed him moments before. The deputy walked back to the park office through all the people he and Charlie had dislodged from their picnic spots. Some of the people laughed, but most were concerned and asked the deputy if he was okay. He was limping slightly and wasn't smiling. I was thinking of clever things to say, but I thought better of it. We were about the same height; however, he was solidly built and was a rough and tumble kind of guy. I didn't want to be the cause of him becoming more pissed, and mostly I didn't want him to beat me senseless.

The incident happened so quickly none of us had time to react. We stood there and watched the drama unfold. When the deputy reached us, he asked if we saw what happened. "Sure did," we all responded.

"That horse is crazy, I had to step off of him," he told us. The crazy part I already knew, but I didn't say anything. The stepping off part didn't jibe with what we saw.

One deputy mumbled, "He got throwed!" No one had the heart to contradict the poor deputy's face-saving effort. Years later I would hear him tell the story about the crazy horse Charlie, and how he had to step off the horse when it broke and ran.

Like Charlie's rider, I had some embarrassing incidents on horseback as well. I enjoyed police work from high atop a horse. One of my first forays as a sergeant with mounted crowd control came on a busy holiday in the same park. By mid-morning, the crowds were so large that county officials closed the park. There wasn't any more room for more cars.

There was a long line of cars at the park entrance waiting for vehicles to leave so they could drive in. Others had parked along the rural road leading to the park and were walking in carrying their picnic supplies, blankets, coolers, small BBQs, and children. It was easy to keep the cars out, but there was no effective way to stop people from walking into the park.

Alcohol wasn't permitted in the park, but we weren't able to keep it out either. As the sergeant, I was riding alone taking stock as to what was happening in the park and the state of the crowd. I could see lots of drinking and obstreperous behavior. I was noting where to concentrate the ten mounted deputies already patrolling. My attention was drawn to a loud gathering of young men not far from the park entrance who were arguing. Some picnic tables had been moved from one picnic site to another to accommodate a large group of people who were occupying the tables. The young men were all shirtless, drinking beers, and arguing with some of the men at the picnic tables. The two groups were in various states of intoxication. One group wanted some of the picnic tables, accusing the men of having stolen the tables.

I moseyed over with my horse, a large and well-trained animal unflappable in crowded situations. My thought was to ride between the two groups and break the whole thing up. As I approached, the head picnic table thief yelled at me to get my horse out of his face. Yep, sure, I thought, as if that was going to happen. I rode past him, and he grabbed my leg and tried to pull me off the horse. I side-passed the horse into him and broke his grip on my leg. He stepped back, threw his beer on the ground (now I knew he meant business) and said, "Get off that fucking horse and I'll kick your ass!"

"Done," I responded as I dismounted.

By the time both of my feet hit the ground I was hit six or seven times by fists coming from every direction. I fell to one knee, covered my head with one hand to protect it from the blows, and held onto the horse's reigns with my other hand. Both groups seemed to want a piece of me. This wasn't good. Fortunately, within seconds, two mounted deputies who saw me heading into the crowd were on the scene breaking things up. Deputies on foot patrol ran into the crowd, and the guy who started the whole thing was arrested. I was shocked at what happened. Except for my pride, I was uninjured. "Why did you get off your horse?" was the constant refrain that day whenever I recounted the incident.

When I acted cocky as a teenager, my mother would tell me to "get off my high horse." It was good advice at the time, but I learned when you're already on your high horse doing police work, don't get off.

Shoeless and Clueless

In January 1975, a newly elected administration took over from the previous sheriff who had served the county more than twenty-five years. The department had been rampant with rumors about what changes the new guy would make. There was talk about which captains would retire, be promoted, or transfer to other assignments. This was heady stuff. I had never heard of a captain being transferred; captains usually were promoted from within the division they were working and spent the rest of their careers heading those divisions. Everyone was anxious about the potential changes.

Many people believed that the retiring sheriff had spent his last years in office going forty mph in the fast lane. The only changes were those that couldn't be avoided. Innovation usually didn't find fertile ground in his administration, but I had found the old sheriff receptive when, along with another deputy, I proposed putting deputy sheriffs in high schools to teach the Student and the Law program. Nevertheless, I was looking forward to what the future would hold with the new, younger, and more enthusiastic administration. But I didn't think anything was going to happen right away to me.

In February, a month after the new sheriff took office, I was rotated out of Records to supervise the Identification (ID) Bureau. The Records captain decided that one year of me in Records was enough for him. I felt the same. My impression was that he thought I was a little too familiar with him, and I had failed to demonstrate sufficient fear during his far too frequent outbursts of anger. He tired of me telling him to stop yelling, calm down, and cautioning him about the potential for a stroke.

My position in Records was filled by a long time ID Tech Supervisor whom most people believed lived in genuine fear of the captain's tirades. A more studied observation, however, revealed a decorated war veteran whose passive-aggressive nature served him well when dealings with the captain. He avoided the captain as much as possible, and the captain, in my opinion, preferred his new sergeant's behavior over mine.

I was in my new windowless cubbyhole of an office in the ID Bureau on my first evening shift when the Patrol watch commander appeared in my doorway. I was unpacking a few personal items into the small cabinet I was allocated, as the office was used by me and two other sergeants. The watch commander said, "Don't unpack."

Earlier in the day there had been a large staff meeting with the new administration and all the captains. A big transfer and promotion list was expected in a few days. To my surprise, the watch commander had the rough notes from the staff meeting and a penciled copy of the yet-to-be-published transfer list. Sure enough, in a scrawled penciled hand was my name. "You're going to the academy," he said with a smile. There it was on the list, me to the training academy as a tactical sergeant.

The watch commander was grinning, I supposed, because he was in possession of information to which no one else was privy. Nothing excited him more than the ability to demonstrate he was in the know. It was doubly exciting if, after sharing the information, he labeled it as confidential. He asked me not to tell anyone else. This ensured he was able to share his secret with others and pledge them to secrecy as well.

The watch commander, who had keys to every door in the headquarters building, had gone into the conference room where the staff meeting had been held. He rifled through the wastepaper baskets and retrieved the rough notes from the meeting. I had two concerns. Did the rough notes accurately reflect what the final transfer list would show? My other concern was not being able to share this new information as the watch commander had pledged me to secrecy. My latter concern was mitigated later in the evening when I saw the watch commander showing one of the Patrol sergeants the transfer list. Upon seeing me, the Patrol sergeant congratulated me on my transfer. So much for confidentiality.

When the list was published, it was exactly the same as the rough draft I'd seen a few days earlier. The only woman lieutenant in the department was promoted to captain and transferred to the Personnel-Training Division. The academy fell under her new command. She had been the first and only head matron in the women's jail, then the only woman lieutenant on the department. As of her promotion, she was then the first woman captain in the department. Upon her retirement in later years, she would become the last female captain we had throughout my tenure with the department. Ironically, today a female sheriff heads our force.

There were three tactical sergeants assigned to the academy who supervised the basic recruit training, reserve officer training, and in-service training. A fourth sergeant managed the firing range and supervised all firearms training. Tactical sergeant was a plum assignment. With my penchant for spit and polish and my interest in lifetime physical fitness, it was an ideal place for me. I couldn't wait.

In my view of the police world order, tactical sergeants were role models. They were, in my vision of things, in good physical condition and well turned out in their uniforms. The tactical officers (seasoned patrol deputies) were responsible for the daily training of the classes. They would make sure instructors arrived on time, supervised the trainees during breaks, instructed them on physical training, and made judgments about the trainees' potential as law enforcement officers. The sergeant's job was to supervise the entire recruit training process, considered the major component of the selection process for newly hired officers.

Not everyone subscribed to my view apparently. The reality of the academy was different. The lieutenant who served as the academy commander was anything but spit and polish. He did have a clean and pressed uniform, but his belly hung over the front of his pants. He liked to wear a "janitor" type of silver metal retractable key holder with a large number of keys attached to it. When he walked, besides jingling, he had a tendency to lead with his stomach, projecting anything but a commanding presence. Exercise wasn't part of his daily regimen. He didn't like our new captain and gave the impression that it was somehow demeaning for him to work under a person he considered less competent. Mostly he didn't like working for a woman.

This was troubling to me since I knew it would never bode well for the academy leader to be in a pissing contest with his boss. The commander had much more experience than I, but I had learned early on that while it was perfectly acceptable to think I was better, smarter or more deserving than my boss, it was incredibly stupid to let them know I thought so. Within the first few weeks of my arrival, he told the staff he thought the captain was stupid, yet he had no clue as to our loyalties.

One of the other two tactical sergeants had spent a long time as a detective before his promotion to sergeant. He had worked as a supervisor in the jail and, at one time, was one of my patrol sergeants. He wasn't one of my favorite patrol sergeants. Now we were of equal rank, and I wanted to tell him what I thought of him when I was a patrol deputy. I thought I was better, smarter, and more deserving but I didn't tell him.

This guy was a mess. He had a reputation for laziness. He didn't spend much time putting his uniform together and even if he had, he was the type of person who always looked dumpy in a uniform. He wasn't a role model for the trainees. The term "soup sandwich" would be an accurate way to describe his appearance.

Besides his appearance, he had the galling habit of working hard to get out of work he was supposed to do. He'd leave work early, having spent the day doing as little as possible. He didn't exercise, and loudly distained those who did, which didn't encourage trainees to keep fit throughout their careers. Although retirement was some time off for him, I think he spent his days dreaming about it. Comfort was always his first priority, and he would sit in his office with his shoes off and his stocking feet perched up on his desk. If he needed to go into the classroom to speak with the recruits, he would do so without his shoes. He and the lieutenant got along well.

The other tactical sergeant looked good in his uniform and was well skilled in the field of weaponless defense. He assisted another instructor most afternoons teaching the trainees the use of the police baton, how to disarm someone, handcuffing techniques, and general self-defense. He had a reputation as someone a cop would want in his corner, and he impressed the trainees, who weren't always impressed.

During his tenure at the academy, he was involved in the forming of a bargaining unit for the deputy sheriffs. The union eventually ran a candidate against the incumbent sheriff when he ran for election after his first four-year term of office. The union and the administration had a tenuous relationship and, because of this, the sergeant's career prospects suffered. When I arrived at the academy, he was looked upon with some suspicion by the new administration.

There I was, now the new kid at the academy, surrounded by a boss who openly disliked the captain, one colleague who was lazy, another who wasn't trusted. I was probably considered the one who didn't know what he was doing. I soon learned my role there was to keep an eye on things. I was never told that exactly, but both the captain and her boss called me directly about issues at the academy bypassing the lieutenant. To cover my bases, I always told the lieutenant about who called, what they wanted, and what I told them. I think he appreciated my position and my honesty with him.

One day the lieutenant and the shoeless sergeant disappeared. One minute they were in their offices, the next they were nowhere to be found. The captain called me and asked if I knew where they were. I didn't. A few minutes later, the chief deputy (the captain's boss) called and asked me the same question. I told him also that I didn't know where they were. He pressed the point, but I convinced him I really didn't know.

Around six o'clock, I heard the two of them come into the building. They were both in civilian clothes, and it was nice to see the sergeant was wearing shoes albeit tennis shoes. He didn't look much better in civilian clothes. They were laughing and joking with each other and talking about baseball. Since the academy was only a few blocks from a baseball stadium, it wasn't difficult to figure out where they spent their afternoon. The short time I spent in detectives was paying off. I told the lieutenant about the calls, but he wasn't concerned. They each went to their offices, picked up some items and clocked out for the day, satisfied with a hard day's work done well. I never learned why the captain and the chief deputy were looking for the lieutenant, I don't know if the lieutenant called them back, and I never found out if either of them got in trouble.

I spent the next fourteen months at the academy working with the recruit officers, the reserve officers and, for a period of time, dealing with the in-service training requirements for the deputy sheriffs who had graduated from training. Within a short period of time, the two sergeants were replaced with more appropriate supervisors and a little later the lieutenant was also transferred. I wondered if the lieutenant's transfer was the result of the day he ditched work for a baseball game, his often-scathing comments about the captain, or the bosses recognizing that he was miscast at the academy. I think it was the latter. The academy began to take on a more professional appearance, but then we were attacked.

FIVE

LICKSPITTLE AND OTHER MANAGEMENT STRATEGIES

✯ ✯ ✯

This above all: To thine own self be true,
And it must follow, as the night the day,
Thou canst not be false to any man.

– Palonius to Laertes, Act I Scene III *Hamlet*, Shakespeare 1602

Sucking Up

I was young and impatient, and while I had a great assignment at the training academy, I was fearful my career was at a standstill. In addition to my duties at the academy, I was still on the Mounted Squad, and this required monthly daylong training sessions during which we tried to hone our riding skills. During one of these training sessions, a deputy in a patrol car came by our training site and told me to report immediately to the sheriff. I rushed off to the headquarters building and located the sheriff and his three chief deputies in a conference room. I knocked on the open door and stood in the doorway sweating, dirty, and smelling of horses. One of the chiefs asked, "Is this how you dress for a meeting with the sheriff?"

I was wearing jeans and a tee shirt, which was what we normally wore during our training days. Stammering to answer, I managed to explain where I had been and why I was dressed as I was. "They told me to get here right away," I explained. "They said it was important and to hurry," I continued to ramble. They were all staring at me, and then they smiled, and I realized they were having some fun at my expense.

They continued to joke with me about how I smelled, how I was dealing with my colleagues at the academy, and the wordiness of a report I had written for the captain suggesting ways to improve our training process. The captain had shared the report with them. I kept wondering what they wanted. I knew I wasn't getting promoted, as I was number ten on the lieutenant's promotional list and, so far, only two people had been promoted off the list. Transferring out of the academy was a possibility, but why would they call me in to headquarters to tell me? Transfers were done in writing and weren't handled personally by the sheriff or his chiefs.

They had a special assignment for me. A highly charged political issue had arisen involving the command of eighteen district attorney investigators. The county board of supervisors wanted to transfer the investigators out of the district attorney's office and into the sheriff's department. The district attorney had irritated the board by pursuing some legal action that the board felt impinged on its authority. Naturally, the sheriff was mildly empathetic about the district attorney's plight, but we wanted to have those investigators in our shop.

My assignment was to draft the arguments and legal authority for the transfer of the investigators. The sheriff asked me to report directly to the chiefs, who would review and approve my work. I worked out of my academy office. My lieutenant and captain were told that my special assignment was a high priority and my other academy duties were to be borne by the two other sergeants. This didn't endear me to the sergeants but my discomfort was overshadowed by the enjoyment of working directly with the big bosses.

The chiefs liked my work, and I held my own against whoever the district attorney had writing rebuttals to the reports I wrote. Ultimately the courts sided with the district attorney and prevented the board of supervisors from transferring the investigators. I was told that, despite the loss, I had impressed the sheriff and the chiefs. Soon they sent other specialized staff work to me. It wasn't unusual for one of them to call and speak with me about a variety of issues confronting the department. For the first time in my law enforcement experience, I had the benefit of hearing directly what the key department administrators were thinking. I liked the rarified air of corporate decision-making.

Messages from the top often become completely and utterly detached from their original meaning and intent by the time they've reached the rank and file. A police force is no different from a large organization, and seeing this communication artifact first hand and its negative effect on the organization shaped many of my ideas about management theory. It was one of the prime factors in choosing communications as a course of study in graduate school.

In a large law enforcement agency, promotions within the lower ranks are generally a matter of testing and time. Officers who were good test takers, were well spoken, presented a good corporate image to the interview panel, served the appropriate amount of time in rank, and who had done a good job, always scored well on promotion lists. But, in climbing the law enforcement corporate ladder, officers can discover that higher ranks are elusive and not so straightforward.

People can get lost in a large organization. Showing up each day and doing a good job won't necessarily garner you the favorable attention of the bosses who make the promotional choices. Exposure, however, can be troubling if the bosses don't like what they see. In my case, I was fairly certain the chiefs and sheriff liked me and judged my potential with the department in a positive light.

In the mid-seventies, the department was poised to expand, and our county of 1.2 million residents would explode over the next twenty-five years to a population of more than three million. The subsequent expansion of public safety resources, my incredible deftness at "sucking up" and taking advantage of my exposure to the big bosses, and the good luck of having joined the department at the right time provided the opportunity for rapid promotion.

Even with only ten years on the force, I saw all of this clearly and vowed to productively utilize each opportunity coming my way. When the old lieutenants' list expired and my name died on the list still seven candidates away from promotion, I applied for lieutenant a second time. I studied hard and passed the written test with a high score. I felt I had done well during the interview panel, but I wouldn't know the results until the new promotional list was distributed. Two weeks after everyone had finished with their interview panels, the list failed to appear. Three weeks passed and still nothing.

Something was going on, but none of the other sergeants who had taken the test with me had any information. I received a memo one day directing me to report to a conference room in our main building. I had studied for the test with a friend who was also a sergeant. He had received the same memo, but had no other information. On the designated day and time, I walked into a conference room to find nine other sergeants milling around all discussing why they had been called together. They had all taken the promotional examination, and some were speculating that maybe someone cheated or stole a copy of the test.

The chiefs walked into the conference room together, sat us down, and congratulated the ten of us on passing the lieutenant's test. We were all rank ordered on the promotional list, but they didn't tell us our ranking. They told us this was the final list, and it would be distributed in a few weeks. Regardless of whatever happened the following week, the list would remain the same.

Our attention was riveted. What were they going to do to us next week? We wondered. The ten of us were going to an assessment center. Our assessment center would be a three-day process during which outside evaluators would put us through a battery of tests and simulation exercises designed to test our ability to competently perform the duties and responsibilities of a first line police management position. I knew several police forces had used this process to select their lieutenants and captains. They were also used to help guide city managers in choosing police chiefs. We were told this was a grand experiment. The administration would compare how they rated us on the promotional list with the outside evaluators' rating.

The following Monday we candidates were standing tall in a conference room of a local hotel trying to look confident as we made introductory small talk with a college professor who owned the company doing the assessment, a city manager from a large city, and a local police chief. These were our assessors. There we were, all freshly scrubbed, being careful not to spill coffee or say something stupid before the assessment officially began.

As I looked around the room, I realized that, with the exception of a friend who was about three years older than me, the rest of group was five to ten, and in one case, fifteen years older. Nearly all had military experience and they all had far more experience in either patrol or detectives. They had been sergeants much longer than my two and a half years in rank. In trying to put a good spin on things and keep some positive energy flowing, I reminded myself that I was quick on my feet. I had had some great experiences doing specialized staff work for the administration, and I thought the work I had done for the sheriff and chiefs would be considered important. My competitors didn't have anything similar in their backgrounds.

The three days went by in a never-ending series of psychological, managerial, and self-assessment tests of various types interspersed with complicated group problem-solving scenarios. There were also three one-on-one interviews for each candidate with each of the assessors. At the end, I was exhausted, but felt I had held my own and was sure the assessors would beatify me. I knew that self-evaluations were, as Sam Goldwyn once quipped, like a verbal contract and not worth the paper they were written on. Nevertheless, my personal assessment of my performance kept me sane for the next two days while waiting for Friday when the original promotional list would be published.

I was number one on the list. I was beside myself with happiness, or maybe just full of myself. I humbly accepted congratulations from around the department and worked diligently not to act too arrogantly. When the excitement wore off over the weekend, it occurred to me that there weren't any openings for lieutenant so my promotion wouldn't be immediate. One of the chiefs spoke to me about the assessment process I had gone through. He assured me I'd be promoted in a few months, but that I should know I wasn't one of the top candidates chosen by the outside evaluators.

They had selected three sergeants whom they felt had the type and variety of experience that would serve them well as lieutenants. Poor me; I was in the middle of the pack because of my lack of experience. They thought, I was told, that while I had some highly specialized staff experiences there was a lack of sufficient field experience to be a lieutenant. At first I was devastated, then realized they were right, then thought, screw it, I'm number one on the list, and I'm going to be promoted regardless of what the assessors thought. I never thought about promotional assessments until a few years later when I was asked to be an assessor by the college professor who owned the company we had hired for our grand experiment. Our force never used an assessment process to assist us in our promotional decision-making while I was there.

I went back to work at the academy, but stayed alert for news of any pending new lieutenant openings or of any captains or lieutenants who might be contemplating retirement or be near death. In the meantime, I continued to practice my "sucking up" skills.

The Wall

A new lieutenant was assigned to the academy. He was a contemporary with whom I had worked in patrol. He was a rising star in the department and was on the top of the captains' promotional list. Those of us at the academy didn't think he would be with us long. I certainly was hoping his time would be short since I was at the top of the lieutenants' list. If he were promoted, I would be promoted and probably be assigned to one of the jails. Most sergeants, lieutenants, and captains rotated in and out of the jails with each new promotion to a higher rank.

Even though the lieutenant understood his time at the academy would be short, it didn't dull his enthusiasm. Right away, he began making appropriate and long overdue changes to the curriculum and the procedures by which the academy operated. No one had ever taken the time to look at our training procedures from a systematic point of view, and no one had ever tried to make significant changes.

We were all pleased when initial changes were underway. We were ready for change. When the state made the decision later in the year to completely revise the entire basic peace officer course of instruction, our academy staff was well positioned to assist the state in its efforts. There was one thing, however, that drove me crazy, and it didn't appear as if it were going to change.

The entire training staff was housed in a modular building. The three tactical sergeants and the lieutenant each had small, dark offices. The lieutenant's office was a littler larger than the sergeants' offices, but it was cluttered, making it appear darker and smaller. On the left side of the lieutenant's office was a nine-foot wall covered with cork. On every inch of the wall were memos, calendars, procedures, newspaper clippings, cartoons, rosters, and various bits of paper. Each academy commander had added to the collection, but none had ever removed much of anything.

When there was a question about a policy or a procedure, I had watched the commander turn to his paper-strewn wall, look around, and finally locate the appropriate page of ephemera for the answer. There was no order to how things were posted on the wall, there was no priority as to where material was posted, and there clearly wasn't any discernible criteria used to determine what would or would not be posted. I suppose, for most of the commanders, it had to do with how frequently they thought they would need the posted material. Maybe it was something they didn't want to forget.

I wondered why they didn't have nice, orderly files in their desk drawers until I saw the drawers too were chock full of files and miscellaneous papers. The top of the desk was littered with stacks of files and a jumble of detritus. Anyone who entered the lieutenant's office wouldn't be imbued with a sense we were an orderly, well-run training facility.

I was promoted to lieutenant at the same time the academy commander was elevated to the rank of captain. He was transferred to the jail where he assumed the duties of the Jail Division commander. It was difficult to explain how the entire department or I reacted to the news that I would move into the academy commander's slot. Something like this had never happened.

I knew the job and thought I'd do well. But I also knew several senior lieutenants had been vying for the position. There wasn't much chance I was going to turn it down and ask to be sent to the jail with the new captain. The chiefs and sheriff must have believed I was the right choice. I wasn't about to argue with their assessment of my abilities. I had spent a lot of time at the academy working all three of the sergeants' positions, so I knew there weren't many training issues I couldn't handle.

The tactical sergeant's position was a plum assignment but this was a dream assignment. The academy trained nearly every law enforcement officer in the county. It was housed on the grounds of the shooting range used by many of the police agencies. The operation of the range was the responsibility of another sergeant, but the administrative responsibility rested with the academy commander. I was moving into my new position when the state was completely overhauling the basic peace officer course. It was a major undertaking for the sixteen or so law enforcement training centers scattered throughout the state. As the academy commander, I was to be the sheriff's representative on a statewide committee established to oversee the changes. I was ready for this new prestigious assignment, or so I thought.

My first order of business was to tackle the offending, irritating wall of paper. I knew I wouldn't be able to sit in the office with the oppressive wall of irrelevant ephemera bearing down on me each day.

One of the secretaries wheeled in a large trash barrel and within an hour, I cleared the wall of every scrap of paper. I tossed about 90percent of the material, including several outdated calendars, numerous outdated memos, a recipe for Yorkshire pudding, old promotional lists, a cookie of unknown vintage or ownership wrapped in a sandwich bag, several tasteless and inappropriate cartoons, a current and obviously well-used baseball schedule, and many old class schedules and rosters.

Next, I turned my attention to the desk drawers. I didn't know how many pens and pencils I would need during the course of my daily routine, but I was fairly certain forty-five was far too many even though half the pens no longer worked. The file drawers were completely full, and it looked as if adding even a single sheet of paper would cause the drawers to burst. I took everything out of the drawers and, after carefully scanning the files for importance, put it all in boxes and placed them in a small warehouse building used as a storeroom for the range. I did the same with the piles of paper, which had nearly covered the top of my desk. The range sergeant wasn't happy about me storing the boxes as he felt his space in the storeroom was filling up and he would run out of room.

In the storeroom there were boxes piled floor to ceiling, filling nearly three quarters of the room. The boxes contained, the sergeant explained, the shooting scores of every law enforcement officer's visit to the range since 1954 when the range first opened.

This represented a large amount of what I considered useless information. When I asked why we kept all these scores, I expected the answer to center on the fact we had always kept them. But the sergeant surprised me by telling me the scores may be needed in court someday if an officer shot someone. My thought was, if an officer shot a suspect, that was a pretty good indication of his shooting skill. Perhaps these shooting records were often called for in court, but when I asked how often we had to bring a shooting record to court in any kind of case, the sergeant said they had never been asked to take such records. "Never?" I asked.

"No, never," he responded. Though such a thing could happen, he reminded me. Indeed.

I directed the range sergeant to keep the shooting records dating back for three years only and to throw the rest of them away. I thought, from the look of him, the sergeant was going to have a heart attack. He didn't have a heart attack, but my youth, lack of experience, my enthusiasm, and what he believed to be my cavalier attitude about his carefully preserved treasure trove of bureaucratic record keeping deeply wounded his psyche. I blissfully moved on to more troubling challenges.

Night Problems

Our trainees didn't learn how to be a cop by simply sitting in a classroom listening to lectures. Academy training was a vital part of the overall selection process. To evaluate trainees effectively, the training staff had to observe the recruits apply their classroom theory in reality-based training scenarios. We called these life-like training events "night problems." They were standard fare in police training programs throughout the country.

Our night problems were scheduled on Friday nights and happened six or seven times during the four-month-long basic training program. Each session of night problems was designed to test the recruit in various aspects of police work. During the course of an evening, each recruit faced scenarios testing decision-making skills, knowledge of the law as applied to the situation, discretionary use of force, car stops, problem-solving ability, and, always, the recruit's people skills.

The first set of night problems tested the recruits' ability to make decisions in some of the worst possible decision-making environments. The problems they faced unfolded in tense and emotionally charged circumstances similar to what they would experience in patrol.

There were ten quick problems during which the trainee had to make one critical decision. The decision could be as simple as to arrest or not, sometimes the decision might involve discerning if a crime had, in fact, taken place. In other cases, the recruit would have to decide if more resources were needed, if a citation should be written, a verbal warning given, if drawing a weapon was necessary, or if retreat was the safest and most appropriate action to take. Veteran officers were stationed at each location to evaluate the recruits. They graded the recruits' performance, maintained safety, and directed the civilian volunteer actors.

These night problems were a major production. They required a safe location where various different "problems" could be played out. We chose large parking lots in industrial areas where we were able to limit access. A cast of sixty or more actors, evaluators, training officers, and support staff assembled at the location an hour or so before the trainees arrived. It was a logistical and managerial nightmare.

The actors were all volunteers and I learned punctuality wasn't necessarily a core value of volunteerism. We drew our volunteers from our extended police family of civilian employees from our force and other police forces, family members of the training staff, the evaluators, reserve officers, and recently graduated officers. The recent graduates arrived for the sole purpose of making sure the trainees experienced the same level of hell they had gone through.

The high point of night problems occurred near the last quarter of the training program and tested the recruits on stopping cars. To the untrained eye, stopping a violator may seem a simple procedure. The officer pulls up behind the car, turns on his emergency lights, follows the car to the curb, gets out, obtains the driver's license, writes a ticket or gives a warning, and then starts looking for his next victim. Car stops, however, aren't always about traffic violations. The officer may initially stop a car for equipment or moving violations, but the officer must nevertheless be vigilant about who's in the car and what they may be doing.

We taught our officers to check out the license plate for alterations and the deck lid to assure no one was hiding in the trunk. At night, we taught them to focus their flashlights on the *backseat*s and around the interior of the car to learn where everyone was located. There was a procedure on how to park the patrol car to afford the best possible safety position while illuminating the suspect's vehicle interior with the patrol car's headlights and spotlights, giving the officer a greater tactical advantage.

If there were two officers, they had to time their approaches to the suspect's vehicle or, if they perceive danger, they needed to decide where to position themselves to avoid peril.

It wasn't unusual to see seasoned patrol officers make simple, but potentially dangerous, mistakes during car stops. On nearly every episode of *Cops* (the popular TV reality show) viewers can see officers who approached suspects with flashlights in their gun hands. A basic and consistent rant of training officers to recruits was, don't carry anything in your gun hand. This was something drilled into all officers during their initial training. But over time, officers drop their guard and make mistakes.

It was our job at the academy to drive home the importance of caution when stopping cars. Since there were so many things for the recruits to remember, they were nervous when they arrived for the car stop during night problems.

A viable cadre of actors was critical to the success of night problems. We tried to make their experience enjoyable and show them the value of their participation. But we also had to maintain stringent safety controls. The training staff demanded compliance with a few but vital rules.

The first rule dealt with guns. Half the people there carried guns. We'd disarm them and lock the weapons away before training took place. It was fairly straightforward with the recruits. We took their guns and gave them play guns capable of firing only blanks. The play guns had brightly painted red handles and the barrels were plugged so a real bullet couldn't be used. Evaluators, reserve officers, and recently graduated officers were a different matter. They were sneaky. For some reason, a few of them behaved as if giving up their weapon during the night problems was a form of emasculation that would forever stigmatize them.

After wrestling the evaluators and actors to the ground about carrying weapons, the training staff made sure the evaluators knew what we expected of the recruits. The actors had to fully understand their roles and the teaching points involved in their scenario. There were times when an evaluator didn't know what the correct procedures were for the trainee. In some cases, an evaluator held their own opinion of how a situation should be handled.

When an evaluator's opinion about the proper handling of a problem was different than the one the training staff prescribed, another wrestling match would ensue. Actors were always problematic. With all good intentions, they would get into the spirit of the training scene, get carried away with their fledgling thespian efforts, and completely lose the training point that had been carefully woven into the event.

Despite these annoyances, the real-life training events were usually successful. Occasionally there would be an injury to a trainee or actor, but generally, everyone felt night problems was the most critical part of the training process. They were also fun for everyone who participated. Some actors were standouts in their ability to test the trainee's applied police skills, but only one shot up an academy classroom.

Crazy Mary and the Night the Lights Went Out

Crazy Mary and her husband Dennus (the "u" in his name led us to say that he was living life as a typographical error) were the next-door neighbors of Vince and Susan who were both deputy sheriffs. Vince and Susan were longtime friends of mine and were always willing to help at the academy by volunteering their services during night problems. Since we had an ongoing need for actors, they suggested their neighbors, and so Crazy Mary and Dennus arrived one night to act in our decision-making night problems.

Crazy Mary wasn't actually crazy, but she realistically played a crazy woman in one of the problems. She was convincing and received her sobriquet when, during debriefing, one of the recruits referred to her as "that crazy woman." I corrected the recruit and said, "Her name is Mary."

The recruit responded, "Right, that Crazy Mary."

We all started calling her Crazy Mary, and until her recent death, I think she takes pride in the nickname. Mary was a tall, slim woman with unbridled energy. Her enthusiasm for life was boundless.

When she was asked to play the role of a crazy person involved in a domestic dispute, she smiled and said, "I can do that." She played a crazy person like every evil contained in Pandora's Box, and when the poor trainee entered the scene, the box of emotion was opened. The force of Mary's personality created havoc for the inexperienced recruit officer. Mary would scream profanities the likes of which not only the recruits, but also most of the training staff had never heard before. No matter where I was on the academy grounds I could hear Mary yelling at the poor trainee whose turn it was to deal with the scenario, which starred Crazy Mary. Only a few of the trainee's did well with Mary. They often left the scene in a state of shock having experienced for the first time someone who could make them feel powerless. It was a great training event whenever Crazy Mary was able to participate in our night problems.

Dennus was a self-assured, easygoing kind of guy. He was the perfect foil for Mary's exuberance and always seemed happy. He had a keen interest in people and wanted to learn more about police work. When he asked to participate like a trainee in one of the training scenes, we thought it would be interesting. Dennus wanted something during which he could use a gun. What could make him feel more cop-like than a training event where he would draw a weapon?

In our decision-making exercises, we had a brief event that tested the recruit's judgment about whether to shoot or not. We projected a 16mm film onto a large roll of butcher paper. The film would depict various scenes with possible suspects, some of whom would draw weapons and attempt to shoot. The recruit would stand to the side, watch the film, and if appropriate, draw and fire a weapon loaded with plastic bullets. The noise of the discharge would stop the projector, and the plastic bullet would tear the butcher paper. We were able to hear if the recruit shot first, see where and if he hit the suspect and, if he should have shot at all. Each recruit would be exposed to six of the scenes on the film.

Dennus was excited about trying this and told us he had some experience with firearms. Even before we could explain how the system worked, he was waving the weapon with the plastic bullets around. We were all grabbing at him and telling him to keep the weapon down at his side. Even though they were plastic bullets, none of us wanted to be struck by one, as they hurt and could do some serious damage if hit by one at close range.

As the film rolled, Dennus, reliving something he must have seen on a television cop show, pointed the gun in the air. On the film a suspect jumped out from behind a dumpster, a loud shot was heard, and the lights went out. Everyone in the room was sprayed with shards of glass from the light bulb above Dennus's head. We were safe. Dennus's flaming red hair was covered with pieces of glass and he looked as if he'd been out in a snowstorm. We found a breaker switch and restored the lights. We took Dennus's gun away and ended his police training.

They Couldn't Say Anything Nice

It was easy to settle into a great lieutenant's position like that of academy commander. It had many benefits over other police management jobs. I was away from our headquarters and all the bosses for most days. My domain was clearly defined, and my job was straightforward (i.e., to turn out a cadre of well-trained police recruits three or four times a year). Although my decisions about terminating poorly performing recruits were reviewed by my captain, they were seldom overturned. The work wasn't difficult, but the days were long. There was a sense of accomplishment the staff and I shared each time we graduated another class of new law enforcement officers.

Time passed quickly, and before long, the new sheriff was up for re-election, and my tranquility was jolted into a new reality. The recently formed bargaining unit for the deputy sheriffs decided to run one of their founding members against the sheriff. He was a sergeant, who happened to have been a fellow recruit when I went through training. Most of the deputies supported the sergeant. It took courage for him and the union to oppose a sitting sheriff. The campaigning turned nasty.

The FBI opened a criminal investigation of the sheriff involving allegations of corruption and racketeering. I never knew the source of the allegations, but it was rumored that someone within our own force had provided the FBI with lots of unfounded information suggesting the sheriff was corrupt. Of course, that wasn't my view of the man who had been good to me. When something like this happens, crazy people come out of the woodwork and are always willing to pile on a person whom they think is down. Much later in my career, I too was on the bottom of a pile that included the sheriff. I was surprised he didn't seem to remember the anguish one feels in that position.

A short time after the FBI investigation became public, a state regulatory commission charged with assuring law enforcement training met certain standards began to investigate the academy. They wanted to know if we were doing the training correctly or if we were being too "hard" on the recruits. One of the employees of the commission was a retired police chief of a small police force. He began showing up in my office more and more frequently. It was easy to see this was a "put up" job and that he was doing the bidding of others. His sole purpose was to make our force and the sheriff publicly look bad. My discussions with this man turned into arguments.

The training issue for the commission centered on a recent study about stress (military style boot camp-like training) versus a more collegial style of training for police recruits. The study, completed by a high-ranking law enforcement official as part of his doctorate of public administration degree, hypothesized that stress training was less effective on a number of dimensions involving a police officer's skill in dealing with the public. The concept had great sex appeal and the news media gave it wide coverage. Most police managers and executives read the news stories, but never read the actual dissertation. Yet, across the country, many police academies changed their training style.

I read the dissertation and several reviews of it presented in professional journals. These reviews suggested the conclusions reached in the study weren't supported by the data; that the correlations drawn in the study were suspect and there wasn't any indication of a causal relationship. Subsequently, we continued training our recruits in a disciplined style patterned after a military boot camp, but geared for police work. The military wanted people to follow orders, the police needed people who could seize the initiative and solve problems on their own.

We weren't ashamed of our training, and we weren't willing to compromise it for the sake of a new training regime that happened to have caught the eye of the news media. These new training methods were becoming the flavor of the month for many police agencies in the United States.

Police academies in California are always affiliated with local community colleges. This works out well for the police academy and the college. The academies gained academic credibility, and the colleges were able to enroll the recruits as students and thus were able to apply for state money. The recruits earned college credit for the course. The college paid the academy instructors. The relationship was mutually beneficial.

In our case, during this time, the relationship between the college and the academy became strained. The college applied to the state commission to operate its own police academy on the college grounds. Since the certification for the academy was given to the sheriff's department, not the college, this wasn't going to happen. This attempt by the college put us through many months of needless aggravation.

Several members of the college were supporters of the sergeant, who was running against the sheriff. In fact, a few years later, one would run against the sheriff in another election. They felt that, since the state was looking into how we ran the academy, they would take advantage of the situation in an attempt to take police training out of the hands of the sheriff. In one meeting, they presented their proposal to the local representative of the state commission. For the most part, it was taken nearly in whole, in many cases word for word, from our training manuals. I couldn't believe they were presenting a proposal duplicating the training we were doing. It was the training the state was investigating. No one seemed to get the irony.

When the sheriff was reelected, the FBI investigation was concluded without any findings of wrongdoing, the state stopped investigating our training methods, and the college dropped its request to the state to operate its own police academy. I spent the entire time being angry that these kinds of groundless accusations could so easily be made and taken seriously. It was nice that it was over, but it ruined a perfectly good assignment or at least a chunk of it for me. Being in the heart of all this controversy also taught me how completely misinformed the news media can be and how headlines and subtly worded paragraphs try to shape public opinion.

Where Are They?

After the election, it was back to normal for the most part. I had been able to get people assigned to the academy staff whom I trusted and relied upon. The tactical officers were particularly pleasurable employees to have working at the academy. One was older than I thought was prime age for a tactical officer. He was in his mid-forties. He seemed to be ambulatory from my thirty-four-year-old perspective of things. He was handsome with dark graying hair, a shade under six foot, stocky but not heavy with a youthful exuberance that projected a more youthful appearance. He was emotional and dedicated to doing a good job.

His partner was a few months older than I, slim, over six feet tall with a full head of thick, dark hair, and a devastating sense of humor. They made a good pair with the older officer falling victim to the younger officer's quick wit and penchant for giving no quarter whenever people exposed their foibles or were disingenuous.

The duty of supervising them fell to a sergeant of limited capacity who projected a serious demeanor. The two tactical officers were a difficult supervisory task for the most experienced, cunning, and capable supervisor. Together, they made the sergeant's life at the academy hell. Personally, I found them entertaining and no one questioned their ability to handle the recruit classes. They wrote excellent evaluations of the recruits. These were helpful to the staff in making our decisions about the recruits' propensity for success in our organization, and their evaluations were also helpful to the recruits in identifying those areas in need of improvement.

For the most part, it was a happy and productive time for all of us. Every four months we'd take on the task of organizing an academy graduation. The two major things were to find a nice location and a good commencement speaker. The rest of the logistics were routine and simple. We had conducted many academy graduations and each seemed to get better. Near the end of my tenure at the academy, we tried to top all the other graduations. We decided we'd ask Jack Webb of *Dragnet* fame to be our keynote speaker. Surprisingly, we were able to get right through to him personally, but there was conflict with the date and he wasn't able to do it. We ended up settling for the Los Angeles County sheriff. He was honored to be asked and readily agreed. No one told him he was our distant second choice.

Now the pressure was on to make the graduation perfect. Our sheriff didn't want to be embarrassed in front of the sheriff of the largest sheriff's department in the United States. We decided to have the graduation outdoors in front of a police memorial in the civic center. It would be the first time we held a graduation there, and we learned many of the logistical issues we took for granted required much more effort. Amplification, awnings, seating, and parking were more difficult at the new location. It was a beautiful setting, and what could be better than to have brand new officers beginning their careers at the police memorial honoring those officers who had given their lives to the law enforcement profession?

It was a twenty-minute drive to the graduation site, primarily along busy surface streets. The academy staff spent time primping before heading to the location, which had been prepared by others. The chairs were arranged, a lectern placed on the stage, an awning was erected over the stage so the sun wouldn't burn the two sheriffs, and everything seemed at the ready. We rushed through our primping behaviors so we'd arrive in plenty of time to make sure everything was in place and set to go. The entire staff left, leaving only a secretary to hold down the fort.

When we arrived, the Marine Corps band was playing music for the early arrivals. The place looked great. We had fifteen minutes before the ceremonies would start. The graduates arrived on a bus from the academy right after we arrived. We needed only the two sheriffs, then we'd be set. I saw our sheriff walking toward the stage, and I rushed to do my usual ass-kissing. He could be volatile if things didn't go well. His first comment to me wasn't "Hello, the place looks great," but rather, "Where's the sheriff?" I didn't have a clue.

I assumed he was on his way, but the question served only to unnerve me. I could feel the perspiration running down the back of my neck. Before I started blubbering, one of the tactical officers approached to tell us the other sheriff had arrived. Yes, now we could start.

The recruits marched in as the Marine Corps band played "Pomp and Circumstance." The flags on the stage were fluttering in the gentle breeze, it was seventy degrees on a bright, mild California kind of day, and I was feeling proud. This was going to be our best graduation ceremony ever. Future academy commanders would strain to equal the pageantry we had orchestrated that very day.

I was on a roll, as I made the traditional introductory comments. I could feel the excitement in the air as parents, family, and friends listened in complete and utter fascination while I introduced the academy staff and the guests of honor on the dais with me. I presented the special awards to the most physically fit trainee, the best pistol shot, and the trainee with the highest academic score.

The audience held their breath as I announced the overall outstanding trainee for the graduating class. The applause was sustained for this trainee who had done a remarkable job throughout the training process. No one, except a couple of the staff members and I, knew who the outstanding trainee was going to be, so this announcement was greeted with much anticipation. I noted that even the trainee's competitors for the honor did a notable job of faking enthusiasm for the winner.

I introduced the sheriff who introduced the Los Angeles sheriff. It was obvious the sheriff hadn't read the remarks we had prepared for him, but he managed to stumble through it. The Los Angeles sheriff had been sheriff for a long time. He was a senior politician and had a reputation for being petulant if things didn't go his way. He apparently overlooked the poor introduction he received, and his booming voice reached out to the recruits. He said things none of the recruits would ever remember. This wasn't the sheriff's fault. There had been few memorable graduation speeches. This was no exception and, as he spoke, my mind wandered.

Suddenly I had a mild sense of something being wrong. I looked around and couldn't discern anything out of the ordinary. When I looked over at the staff sitting next to the trainees, they smiled and nodded. I was getting a distinct sense of trouble coming my way, but I didn't know what it was. While I wasn't quite at the panic threshold, I was approaching it as I began to look around the stage.

The sheriff was droning on about how important police work was, our sheriff was pretending to listen, and the other guests on the dais all appeared to be awake. My eyes were dotting about when I caught a glimpse of the shelf behind the lectern. The diplomas were normally placed there. The shelf was there but there was nothing on it.

A trick by the staff was my first thought. I looked over at them again and received more smiles and nods. In the middle of the sheriff's speech, I got up, walked off the stage and over to the tactical officers. I whispered, "Where the fuck are the diplomas?" They appeared to have been struck dumb. People began to notice something was wrong. I could all but keep my hands from throttling both of them. They said they left them on my desk thinking I might want to bring them with me. Although I had never done such a thing before, I guess they decided bringing the diplomas was a task I should start to do.

My perfect graduation was crumbling before my eyes. I looked back and saw our sheriff looking directly at me with his beady little eyes. He didn't look happy. Well, crap, I thought, they can kill me, but they can't eat me. I marched back up on stage, walked over to our sheriff, and nervously confessed.

I told him we would call each recruit to the stage where they would salute him and he would shake hands with them. They would get their diplomas at their graduation party later that night. Surprisingly, the sheriff didn't seem concerned. When the Los Angeles sheriff finished his words of wisdom, I took center stage. I explained that I (although, to this day I don't think it my fault) forgot to bring the diplomas. People laughed thinking it was a joke. Then I think people laughed because I was so embarrassed by the circumstances.

We finished the ceremony. It looked as if everyone enjoyed it despite the foul up. The tactical officers left immediately afterward in an attempt to avoid me. I didn't see them until the graduation party. Well into the party, after they had consumed a manly amount of alcohol, they made their way over to me to test the waters. I told them the sheriff wanted to see them both the next morning in his office. They were shocked. I wouldn't tell them anything more. Of course the sheriff didn't want to see them. I told the sheriff I had forgotten the diplomas, not them. I let them stew about it until around midnight when I let them off the hook.

Going South

I had been a lieutenant a whole two years, and I was anxious about moving up in the organization. It didn't matter that most people spent many years as a lieutenant before making captain. I had a friend in a police force overseas, and he'd spent nearly twelve years as a sergeant before promotion to the next rank, which for him was inspector (the rough equivalent of lieutenant). My captain had been a lieutenant for ten years prior to her promotion, but none of this mattered to me. I liked my position at the academy, but I also liked the idea of being one of the big bosses. Whenever I reached a certain rank, it always appeared that the next rank up the promotional ladder was better. I guess I wasn't so much interested in what I was doing, but rather in what I could be doing.

That's not to say I didn't pay attention to my work. From the feedback I received in the form of yearly evaluations, I was, according to my bosses, doing a good job. The chronic problem was, of course, that if I were promoted, I'd be assigned to one of the jails. I didn't want to work in a jail. I thought my ten weeks of jail experience, as a temporary sergeant and my corrections officer experience, were more than enough for any law enforcement career.

As the year drew to a close, there were rumors about a big transfer list in the offing. This primed my interest and I searched around looking for anyone with information about who was going where. There were no promotions scheduled, and I figured I was irreplaceable at the academy so my interest was purely academic.

Then I started thinking about what a tough time we had had at the academy with the state commission giving us aggravation, the community college wanting to start its own academy, and the news media portraying our training methods as unsophisticated. My response to these attacks was always volatile and lacked finesse. Maybe the department wanted someone at the helm who was more mature and not prone to fits of pique and who didn't see criticism as a personal attack.

Before the list was published, I was ushered into the chief's office. He informed me that I had been doing a good job but I lacked field management experience. This was what the evaluators at the assessment process had told the department as well. This sounded ominous. Was my time up? Was I going to become a jail watch commander? It was a crappy job in my opinion. But it was true that I had neither supervisory nor management experience in any field operations. I had been a sergeant in Records and in Training and a lieutenant at the academy. I did have an ancillary duty as a sergeant working our mounted patrol, but this didn't add up to much field experience.

I braced myself for bad news. But the news turned out to be good. I was going to be the commander of our South County patrol station. This would place about a hundred patrol personnel under my command, and I would also have administrative supervision of twenty investigators housed in our patrol station. The station was responsible for all patrols in a vast ranging and fast growing portion of unincorporated land with about a hundred thousand residents.

Again, I had lucked out with a great assignment. I was also told in confidence that in a short time the intention was to make the station commander position a captain's level assignment. As the incumbent, I'd be promoted to the new rank when the department received approval of the plan. The final decision about whether to upgrade the position hadn't yet been made by the sheriff. I was told to say nothing. This killed me. I wanted to tell everyone. I was to be transferred to a lieutenant's position in patrol at the south station, knowing it would eventually be upgraded to a captain's position. I had to act as if this was a lateral transfer from one lieutenant's position to another.

At the start of the New Year, I began my first managerial field assignment full of trepidation and excitement.

SIX

A SOUTHERN EXPOSURE

✫ ✫ ✫

Nearly all men can stand adversity, but if you want to test a man's character, give him power.

– Abraham Lincoln, 1862

Aren't They Special

In the late seventies, the department decided to open a patrol station in the southern part of the county. The area had grown rapidly, and while there were only a few cities, there were many unincorporated communities well on their way to becoming cities. Having a patrol station located there made perfect sense as the patrol cars would deploy from a closer location, and the residents didn't have to drive to the county seat whenever they might have business with us.

Before the existence of the station, all patrols deployed from the headquarters building to their assigned areas. For the patrol cars heading south, this often meant a thirty- to forty-minute drive. In some cases, on certain days at certain times and with traffic building on the freeways over the years, patrol cars could take up to an hour to reach their patrol beats.

When I was a patrol deputy, there was less traffic and my partner and I could make it to "South County" in twenty minutes. Often we'd turn on our headlights in daylight hours or our high beams at night, tailgate the unfortunate driver in the number one lane until he moved over, zoom by, and jam along at about eighty-five mph to our patrol area. In the late seventies, it was too crowded on the roads to drive fast. The newer deputies, for the most part, had a better sense of responsibility and public image than I did in my earlier days in patrol.

The cost of the new station was shown to be a savings in man-hours and gas. I don't suspect that was actually true, but to the casual observer, it appeared to make sense. So approval for the station was received, and it was soon announced that we'd be moving temporarily into an unused courtroom in South County's court building. We were still in those temporary quarters when I received word of my transfer.

I was ready to start, but it would be three weeks before I would officially take over the station. I had only been there once shortly after it first opened. This was a chance to get a sneak preview of my new office without a lot of people around. It was the Christmas holiday season, many of the employees who worked in the office would be gone, and the patrol deputies would be out in the field.

The courthouse consisted of four courtrooms. Two were upstairs and two were downstairs. We were assigned to one of the downstairs courtrooms. When we moved in, the department refurbished the courtroom but with severe limitations that the judges imposed on us. Of course, we couldn't make any significant changes. They would be using the space as a future courtroom. We were limited to moving walls around and making do as best we could. So as not to offend, the judges declared we couldn't use the front door of the courthouse. All the officers had to use the back door that led directly into our space. We never knew whom we might offend outside of the judges, who clearly didn't want us housed in their building in the first place. We complied, if for no other reason than to keep the peace.

Unaware of the back-door rule at the time, I boldly marched through the public entrance, passed the district attorney's office and the clerk's office, hopped down the stairs, and into our space. If I didn't know where I was going, I could've missed the station. There was only one small sign on the front door to indicate it was the sheriff's department.

When I walked in, I noticed there were few people working. I expected a small staff presence in the office during the holidays since many people took their vacations during this time. One clerk was sitting near the counter. She continued doing some work at her desk while I stood at the counter. She looked up once, but then went back to what she was doing. Rather than make a scene, I stood waiting.

I could hear people talking in the next room. The rooms were constructed of cheap, simulated wood dividers that didn't go all the way to the ceiling, so sound traveled easily throughout the station. Toward the back of the clerk's area, I saw the Investigative sergeant emerging from one of the rooms. He looked over at me, smiled, and said, "Hey, Dennis we weren't expecting you." I'd known the sergeant for many years; we were contemporaries and were on a first-name basis.

The sergeant was a tall, good-looking man. We were about the same age. He had joined the department a few months after me. He had an easygoing manner and a quick smile. During his time with me at the station, he ran interference for me with his lieutenant with whom I had a contentious relationship. He was the first contemporary in my life to die when he succumbed to a brain aneurysm several years later. This happened after he'd been promoted to lieutenant and was working as the academy commander.

I told him I was in the area and decided to stop by at the last minute and see what my office looked like. With that, I had the clerk's undivided attention. She introduced herself and apologized for not knowing who I was. She didn't apologize for ignoring me. She didn't grasp the fact that ignoring anyone who comes to the counter doesn't lend itself to building good community relations.

The sergeant took me into the investigators' room. It was a simple bullpen arrangement with one desk shoved against another. Each desk was a rat's nest of reports. I recognized one of the few investigators in the office. He was reading the paper with his feet on the desk when I walked in. He put the paper down, jumped up, and hurried over to me to shake my hand and congratulate me on my new assignment. He took this time to tell me how different this station was from the rest of the department.

"The detectives here really work, it's not like it is at headquarters where they have time to screw off," he lectured me. "The guys here work hard," he explained.

I said, "The more people have time to talk about how hard they work, the less work they do." The silence in the room became oppressive. Several of the few other detectives looked up, then back down at their paperwork. They didn't want me to think they had been listening. I swear I thought I heard an audible gasp at one point. I imagined I was being dropped from many of their Christmas card lists.

I was ushered out of the room and away from the detectives by the sergeant. He showed me around the rest of the station. There wasn't much to it. The entire station consisted of a small briefing room for the patrol deputies, an office for the detective sergeant, my office, the detectives' bullpen, and the clerks' desks that were stationed behind the public counter. There were a couple of storage rooms in the back and only two, single-stall bathrooms for the entire staff. The station didn't have locker rooms and deputies came to work dressed in their uniforms.

During the tour, the sergeant took a stab at speaking about the workload. He was more diplomatic saying everyone there was chosen especially for assignment to the station. The sergeant didn't know nearly all transfer requests to the new station were granted. A few, because of prior internal investigations, were turned down. I think since everyone at the station was, in fact, a volunteer, they felt special.

I would hear about how special they were many times. As far as I could determine, we had about the same percentage of excellent deputies, average deputies, and marginal deputies as were deployed elsewhere. We even had a few poor deputies. But they were all imbued with the idea that, because they were selected to be at the new station, they were somehow better than deputies in other assignments.

It didn't hurt anything, and I didn't disabuse them of the idea. They all had a remarkable sense of *esprit de corps* and, while this may have only been an illusion, it was real to them. Perceptions were real in their consequences and for the cadre of station deputies those consequences manifested themselves in a willingness to work hard and take pride in the work they were doing. For the residents of South County, the consequence was a more helpful and caring patrol force.

Bad Dog

I liked being back in patrol, even if my days were spent behind a desk and in plain clothes. Lieutenants, at that time, didn't often wear a uniform. Nevertheless, the issues I dealt with daily involved deputies doing real police work, and I enjoyed the challenges. As an administrator, the actual police work was relatively simple. It was the peripheral stuff that detracted from the work, things such as dealing with personnel matters, budgets, and the daily politics of the area.

The population in our patrol areas was growing fast and many were destined to become cities. We wanted to continue patrolling those areas when they incorporated as cities. That meant I had to be active in many local organizations. Some days were spent attending one meeting after another. Some of the meetings were during the day but others were after work. These nighttime meetings were killers.

We were patrolling one small city and the city council wanted the station commander to attend the weekly Tuesday night city council meetings. They started at seven, took a break around nine thirty, and then continued late into the night. Fortunately, the city manager allowed me to leave after the break. The entire time I spent as the station commander, I was never called upon at that city council meeting.

There were many other meetings in which I was expected to participate. These included chambers of commerce meetings, local advisory board meetings, occasionally school board meetings, traffic committee meetings, special events planning meetings, and the list went on. Except for the long hours and the sometimes incredibly boring nature of the meetings or the long-windedness of some speakers, I enjoyed meeting all the people in the area who were considered the movers and shakers. They were, to me, the stakeholders in the future of the area and, if the sheriff's department wanted to be the police force for any newly created city, my presence at these meetings was critical.

I spent so much time on this grip-and-grin circuit that for the first time in my life I was referred to in a small local paper as "popular!" Never before and never since has anyone ever used such a word to describe me. These were heady times for me. I relished the good press when it occasionally came my way. I was proud that, for the most part, the department was portrayed positively in the press.

Once in a while, I would suit up in my uniform, grab a patrol car, and work with the deputies on busy Friday or Saturday nights. This usually happened when my personal social life was at low ebb. The station kept me informed of emerging events during my off-duty hours. From this time and for the next eighteen years, the sound of the phones ringing at two o'clock in the morning held no dread.

I learned to swing my feet onto the cold, hard floor, clear my head, and prepare myself for whatever event, sometimes dire, sometimes unusual, would spew from the phone. Many times the caller was only informing me of events and no action would be necessary. The callers were seeking advice or approval or maybe getting the monkey off their back by telling someone in higher authority about what had happened.

Around five o'clock one morning, I was told that there had been a shooting at a fast food restaurant during the late evening hours. Another police agency had been following some suspected robbers and had information the robbers had targeted this particular restaurant. The police hid inside the restaurant before closing hours when the robbery was expected to happen. Protocol required any law enforcement agency working outside its normal jurisdiction to advise the local law enforcement agency about what they're doing. In this way, mishaps were avoided, especially when officers weren't in uniform. The officers, prior to entering the restaurant, saw a sheriff's car and told the deputy what they were doing. Then things unfolded quickly.

The deputy took his car out of the immediate area so as not to scare off the would-be robbers. The police secreted themselves in various locations in the restaurant. The three robbers arrived at the back door of the restaurant minutes after closing. They were let in and were confronted by the police. All three suspects were armed with handguns. Two of the suspects fled out the back door, but one leveled his gun at one of the officers. The officer fired at the suspect and struck him once in the middle of the chest. The suspect turned and also fled out the back door following his compatriots.

With the officers in pursuit, the suspects disappeared into a large field next to the restaurant and the freeway. The field was practically a bog from recent rains in the area. In some parts of the field, the water was two or three feet deep. A party of reserve deputy sheriffs who specialized in search and rescue responded to the scene. Nothing was found during the evening and, with daylight, it was decided a full-press search was needed.

When I arrived, the crime lab was processing the scene, deputies were still writing reports, our robbery-homicide team was there (behaving as if they were the only true cops at the scene) emitting a fowl stench of self-importance that pervaded everything they did, and the poor volunteer reserve deputies were wandering around looking for guidance. The reserve deputies from the search and rescue unit were a hardy, well-meaning bunch of guys who would drop everything and respond to any call for help at any time. They were dedicated to their particular form of volunteerism, but weren't always appreciated by the regular deputies.

The reserves had reinvigorated their bloodhound program recently, and one of the dogs was at the scene with a handler. I watched the handler prepare the dog with a long lead. The scent was provided to the dog from a glove dropped by one of the suspects as he fled. The dog took off quickly.

Immediately, the dog went to the edge of the field where there was a large body of standing rainwater. Several witnesses had thought they saw the suspect flee up an embankment to a street leading across the freeway. The handler knew this and thought the dog was looking to have some fun in the water.

The handler jerked the dog back out of the water and lightly smacked him across the back, practically dragging the dog across the parking lot to the embankment. Once at the foot of the embankment, the dog took off up the hill with the handler running behind. The rest of the search and rescue deputies fanned out across the field but, for the most part, avoided the watery parts.

I went on to my office, as it seemed there wasn't much to do. The officer who shot must have been mistaken about hitting the suspect or, if he had hit him, the wound wasn't fatal. It appeared as if the suspects had escaped. Toward the end of the morning, I received a phone call telling me one of the suspects was found near the scene, dead. I returned to the crime scene and was directed to the edge of the field where the bloodhound had first taken his handler. There, in about two feet of water, you could see the suspect lying face up. Indeed, as the officer had said, there was a single gunshot wound in the center of the suspect's chest.

The dog had been right. The handler had a preconceived idea about how the suspect made his getaway. We hadn't let the dog do the work he was trained to do, and we all learned a valuable lesson. I thought everything was over for my part, but I was to learn how little some people felt about my style of management and about how hubris fueled some detectives.

Late in the afternoon, I received a call from a detective with whom I had worked in the past and with whom I had a good relationship. This detective was "slick." He was several years my senior with more field experience. He had a nice style about him and was a smooth talker. Apparently, during the morning, I was a little chagrined about the other police agency coming in at the last minute and upsetting our nice quiet community. I had expressed this to one of the other robbery-homicide detectives.

The other detective was a sullen man who had been in an investigator for a long time. He took umbrage at my assessment of the situation. He lacked the courage to speak to me about it. He believed I'd complain to the officers' agency about their actions at the shooting scene. He pressed his workmate to call and dissuade me from getting the officers in trouble. It hadn't been my intention to do that, but there'd been a certain cowboy-ish, fly-by-the-seat-of-their-pants kind of style to the officers' behavior in my opinion, and it didn't set well with me.

I guess it was the detective's job to school me about my job. I listened patiently and tried to explain things from my perspective. Then I realized what was happening. Here was a man with a great deal of field experience, but no management experience, telling me how I should manage my bailiwick. I had become the dog leading the handler in a direction that the handler perceived as wrong. The caller was jerking me back from the edge of the water and smacking me on the back, trying to drag me off in another direction.

I told him I understood his perspective, but I had to manage my area of responsibility in the best way I knew how. I reminded him I wasn't a junior detective under his tutelage but a manager. I also reminded him he had no management experience and he seemed to be trying to tell me how to do my job. I explained I would have to make my own decisions about what was or wasn't the correct way to proceed.

Fortunately, I think our conversation cleared the air. The older detective, never a warm and friendly guy in the best of circumstances, usually avoided me whenever possible. The caller and I remained on good terms even though he tried to beat me like the handler had beaten the dog.

Cars

Even though most of our police cars looked the same, they weren't. It wasn't surprising for me to learn how important even the smallest innovation in a police car could initiate a mad stampede at the end of patrol briefing for the keys to the car with the newest gizmo or gadget. It was often heard around our force that "if a deputy can't make love to it, he'll crap on it." Patrol cars were no exception. I'd find cars damaged in ways seldom seen in private vehicles.

It wasn't unusual to find the dashboard of a unit marked up with various license plate numbers and other notes. I wondered how many people who needed to make a note of something and couldn't find a piece of paper wrote on the dashboard of their car, not many. Yet this was a common practice for some, and if not the dashboard, then the seat. We would discover patrol cars with headliners ripped, chunks of steering wheels missing, glove box doors broken, inside door panels loosened, and often the cars were covered in a plethora of unreported small dents and scratches. In one particularly egregious case, a deputy cut out the seat belts in the car to make a towing strap for another patrol car stuck in some mud.

Rather than throw trash onto the highways, deputies tossed things onto the *backseat*. This wasn't a bad idea if they threw the trash away at the end of shift, but many didn't. Most of the on-coming deputies refused to clean another deputy's mess. This would continue until finally a deputy starting his shift would be overcome by the smell and resign himself to clean the inside of the car.

We kept a stockpile of spare hubcaps for the many patrol cars starting a shift without one. A car without a hubcap looked as if it were in bad repair. There was no report needed when a hubcap went missing. There was a simple requirement: the deputy had to pick up a replacement and put it on the car. Nevertheless, nearly every day one could spot one or more of our patrol cars driving around with missing hubcaps.

Once the county purchased patrol cars with smaller engines encumbered with new smog-control devices, an urban police legend circulated around the patrol stations. Officers believed turning the air filter cover upside-down would make the car go faster. In reality, this caused more problems for the car, but deputies were convinced this was the only way to get any speed out of the cars.

Then, instead of looking for the newest patrol cars (the perceived slower ones), deputies rushed to get the keys to older patrol vehicles with the larger engines. This was a complete reversal of the norm. New cars had newer emergency lights and sirens, along with other creature comforts previously not found in our police cars, such as air conditioning, adjustable and more comfortable seats, and more secure screening between the deputy and the *backseat* where prisoners were transported.

In an effort to overcome the mad scramble for patrol cars, I assigned cars to each patrol area. A patrol car would be the responsibility of the same three or four deputies. If they damaged a car, they knew they were going to have to live with it. While this didn't solve all the problems, it was an improvement over the old system. We saw fewer incidents of damage to the vehicles.

There was one deputy who was abnormally particular about his patrol car. He took great pains to ensure his patrol car was clean and in good operating order. He would, on occasion, take the car home and wax it. Well, this was my kind of guy since I never liked working in a dirty car. We used him as an example. Whenever we received a new car, he had the right of first refusal. Other deputies would howl. They perceived this as disparate and unfair treatment. We told the deputies they could receive like treatment if they took care of their vehicles in the same way. They claimed the deputy was nuts, but I saw him as fastidious.

Plain units, or E plate cars, were one step down from our patrol units. These cars were white, had easily recognizable government plates, and were stylishly topped off with two chrome spotlights. The driver's side light was red. Under the hood stood a weak six-cylinder engine and a mechanical siren driven by a compressor. These cars did not lend themselves to undercover work.

Lieutenants, like me, drove these cars, along with a whole host of other officers not engaged in primary police work. Occasionally, when there was a shortage of black-and-white patrol cars, an intrepid officer might use one of the plain units on patrol. Even though in the cold, clear light of day it didn't take much to notice it was some sort of police car, at night they were much more deceiving. People would sometimes commit crimes right in front of an officer driving one of these cars.

There were full and midsize cars. The main problem was the small, six-cylinder engine. Additionally, with no screen between the front and rear seat transporting a prisoner was more problematic. Since the cars weren't designed for patrol work, there was no place to mount a shotgun, and they were mostly equipped with older style police radios.

If the car hadn't been recently tuned-up, and if the car did not have a perfectly good battery, it was impossible to turn on the red light and sound the siren without the headlights dimming and occasionally the engine dying. Receiving a hot call was exciting; receiving one while driving a plain unit made it more exciting. Whizzing pass unsuspecting motorists in an unmarked car was fun. It was, however, disheartening if the car died in the middle of an intersection, as these cars had been known to do.

Detective cars were referred to as undercover cars. Actually, when I first started working, there were undercover and super undercover cars. The latter had white side-walled tires. By the time I commanded the patrol station, the investigative units were fairly nice. Most were full-size cars and were well equipped with V-8 engines.

For a time, we experimented with buying a wide variety of low-mileage rental cars. The purchase price was less expensive than a new car, but other manufactures of police vehicles began to provide high-mileage warranties, which reduced the total lifetime operating cost of the vehicles significantly. This made the purchase of low-mileage rental cars less cost effective.

Naturally, detective cars didn't accumulate the kinds of mileage patrol cars did in a year. The replacement of a patrol car occurred when it reached the first major repair after seventy-five thousand miles. This happened in two to three years. A detective car was replaced around a hundred thousand miles, but it took many more years to travel those miles. The white, plain units usually fell apart before too long and were eventually replaced by cars with more powerful engines.

As the station commander, I was the proud recipient of a midsize plain unit with fifty thousand miles on it. It could best be described as a "piece of shit." I drove my personal sports car back and forth to the station each day, and the transition to my little white unit was annoying. If I attended an evening meeting, I had permission to take the car home for the night. While this saved on gas (we were in the middle of the second gas shortage), it wasn't a pleasant vehicle to drive.

Once, when a city council meeting went late into the night, I drove the car home. The next morning when I started the car, I thought I smelled gas, but the car started without difficulty. I had gone less than a quarter of mile when I saw smoke coming from under the hood, then saw flames. I pulled over and called for the fire department via the police radio.

I was standing by the car watching it burn when one of my neighbors came running to the rescue with a garden hose. I told him help wasn't necessary, as I had already called the fire department. Unfortunately, he wouldn't be deterred. He probably envisioned himself on the front page of the newspaper as the hero who saved the day for a sheriff's lieutenant. By the time the fire department arrived, the car was smoldering but the fire had been contained within the engine compartment thanks to my enthusiastic neighbor. Overall, the rest of the car looked fairly good. *Damn it*, I thought.

I had heard my chief was getting a new car, so instead of hitching a ride from the patrol sergeant to my station, he took me to headquarters. I marched into the chief's office, said I needed a new car, and asked him if I could have his old one. I learned early in my career that if I didn't ask, I'd never know. The worst thing that could happen was to be told no. The chief said yes. In a matter of a week, I was driving a low-mileage, full-size Chevrolet Caprice detective unit. It was air-conditioned and had the same engine as our patrol cars. It was a nice-looking, fast car. I felt it befitted a man of my rank and position.

Somewhere in the nether world of organizational communication, however, there was a breakdown. One day I went to retrieve the keys to my new car from the board near our briefing room. My keys were missing. When I looked in the parking lot, my car was gone, although many of the other detective units were parked there. One of the detectives decided the new car wasn't meant for me. In his mind, the car was sent to replace another detective unit that had reached its hundred thousand-mile apogee. When I spoke to the detective sergeant, he told me his lieutenant informed him the car was assigned for investigation and wasn't at the station for my use.

The detective sergeant's lieutenant was a little, round, short guy with an overactive imagination, lots of nervous energy, a tendency toward verbal dominance in any conversation, and he was an aggressive kind of guy. He was in the top group of lieutenants in contention for a promotion to captain. He didn't know about my pending upgrade. This was a scrimmage he was bound to lose, but he was blissfully unaware.

I spoke to the chief to make sure I had the facts right and that the car was assigned to me, he told me that it was. The lieutenant was housed at headquarters so before heading to the station one morning, I stopped by to see him. I must admit I was surprised he hadn't contacted me if he felt I was using some of his resources inappropriately. I realized the main problem was that he saw me as a competitor. I didn't want him to think of me that way. I wanted to give him an out so he could gracefully allow me to use the car. I didn't want to tell him I'd spoken to our boss.

We had a nice chat. I explained my tail of woe about the car I had had to drive until it caught on fire. I sniveled about there being no replacement and asked if he could help me. And here was the stroke of genius I came upon. In all seriousness, I said, "Look, you're going to be a captain here pretty soon, and you'll get a nice car that you'll even be able to take back and forth from home to work each day. Can't I use the detective car until they find a replacement for me?" He agreed and my troubles about the disputed ownership of our boss's former car were over. When I was promoted to captain, I noticed the lack of a congratulatory phone call from the lieutenant.

Crime Fighters and Problem Solvers

During graduate school, I read many books about crime and delinquency. The one that impressed me most was *Criminal Violence, Criminal*

Justice by Charles E. Silberman (Vintage Books, 1980). It became the foundation upon which I based my theory and practice of law enforcement. As the station commander, I had an opportunity to instill some of these ideas in the officers with whom I worked. I was also teaching this theory of policing to many training academy recruit officers in a class entitled "Interpersonal Communications for the Patrol Officer." I'm sure when the recruits would look ahead in their syllabuses and see the title of this class, they probably wanted to call in sick for the day. How boring can such a class be? It didn't touch upon all the excitement they expected in police work.

Recruits were interested in classes about criminal law, felony car stops, weaponless defense, arrest laws, and search and seizure. These were the heart of police work. I'm sure most thought my class was going to a complete snooze. But with practice, I made it interesting and fun. The students always gave me good evaluations.

I've been fortunate to travel a great deal in my life and visit with many international colleagues throughout the world. From time to time, I would be invited to speak to some colleagues in these countries. I was fond of saying that, throughout the world, regardless of the political regime under which cops may labor, our main job in police work was the same, "to throw assholes in jail." Obviously, an academic would say this in a more sophisticated way. I think, though, for the most part, the point was made in a simple and understandable way. However, I always knew that that statement belied the much more complex nature of police work.

In his book, Silberman posited that cops played two roles: crime fighter and problem solvers, the latter he identified as a social arbiter. But the crime fighter and the social arbiter don't behave in the same way, and they practice different sets of skills. Where the crime fighter could be identified by an aggressive and dogmatic approach, the social arbiter would more likely be communicative, open, and inclusive. A crime fighter must be willing to draw a weapon and be prepared to use deadly force in the right set of circumstances. The crime fighter's skill in the use of less-than-lethal weapons, thoroughness in searching suspects, and a penchant for keen observations of those things that appear out of the ordinary mark him as a diligent cop. He must be able to analyze in seconds a set of circumstances crossing his path and respond to those circumstances with an appropriate amount of force.

Recruit officers, even today, spend substantially more hours learning about crime-fighting skills than about skills involved in decision-making and problem solving. The majority of hours in any entry level training program are taken up with firearms training, weaponless defense training, criminal law, car stops, traffic enforcement and accident investigation, interrogation, note taking, and many other classes focusing on officer safety, searching suspects, handling crime scenes, and a host of specific crime-related skills. Much less time is spent on classes such as how to handle a mentally ill person, how to resolve a civil dispute, dealing with family violence, and classes like the one I taught on interpersonal communication.

More time should be spent on the former rather than the latter. In dealing with firearms, for example, everyone knew the consequences of misuse due to a lack of training would be severe and could result in death. Recruits needed to understand their authority and how to apply it in the field. If not, new officers could make unlawful arrests resulting in the illegal detention of people. Not knowing how to properly search could cause an officer to miss evidence and allow a felon to escape justice.

If a recruit fails to develop good social arbiter/problem-solving skills, the results may be less severe. What if recruits never recognize the importance of good public relations during their tenure? Their behavior may cause people to file more personnel complaints with the department. The behavior may be vexing, and the department may have to struggle to garner community support, but the consequences of poor performance in these types of skills don't place people's lives and liberty in jeopardy; they may just piss people off.

However, Silberman found a connection and a paradox some have failed to appreciate. Once officers recognize, understand, and practice the skills necessary to become better problem solvers, they will become more effective crime fighters.

The police alone don't solve crimes. Without information from witnesses, many crimes would go unsolved. Most crime happens indoors, or at least out of a police officer's view. The vast majority of crime was solved, not by some arcane police work, but more probably because a witness provided a clue. Witnesses give descriptions of suspects or cars, often providing the license numbers of suspect vehicles. They help point the police in the right direction. Witnesses sometimes simply tell the officer who committed the crime.

With the pervasive use of video surveillance today, we frequently seek the public's help in identifying a criminal caught on tape. The police work hard and play a significant part in the capture of criminals but their effectiveness diminishes without the public's help. The symbiotic relationship between the police and the public must be emphasized. Crime fighting requires a cooperative effort waged by the police and the community.

If most crime happens indoors or outside the police purview, how do we find out about crime? We find out from people who call us and tell us. The critical link between the police and their ability to keep us safe rests with the community. So this communication link must constantly be strengthened and enhanced whenever possible. If people who witness a crime have information that would lead the police to the suspects, the police have to ask themselves what behaviors best encourage these witnesses to come forward and speak with the police. Here are two examples:

An officer received a call about a stolen bicycle. The officer thought of himself as a crime-fighter. The officer was proud of his felony arrest record and the number of suspects who sometimes gave him information about other crooks. He considered himself a fair officer but usually didn't take crap from anybody. He wasn't happy to be dispatched to a residence about a crime in which there were no leads. The only police work involved writing a report.

He arrived at the house and took the information from the mother of the child whose bicycle was stolen from a nearby middle school where the child had been playing. The officer was perfunctory and handed the woman his business card with the case number on it so she could file an insurance claim. The officer did nothing wrong, and overall, his interaction with the young victim and his mother could be rated as adequate.

Under the same set of circumstances, a different officer arrived. This was an officer who understood the importance of encouraging the public to interact with the police. He knew the public has much more information about what is happening in a neighborhood than even the most diligent police officer. Knowing this, he took the young boy for a ride around the neighborhood to see if they could spot the stolen bike. The young boy was excited to have ridden in a police car and, from the mother's perspective, the officer appeared to be genuinely interested in their case. He, too, leaves a business card with the mother, and in so doing, explained what happens with such cases, the importance of having the serial number, and maybe even ventured a guess at the chances of recovery. He assured them he'd be on the lookout for the bike.

Before he leaves, the mother asked to speak with him. She explained about cars coming and going at all hours to the house next door. People stayed a few minutes and left. She suspected her neighbors were selling dope. The officer told her she could help by writing down any license numbers of cars she suspects. He cautioned her that she didn't have to do it continually, but only when she noticed something suspicious. He told her he'd come back in a few days to collect the license numbers. When he returned, he ran the license numbers and checked the criminal records of the registered owners of the ten license plate numbers the mother collected for him.

No one should be surprised to learn that six of the registered owners had previous records for a variety of narcotics violations. The officer could then proceed to make a case against the owners of the house. Several of the car owners were on probation and search and seizure, so the officer could stop them if he saw them in the neighborhood.

Although there was much more that needed to be done before any arrests in this type of scenario, one can readily see how the second officer, by taking time and demonstrating a caring and helpful demeanor, was probably well on his way to making a significant drug arrest. The crime fighter in the first example left without the resident giving him any information about narcotics in the neighborhood. This officer was happy to have the minor report call handled. While he may have spent the rest of his shift looking for a crime, the second officer had information about serious crime, its location, and suspects, all because the mother felt comfortable in speaking with the officer.

Once, I worked a patrol area where a significant number of heroin addicts lived. Unfortunately, in addition to being drug addicts, they preyed on their neighbors to support their habit by committing burglaries and robberies. Most of the people who lived in the area were happy my partner and I patrolled their neighborhood. Both of us had been well schooled on what to look for in this community. In a short time, we made a number of arrests.

Soon people in their front yards would come out and speak with us. We enjoyed chatting with them during the early evening hours of our shift when things were slow. We often gave out our business cards and encouraged people to call if they had any problems. Many years later I still received calls from some of these contacts I made in those early years. They knew my partner and me; they could put a face to a name, and they felt comfortable calling one of us even though we had long ago left patrol and were working other assignments.

People who call the police for the first time can feel uncomfortable. Even today when I have occasion to call the police, the manner and tone of voice of the person answering or, God forbid, they have opted for a voice answering machine can be off-putting. My constant message to the deputies working in my command was to be caring, friendly, and helpful when dealing with residents and visitors.

Though some may have thought the example about the stolen bike was a bit of stretch to make a point, the next story demonstrates a real-life event that helped a bunch of dope cops catch some crooks.

Marilyn and Me

Neither of us remembers for sure when we first met, but it seems to be around the time we were twelve or thirteen years old. It could have been at a skating rink or maybe later when Marilyn was dating my brother's best friend Pete. We lost touch with each other over the years, but I knew that Marilyn married Pete. When Marilyn was teaching in a small private school and I was a patrol deputy, she asked me to give a talk to her fifth grade class. As she moved around in her teaching career, she'd call from time to time for similar talks.

Marilyn was full of energy and imbued with community spirit. She was on many different boards and advisory commissions and worked effectively for the incorporation of her community to become a city in 1988. Later in my career, Marilyn became a project director for a nationally recognized community program run by our force which she still heads today.

When I was the station commander, Marilyn was on the local area traffic committee in addition to her community involvement in other matters. This was one of many nighttime meetings I would attend. I could have delegated the meeting to someone else, but since Marilyn was involved, I felt a certain sense of obligation, out of friendship, to attend personally. Also, I knew Marilyn was not shy and I thought if I delegated the responsibility to someone else, she would call the sheriff personally and snitch me off. I enjoyed working with her because she was straightforward, enthusiastic, hardworking, and dedicated to improving her community.

One day before heading off to the traffic meeting, Marilyn called and asked for a ride to the meeting. It wasn't a problem since she lived near the meeting location. As we headed to the meeting and passed by a house with a large number of cars in the driveway, she pointed to it and said there was something wrong there. Marilyn suspected an auto theft ring was operating out of the garage. When we returned from the meeting, I noted the house address and passed the information along to detectives the next day.

Probably because the information came from me, the detectives got right on the case. They began to watch the house. After a few days, the detectives suspected not an auto theft ring, but rather a dope ring. The case was turned over to narcotics officers, who began to watch the house. When a new Porsche left the house, the officers followed and were able to develop sufficient probable cause to have the car stopped by patrol officers. When the narcotics officers spoke to the driver, he was unusually nervous. After a few questions, he confessed that he was transporting a kilo of cocaine to someone living near a harbor in another county.

Working late into the night, the officers obtained a search warrant for the house to which the suspect had been heading, contacted their colleagues in the other jurisdiction, and searched the house. They found $30,000 hidden away, and a narcotics dog alerted to the presence of drugs on the money. The officers learned the owner of the house also owned a boat, so they obtained a search warrant for the boat. On the boat, the officers found another two kilos of cocaine. The officers seized the money, the dope, the Porsche, and the nice thirty-five-foot boat under asset forfeiture laws.

All and all, this was a great seizure of narcotics that ultimately resulted in many arrests before the case was closed. It was made possible because Marilyn and I had a good relationship, and she felt comfortable in telling me her suspicions. The narcotics officers became better crime fighters because of it. Marilyn had been suspicious about the house for some time before she shared her suspicions with me. She wasn't sure if an officer would truly accept the information and check it out, so she waited until she had an opportunity to tell me. She knew I wouldn't ignore her.

I often used this real life example in my classes at the training academy to illustrate the importance of developing effective interpersonal communication skills that would help officers build good relationships with the general public and victims. Often I would select a trainee and tell him that he had received a radio call to take a burglary report. The victims returned home from vacation to find their home ransacked and various expensive electronics missing. I'd tell the officer to pretend he had just rung the doorbell and the victims have opened the door. I'd ask the recruit, "What do you say?" Until the class, none of the trainees had thought about exactly what to say.

Some responded, "You called us about a burglary?" or some similar remark.

I suggested the trainee extend his hand, and introduce himself and say something to the effect of, "How can I help you?" By this approach, the officer was no longer indifferent, but rather someone with an actual name who was there to help. I cautioned that titles such as, deputy, officer, and detective weren't names and didn't need to be included in the introduction.

When I suggested this to patrol deputies, they were aghast. By shaking hands with a victim, they would be tying up their gun hands. Eventually I was able to convince some of them to at least try this approach when they thought the circumstances were right. Those who did reported good results and incorporated this into their repertoire of behaviors in the field.

One of the deputies who believed I was on the right track was a young man assigned to a remote canyon area. He was a serious-minded person with seven years of experience. He worked his beat starting around ten each morning and ending his shift at six in the early evening. He had worked in the same area for over a year, and the residents knew him and considered him one of their own.

Canyon residents were a clannish bunch of people with strong opinions about everything, including the deputies who patrolled their neighborhood. If our regular deputy took a day off without letting the residents know, we'd receive calls asking where he was. Little went on during this deputy's watch without him knowing about it.

Local residents would size up visitors to determine whether or not they were up to no good. If they thought someone looked suspicious, they would tell the deputy. As a consequence, he always compiled a good number of arrests at the end of the each month.

He didn't have to work hard to be a good crime fighter because the residents did most of the work for him. He endeared himself to the community and in so doing practiced community policing before it became the popular stratagem of police work that it is today. One resident told me the deputy made it a practice to check on an older lady each day and even do her grocery shopping for her since she wasn't able to get out of the house. He never mentioned he did such a thing to me or anybody else, but the residents knew what he was doing. They were able to see this officer, even as an outsider who didn't live in their community, as someone who had a vested interest in them and their welfare.

I wanted this kind of officer/citizen relationship in all our communities. I realized not every officer felt this kind of affinity for the community and the people they served. Many did, but it only takes a few to spoil the good work of others.

Do We Get a Boat?

Eventually my command was upgraded to division status, and I became a captain. There were only about a hundred people working at the patrol station. It wasn't large enough to be considered a division all by itself. Another bureau was added to my command. The Harbor Patrol Bureau was responsible for law enforcement, rescue, and fire fighting in the various small craft harbors in the county. This added another sixty employees for whom I was responsible.

It also required me to learn a new area of police work. At one time, I owned a small sailboat and survived to tell the tale of my many nautical misadventures. But I was far from a sailor and lacked any serious expertise in patrolling harbors, responding to rescues on the open sea, or fighting boat fires. In the latter case, I assumed boat fires were kind of self-limiting since, in the worst of circumstances, once the fire reached the water line, it was pretty much over.

My promotion to captain was a quiet affair. Several patrol sergeants and office personnel took me out for dinner and that was about it. Other than continually pulling out my new badge with the title captain on it and staring at it, someone looking in at the situation couldn't see any changes. During the first several months, I spent a lot of time at the main harbor patrol station trying to learn as much as I could to provide a competent level of oversight.

Luckily for me, the lieutenant in charge of this bureau had tons of experience, having worked with the harbor patrol for nearly twenty years. The big plus was that he was easy to get along with and was an outstanding manager from several perspectives. He knew and understood budgets, he was able to handle personnel matters, even volatile ones, in a calm and deliberate manner, and he was well liked and respected by the boating community.

When I told my family about my promotion, it was well received, and everyone was pleased that I was moving up in the organization so rapidly. Sometimes, though, a family's reaction can be something unexpected. I remember a colleague telling me about his promotion to captain. He had gathered his family around the dinner table. After dinner he told them he had a special announcement. "I'm now a captain," he told his wife and two little girls.

The kids went berserk; they jumped from their seats and ran around the table yelling, "Hooray for Daddy!" The fact his kids were so excited gave him a sense of pride in having reached this august position in the department. But both he and his wife were somewhat surprised at the kids' over-the-top demonstration and the strong emotional investment they seemingly had in his promotion. He expected maybe a, "Gee that's nice, Daddy." Maybe becoming a captain meant more to them than he thought. He and his wife had often spoken of the possibility of his promotion before in front of the kids so it was possible they instinctively knew how important this was to him and they genuinely were excited for him.

After a while, the kids calmed down and returned to their seats. He told them how good it made him feel that they were so happy. He said he didn't realize they knew how important this was to him. The two kids looked at him and then at each other. The youngest one said, "Daddy, I think this is the most exciting thing ever. When do we get the boat?" Of course, he didn't get a boat with his promotion, but I did. In fact, I got a whole bunch of them.

On The Road

My new position was the first new captaincy in the department in thirty years. Word about my promotion spread slowly, and I found people didn't recognize my place in the hierarchy and, as a consequence, would bypass me on some of the issues in my purview. In part, this was due to the inability of people to catch me in my office. Between schlepping over to the various harbors to see how things were going and pick up a little more knowledge about marine safety and driving back and forth to headquarters, I wasn't spending much time in my office.

As a manager, whenever I worked in an outlying facility and away from headquarters, I felt as if I was a step behind. Our headquarters was our police corporate office. For the most part this was where policy was developed, personnel decisions were made, daily working relationships were formed, and the corporate culture manifested itself. Some managers liked being away from headquarters and preferred to be left on their own away from the prying and often critical eyes of bosses. Closeness to headquarters, for them, meant more headaches and aggravation. But for me, my absence meant I didn't get to participate in a lot of the senior leadership decisions.

Law enforcement organizations, especially large ones, are rife with rumors and speculations. When word spreads about a future promotion list, the communication back channels are abuzz with talk about who'll be on the list, where they'll rank, and who won't make the list and why. Providing information to the rabble doesn't slow down the chatter. Once a promotion list was published, the conversations shifted to why a particular person was ranked in this or that position.

The poor person who finds himself in the number one slot on a promotion list may be subject to a tremendous verbal beating. They've reached an elevated position, not because of their good works, but rather because they went fishing with a boss or were good "suck ups." In my case, they were partially right, but I didn't fish.

Transfer lists presented fertile ground for rumors. With three to four thousand employees in an agency, the need to transfer people happened frequently. Transfer lists, while not a daily occurrence, are published quite regularly. They were fodder for many rumors about the people being transferred. The rumors seldom ascribed positive motivations to the managers involved in compiling a transfer list, and the rumors didn't often put the people being transferred in a positive light.

I wanted to be in on the ground floor with promotions and transfers. I wanted to play an active role in the development of policy. In an outlying facility, you're mostly another manager on the fringes. That's not to say I was never asked for my input on matters or my opinion about changes in direction for the department, but this didn't happen with the regularity I wanted.

After my promotion to captain was approved, my boss called me to headquarters often. When I was at the academy, I had established a good working relationship with the sheriff and his three main underlings because of the work I'd done for them on staff projects. They thought my work was good and believed I could be trusted even with sensitive projects. I didn't think it odd to be getting more and more special projects that had nothing to do with my area of responsibility.

Most of the special projects the boss gave weren't difficult, but some demanded a lot of time. I couldn't get through a week without having to get into the car and drive back up a crowded freeway to headquarters, usually the same crowded freeway I struggled down to get to my office. I would sit down, have a cup of coffee, the phone would ring, and there would be a message for me to meet with the boss in his office uptown. The thirty-minute or longer drive on the freeway put me out of communication for that period of time, except for the police radio. There were no cell phones or car phones over which I could check in and see how things were going at the station or the harbor. I couldn't get briefed about any emerging events taking place during my drive time. I might hear patrol cars being dispatched to a hot call, but I wouldn't be able to be briefed about it until I found a phone.

These were the downsides of working at an outlying facility. But they were mitigated because the boss was relying on me more frequently. Having more face time with the boss and the sheriff far outweighed the boredom of driving up and down a crowded freeway.

Sometimes I was needed in the early afternoon. The work I'd have to do would take me until three thirty or four o'clock. This was way too early to go home, but too late to drive back to the station. Rush-hour traffic would start to build early and it significantly lengthened the drive time back to South County. So, I ambled around the building, trying not to make it look like aimless wandering. I came upon the technique of carrying a bunch of papers and a notebook with me as I dropped in on various colleagues to idly pass the time of day until it was safe to leave for home.

One day while employing my best technique of purposeful wandering, I received a call to meet with one of the judges at the courthouse. Since we had been out of our temporary offices on the bottom floor of the courthouse, I didn't think much about the call, although I was miffed that I had to drive back to the station in the late afternoon. This particular judge was a character. Most judges are pieces of work in their own way, but this judge was unusual. He was hardheaded and led the other judges in promulgating many of the rules and restrictions on deputies' behavior in the courthouse.

Parking was at a premium around the courthouse, and this was something he decided to watch over with unsurpassed vigilance. Sheriff's vehicles were relegated to a chained-in area next to our new modular building at the lower end of the parking lot. We weren't allowed to park our vehicle anywhere else. Court employees' vehicles were assigned to special parking spaces close to the court building. With his own hand, the judge designed a parking permit sticker so he could tell at a glance as he walked to and from his car if there were any errant parkers. He ordered bailiffs to patrol the lots and issue citations to illegally parked cars. Of course, our deputies could issue citations as well for these scofflaws, but they had more pressing matters to handle.

When I had first arrived at the station, I went out of my way to befriend this judge. He seldom went out for lunch, and I often went into his chambers during lunchtime and we would discuss a large number of subjects. He was, to me, friendly and outgoing. He had a special hot dog cooker stuck between some of the law books in his chambers, and lunch mostly consisted of a Hebrew National hot dog cooked on his hot dog cooker, placed in a Wonder Bread hot dog roll, and garnished with French's mustard. He seldom missed a hot dog day. I thought perhaps his diet had made him irregular and that was the cause of his perceived crankiness.

It took a while to get back, but I managed to arrive before the court closed. The court clerk directed me into the judge's chambers. He didn't look happy. "What's up, Judge?" was my start of the conversation. I didn't get a chance to say much more. He ranted and raved about parking around the court and how difficult parking was for many court employees, jurors, and people having business with the court.

He carried on about parking being no small matter and certainly not something funny. Funny? Where was this going? From his desk, he picked up a sheriff's traffic ticket and waved it about. He wanted to know if the deputy who wrote the ticket thought it was funny. I asked to look at the ticket. It was a parking ticket for a car parked in the employee only parking area. The car didn't have one of the judge's approved parking permits.

I didn't get it. "What's the deal, Judge?" I asked.

"That's my car!" he informed me in a loud voice. Well, where was his parking permit, I wondered quietly, especially since he was the parking permit CEO of all things.

He certainly wasn't being judge-like in his actions or his language. I thought judges were more judicious and temperate. I knew the deputy who wrote the ticket, and he was a good officer, but he had, in the past, demonstrated a sense of humor that maybe wasn't always appropriate. Nevertheless, I assured the judge the deputy was doing his job and probably didn't know it was his car. In any event, I told the judge, he didn't write the ticket to be funny.

People with legal training seem to have an ace in the hole. I should have realized this when I was speaking to the judge. He handed me a Polaroid of the deputy who was holding up the parking ticket he had apparently written seconds before the picture was snapped. There was a big smile on the deputy's face as he posed for the unknown photographer. The judge explained why his car didn't have a parking permit on it, but to tell the truth I can't remember why. My head was spinning, and all I wanted to do was get out of there and kill the deputy. I took the parking ticket, but the judge wouldn't give me the picture. I said I'd take care of it. It was the first and only time I ever fixed a ticket. How weird that I did so for a judge.

I called the deputy into my office the next day before he went out in the field on patrol. I tried not to laugh. He knew what he was doing and thought it was a funny but valid point to make to the judge. I told him not to do it again. It wasn't his job to point out judges' mistakes.

"You mean don't write judges tickets, or don't take pictures after I write one a ticket?" he asked.

"No more pictures," I told him. Chuckling, we both went out for coffee.

The Night the Princess Peed In the Woods

During my long police career, I had many great opportunities to meet officers from throughout the world. I developed a keen interest in how policing was done in other countries. Several people on my staff shared the same interest. So around this time we began police exchange programs with international colleagues. This expanded my opportunity to meet more officers, and as time went by, I collected a large portfolio of names and addresses of nearly 100 police officers in thirty countries. I would meet them during vacations my wife and I took or during formal police exchange programs or when a colleague from another country came to visit. Most people knew that anytime an international police officer came to our sheriff's office, they could direct them to me and I would gladly play host.

I remember my wife's surprise when we traveled to Europe together for the first time. Entering a police building in The Netherlands, or the UK, or Germany, and displaying my badge, I was met with kindness and enthusiasm. I'd be supplied with police hats, badges, and other types of police memorabilia. These international police brothers would offer advice on where to eat, how to get to where I wanted to go, where to stay, and often proffer an invitation to stay with them. My psychologist wife was amazed at the relationships police around the world shared.

When planning a vacation out of the country, I'd check my contacts. Seldom would their advice steer me wrong. This was especially so when it came to recommended places to stay and restaurants. My wife, a little more than me, had some definite standards that had to be met during travel. As the prototypical Jewish American princess, she believed camping was going somewhere without a reservation.

We both were repulsed if a restroom was dirty and we were, truth told, kind of finicky travelers. We were adventurous, but we liked our creature comforts as well. We didn't display ugly American behaviors when those comforts didn't meet our standards. We quietly endured off putting local customs, and we were outwardly courteous and resolute.

I gained a little more experience than she did in confronting poor circumstances as I had visited some poor areas of Russia. While I didn't enjoy dirty toilets, poor food, cold, smelly rooms, and uncomfortable beds, I managed to work through it. Jews aren't campers and neither am I. Any hotel below a four-star ranking wasn't on our radar. It used to be a three-star minimum but the number of stars rose as our finances improved.

After completing a police-related program in an out-of-the-way town in the middle of Finland, I made arrangements to meet my wife in Helsinki. We planned a two-week trip across Scandinavia. We took a ferry to Stockholm and spent a day or two. We rented a car and drove to Oslo for the night. From there, we moved on to Geilo, in the middle of Norway, for another night. The next morning, we drove four hours to the west coast town of Bergen.

We were entertained in Stockholm by a police psychologist and her geologist husband whom I met a few years before when she came to our force and visited our crime laboratory. I thought this was a particularly clever choice in the use of foreign contacts as she was involved in police works yet still a psychologist, something of interest to my wife. We were shown around Stockholm, feted at a small party, and taken to dinner. The hotel she'd recommended was perfect. It was off the beaten tourist path.

It was a perfect place. Most of the guests were Swedish businessmen and women. Because of this great Swedish contact, we had an opportunity to spend time in a hotel not frequented by most American travelers and enjoyed a sense of the city.

I had no other contacts in Sweden, and we drove across the country at a leisurely pace, stopping for the night in Jonkoping to visit the match museum in the old Swedish match factory of Ivar Kreuger. My police psychologist colleague suggested we stop there to visit. The recent book, *The Match King* by Frank Partnoy has added new significance to the visit of long ago. We wouldn't have had the experience except for the advice of a police friend.

After a few days, we drove down the west coast of Norway toward the picturesque town of Bergen. It took forever to get there because the scenery was so beautiful we kept stopping every few miles to gaze out at the breathtaking views and to capture them with an old film camera. We were excited to reach Bergen. I had corresponded with a young Norwegian officer whom I had met briefly several years before when he came to visit a friend in California. We exchanged business cards, and I followed up with a letter several months before the start of our Scandinavian adventure.

His response to my letter was intriguing. I had asked for a hotel recommendation. He said he owned a cabin by a beautiful lake that was a perfect retreat for a romantic couple. It was located a short distance from Bergen. He invited us to spend a few nights there and enjoy our time in Bergen. This sounded perfect. We met him at the main police station in Bergen at four in the afternoon as he was finishing his police band practice. Hmm. Band. Oh well, European police were different. I guessed it wasn't unusual for a police force to have a band, although it wasn't normally the case in the US.

As directed, we arrived promptly at four o'clock, and he arrived a few minutes later. I had no idea who he was. I didn't recognize him, but then I had only met him for a few minutes several years ago. He took us for snacks at a hillside restaurant with a spectacular view of Bergen. Since it was now a little after five pm, my wife and I ate only a little but he had a full meal.

He never offered to pay and, while that was unusual in my experience, I didn't have a problem paying. We lingered an hour or so, then he wanted us to follow him to visit his mother.

I should have said no, but I didn't want to be impolite. In all my travels, no one had ever taken me to see their mother. Obediently, we followed him out of Bergen for forty-five minutes to some town by a ferry station. To arrive at his mother's house, we drove through the ferry's parking lot, which eventually narrowed to the house's driveway. She was surprised to see him, and us. Apparently, he never told her we were coming, but she was gracious, made us tea, and settled down for a long chat with her son's new friends from America. She proudly went through and explained each page of several family photo albums in halting but understandable English.

Fortunately, it was summertime, and the sun wouldn't set until after 9:45 p.m. I could see, however, daylight was waning. The conversation was not. I was wondering if we were going to have dinner or when we would head for the romantic cabin by the lake. It would be unkind to say the conversation was bizarre or the relationship between son and mother was strange, but I'd be less than forthright to label it any other way. It may have been that my perception resulted from my own lack of cultural sensitivity. I was feeling both strange and uncomfortable.

After an hour or so, my head hurt because it sounded as if dogs were barking at me instead of two nice people trying to entertain me. Finally, we left his mother's house and followed my police friend to his cabin where we were to spend the night.

Almost immediately, we turned off a well-maintained highway onto a narrow, twisty, one-lane road where speeds in excess of twenty-five mph would be dangerous. There were signs cautioning drivers to be watchful for sheep. Good sign, for as we rounded a curve, we confronted fifty sheep wandering on the road. We drove for an hour and daylight was nearly done when we turned off the road to a main highway. A short distance later, we pulled into a parking lot by a beautiful lake next to which was a nice large cabin.

Ewweee. Things were looking up. He suggested we take our luggage, as this was a rural area and cars were often burgled. Traveling with the princess in those days required lots of luggage. I grabbed two of the bags, my wife took one, and we headed excitedly to the cabin we could see from the parking lot.

My friend called to us and pointed in another direction across the highway. We saw nothing. We climbed over a fence and trudged through a muddy cow pasture. Maybe it was a sheep pasture; I don't know. I do know I became concerned about the nice Gucci loafers I was wearing when I sunk into the mud with each step on the trek to his cabin. When my shoes had been completely ruined, we arrived. There wasn't a single cabin on the property, but rather three little cabins of varying quality. A fast-running stream could be heard flowing nearby.

We entered what he called the main cabin as the sun set and it turned dark. It was a musty-smelling, three-room building furnished with hand-me-down, raggedy bits and pieces. There was a kitchen, living room, and bedroom. There was no toilet or bathroom. There was no running water except for the water in the stream we had heard. What had I done? I could handle this, though not happily. I wasn't sure I was capable of handling the simmering rage I was pretty sure my wife was experiencing.

My friend asked us to sign and write some comments in his guestbook. I looked through the book and read the comments of other visitors. It seemed all the visitors had been men. The comments were, suffice to say, odd. My wife later suggested these were the final words of the victims of the mass murderer who was hosting us. In her mind, we were the next victims and our bodies, along with the bodies of previous victims, would be found in the muddy cow pasture we had traveled through. He showed us around the property. The first stop was the outhouse. He opened the door and pulled back quickly. He expressed his sorrow it hadn't been cleaned and perhaps it would be more pleasant for us to use the woods.

I didn't want to look at my wife for fear her gaze would turn me into a quivering mass of jelly. Next, we were shown to the legendary romantic getaway for two. It was a one-room building with a chair and bunk beds. I wondered about the word "romantic" and couldn't quite reconcile romantic and bunk beds. There was a sink in the room with a bucket so water could be taken from the stream.

He left us with a flashlight as he pointed in the general direction of the stream. I walked through the woods and discovered the stream when I felt the cold water washing over my previously muddy shoes. Farther into the stream, the water was deeper and flowed more powerfully. When I put the bucket down to gather the water, the force of the stream wrenched my shoulder and nearly swept me off my feet.

Back in our little cabin, I found my wife waiting by the door. She wanted to leave, but we couldn't since I didn't have a clue where we were. She suggested making a run for it, thinking we'd be better off driving on the main highway where we'd eventually reach a town. I had some sleeping pills and offered one to my wife as a reasonable alternative to get us through the night.

There was a little porch by the front door of the cabin. Before retiring to my lower bunk (I had won the coin toss), I peed off the front porch. For a guy, this wasn't a big deal. My wife took the flashlight and determinedly marched into the woods to pee outdoors for the first time in her pampered, city life. She told me there were lots of things running around out there and sharply pointed out the obvious: she was a full professor at a major university and shouldn't have to pee in the woods. She climbed into the top bunk and waited for the sleeping pill to kick in. It was a fitful night's sleep for both of us. We awoke at dawn.

We concocted a story for our host before we went to see him in the main cabin where, according to my wife's imagination, he had probably spent the night sharpening various cutting instruments to enhance our eventual disembowelment. We told him we had miscalculated our schedule and had to leave Bergen on the afternoon ferry. He was disappointed, but understanding. We followed him back into town to the ferry terminal, and he headed off to the police station for his shift. When he was out of sight, we drove over to a nice hotel and checked in.

We took long, hot showers. Clean, refreshed, and less anxious, we lunched at a seaside restaurant. We walked around town doing touristy things, always keeping an eye out for approaching police vehicles. When we would see one, we'd duck into a store to hide. We made it through the day, had a great dinner at an upscale restaurant, and a fantastic night's rest.

The next morning we drove onto the ferry and headed for Stavanger in the southern part of Norway. We continued our tour of Scandinavia without incident, and while I did have some other police contacts in upcoming cities, I never bothered to touch base with them. Whenever I mentioned that I knew a police officer in a city and maybe I should contact them, my wife strongly objected. It took her many years to get over our Norway experience. Whenever I mentioned it, she'd say, "It was weird. The whole thing was plain weird."

Three years later, my Norwegian friend came to California and contacted me. I arranged a hotel for him and his new wife. I met them for lunch. When I first saw him, I didn't recognize him again. In Norway, he had a butch haircut, and at the restaurant, his hair was grown out. His wife was a classically beautiful, engaging, and funny woman. They had had a child, and we spent two hours over lunch talking about children, police work, and travel. I thoroughly enjoyed the time I spent with him. He was almost like two different people. Perhaps marrying an outstandingly beautiful woman had changed him. It could have been the fact that mass murderers are capable of completely changing their appearance. Who knows? My wife believes that at some point in time, bodies will be discovered in the muddy pasture across the highway from a pristine Norwegian lake.

SEVEN

THE CORPORATE OFFICES

✻ ✻ ✻

Macht get von Recht. (Power trumps justice.)

– Attributed to Otto von Bismark, Minister President of Prussia and later Chancellor of Germany, 1863

Megalomania in the Land of Management

Having been married to a psychologist for so many years, I took on the habit of playing amateur psychologist. I would never do this in her presence, of course; however, I was powerless to stop doing so in the work place.

When I was transferred and placed in charge of the patrol division in our HQ building, I was able to witness first-hand the daily managerial shenanigans that passed as enlightened corporate behavior. It became clear that the main job of a captain was to implement the corporate will.

There were only a few people privy to the decision-making process as it related to policy development or changing procedures. But the more important the policy or the procedure, the fewer the people privileged to participate in the process. In many cases, such as disciplinary issues, transfers, promotions, issuance of new cars, or the logo on a baseball cap, the decision-making authority was held firmly and tenaciously in the hands of the boss and his immediate underling.

Nearly every decision made by a captain necessitated some type of notification to one of these people for ultimate approval. Years later when I wanted a computer for my desk, for example, I was told, "Computers are for secretaries, not for managers." Advocating the promotion of a woman lieutenant to captain, I was told, "The department isn't ready for another female captain." (Our first female captain had retired.) After much cajoling and pestering, I was allowed to have a computer, but during my tenure, we never had another female captain.

I hoped no one had a malignant heart in these matters, but I never knew for sure. They saw their world in a narrow way. For the boss, police work pretty much stopped when he left a patrol car, and he tended to see things as they had been, not as they were currently. For the boss's second in command, his view of police work was shaped in another police agency, and his managerial style and way of doing things were seen as alien to many of the captains, lieutenants, and sergeants.

These bosses assumed that whatever they said was the final word, and the only way to do things. They expected the entire force to mobilize to do their bidding. Many of the managers on the force didn't feel they had even a modicum of control over their own divisions. Managers wanted to play a worthwhile role in shaping the growth of our organization. Unfortunately, this was never the case for the majority of them. The bosses' way of treating them created frustration, indifference, and smoldering hostility on the part of some. It wasn't the decisions they made, but rather the "Moses coming down from the mountain" manner on the part of the boss that created these feelings.

The sheriff was blissfully unaware of these things. As his political power grew, he became more detached from his own organization and demonstrated a lack of trust in his managers, supervisors, and officers. First reports of incidents were nearly always wrong. Nevertheless, the managerial atmosphere was such that whenever any manager received a report about something possibly done wrong, the captain would rush to tell the boss.

The boss usually assumed we were at fault and would comment profanely saying things such as, "Get those sons of bitches squared away." When further investigation revealed the sons of bitches didn't do anything wrong, the boss would still rail against them. It made no sense but he was so verbally aggressive and appeared so genuinely incensed about almost anything, few managers had the wherewithal to disagree. Arguing with him was thought pointless because it was fruitless.

Me, I was lucky. A lot of my input was valued, and I felt I was making a contribution to the direction the department was taking. But I was still amazed at some of the crazy thinking. I was happy to have a computer on my desk, but I felt the need to have e-mail also. When I asked for it, there was no resistance. It was installed quickly before they discovered what e-mail was. I had concluded that they didn't have a clue when they gave me permission to install it.

This proved to be partially right. They knew what e-mail was, but didn't know that, since we didn't have an in-house e-mail system, I had to get my e-mail through an Internet provider. When they found out I had Internet access, they were pissed. I tried to explain how e-mail worked. I could see they were becoming angry. This was frustrating.

These were two guys running a $300 million law enforcement agency, and their understanding of computer systems was, to be kind, unsophisticated. After much grumbling, they said they would speak with the Records captain, whom they believed would give them a better explanation. It was the last time I heard from them about my e-mail. It was the last time I would have any substantial conversation with them about computers. It was a topic I avoided for the remainder of the time I was with the force.

I don't want to leave the impression that these two men were unkind. They could be when they wanted to be, but as their time in with the department grew, they acted more disgruntled about even minor events. They were good to me, and while occasionally they reined me in, my overall relationship with them was excellent. That's not to say they didn't give me heartburn frequently. They considered themselves smarter than everyone else because they were in charge, and their arrogance caused problems. I called it positional intelligence. It was reinforced, for the most part, by the people working for them, me included.

As an elected official, the boss could say with confidence and a certain amount of self-delusion that he was chosen by a majority of the people as being the best of all the candidates for the office. In fact, he was the preferred choice, not necessarily the best choice. Being the head of a large law enforcement agency, didn't mean he was smarter, cleverer, or prettier than everyone in the organization. His best resource was his employees, but he didn't acknowledge it. I don't think he knew it.

Since employees defer to their boss, especially in authoritarian, hierarchal organizations, it reinforces a boss's sense of his/her own self-worth. In our force, it seemed as if the sheriff and his second-in-command lost sight of their own limitations and failed to value their employees.

What they didn't understand was my sense of self-worth and my firm belief in my early managerial career that I was smarter than everyone else. This wasn't based on positional intelligence; I always thought I was smarter than everyone else. So while my two bosses were out of the megalomania closet for all to see, I was safely ensconced behind closed doors. Perhaps, in the final analysis, that was why we got along so well and why I was allowed so much input into the decision-making process for the department.

Not So Big but Still Vast

Unlike my former command, the Headquarters Patrol Division involved several other responsibilities besides patrol. In South County, the division commander was responsible for all the patrols in the area and the harbor patrols. It was straightforward police patrol work. My new assignment was different. In addition to sheriff's patrols in the central, northern, and western parts of the county, the division commander oversaw the SWAT team, the bomb squad, security at the airport, the motor pool, crossing guards, and the transportation of about eight hundred jail prisoners to the various courts and other facilities around the county.

I can't say I really wanted to have command of the Patrol Division. When I was told, I was ambivalent. The good thing was that I'd be right in the heart of things. The number of patrols was smaller, but my overall command strength was larger. I saw it as a promotion even though it wasn't. I'd be closer to home and closer to the heart of our decision-making machinery.

My boss said he transferred me so I would be closer. He said he needed me for some projects. I don't know if he was being truthful, but it made me feel good. They probably wanted to keep closer tabs on me as I was still in my mid-thirties and didn't have a lot of management experience. Being young and feeling invincible was not a good combination for a police manager. All our other captains were in their mid-to-late forties or early fifties. Maybe they wanted to watch over me until I seasoned.

The specialty units, which were now under my command, were staffed with officers who were, in many ways, a cut above the average officer. The SWAT team officers, for example, competed to be on the team and had to continually prove their worth during their monthly training sessions. The big obstacle for SWAT candidates was being well liked by the other team members since members voted for who would be on the team.

This wasn't an official part of the selection process, but SWAT members believed that, as a team, they would have to work with people they liked and who fit their image of how a team member should look and deport himself. I believed if they were on SWAT, they should have the dedication and discipline to work with whoever came out on top of the testing procedures, not who received the most popular votes. SWAT and I were on a collision course, but the SWAT leaders told me they would stop voting for members. Of course, they never stopped voting, but they made sure I never heard about it again.

The bomb squad was a small unit consisting of four detectives and one bomb-sniffing dog. The members were trained at the country's most prestigious military bomb disposal school. Over the years, since the inception of the squad, it grew from a part-time ancillary unit to one of the busiest bomb squads in the US, and the squad members had grown with it in expertise, sophistication, and bravery.

There was a constant battle about the installation of emergency lights on the bomb truck and trailer. The bomb trailer was specially built and reinforced so suspicious devices could be placed in it and transported to a safe location where they'd be destroyed. The truck and trailer didn't have emergency lights. When I asked why, I was told the administration didn't want them driving fast. The fact that a suspected bomb being transported to a safe location in the bomb trailer might accidentally explode while waiting at a red light didn't occur to anyone. I thought it was a stupid position for the bosses to take. They weren't dissuaded even if police and fire personnel would have to wait around for the squad to arrive once a suspected bomb was located. Had my bosses been in charge of the fire department, I suppose fire trucks would be driving to fires without the benefit of emergency lights and sirens.

I always liked airports. They were interesting and required a special kind of policing. In the days prior to September 11, 2001, airport security was a different type of work than today. We had a busy airport in our jurisdiction. Originally it was policed by special officers in the Airport Police Bureau, which fell under the operational management of the airport director. Special officers must have been code for old retired military guys. With little training or enthusiasm they wandered around one of the country's busiest airports drinking coffee and chatting up the girls. By the time I arrived, responsibility for airport security had been taken over by the sheriff. Better-trained and more competent special officerswere under the immediate supervision and direction of deputy sheriffs.

The system was working well except for the inordinate number of complaints we received about the special officers' handling of parking enforcement at the infamous white curb. The airport handled six million passengers each year. Friends or relatives met the majority of passengers when their flights arrived.

Everyone, it seemed, wanted to park at the curb directly in front of the arrivals terminal. The curb could accommodate about twenty cars, but usually fifty or more were jockeying for a position at a choice white curb spot. The area was designed so people could swing into the curb, open their trunks, and throw in the luggage of the arriving passenger who would be standing at the curb. Otherwise, if the arriving passenger wasn't at the curb with his/her luggage in hand, the driver was directed to park in one of the (God forbid!) paid lots or drive around again.

Most didn't want either option. They wanted to park at the curb and wait twenty or thirty minutes for their passenger to arrive. The parking violator was often agitated, having found this convenient position in front of the terminal only to be told to move. Most violators would recite a litany of reasons why they had to park at the curb and remain there for however long it took. When it became obvious to the driver that a parking ticket was forthcoming, the agitation turned to angry words followed by a complaint about the officer's behavior.

After reviewing many of these complaints, we issued voice recorders to the officers to wear on their belts. When people complained, we'd check the recordings. In many cases, while the officers weren't great at calming things down, the drivers sounded angry, foul-mouthed, and were in the wrong.

Crossing guards were a special group of people in my command. They were responsible for helping schoolchildren across busy streets before and after school. In my force, they were hourly, part-time employees. I met with them shortly after taking command of Patrol Division. They were mostly old women with a few even older men.

Thinking back on it, I would say their average age was "deceased." None of them was shy, and they all bitched about one thing or the other that we were doing wrong. I don't mean to make light of an important safety job. Getting control of a bunch of rambunctious boys and girls on their way to and from school wasn't an easy job. Everyone was concerned about the safety of these children.

But their major concerns, at least the concerns they spent the most time on, were the need for a flashing red light atop their hand-held stop sign and the need for us to issue them whistles. They wanted to direct traffic, which wasn't their job. They were at their posts to help the children assert their pedestrian right of way at intersections. Crossing guards held a different view than this and, during my time, we never saw eye to eye. I tried to get the crossing guard responsibility transferred to the Road Department. It never happened.

When I thought about becoming a cop, I never thought about all the things that go into making a police force run efficiently. All I thought about was the adventure and, of course, red lights and sirens. Even as a patrol officer, I didn't think about patrol vehicles. If one broke, I would check out another, and the broken one would be fixed. If one were totaled, a new one would take its place. I envisioned a never-ending supply of patrol cars and equipment.

My assignment included responsibility for a motor pool of three hundred cars of various types. There were patrol cars, detective cars, unmarked patrol cars, rental vehicles, SUVs, and the cool cars the big bosses drove. The motor pool was even responsible for the Cadillac (yep, a Cadillac!) the sheriff drove for two years until he couldn't take the heat any longer. After the Cadillac, he settled, can you imagine, for a Lincoln Town Car. The motor pool kept track of all the vehicles, made sure they received their regularly scheduled maintenance, and kept them clean. The latter duty was performed by a small group of inmate workers from one of the minimum-security jail facilities.

The Transportation Bureau assigned to me delivered these inmate workers to the motor pool. The Bureau's main job was to transport prisoners to the court jurisdictions around the county. On weekdays, the Bureau would move eight hundred to one thousand prisoners on buses to and from courts, medical appointments, work details outside the jails, and other detention facilities throughout the state.

No officer was ever killed on our force while working in the Transportation Bureau, but it was considered a dangerous assignment. We had many officers assaulted while transporting prisoners. For the most part, the deputies working this detail liked it because it afforded them specific assignments with little paperwork. Simply counting the number of prisoners loading on a bus and checking it against a manifest was probably the biggest challenge of the day. The rest of the day would go fairly smoothly as long as everyone was vigilant.

Desperate prisoners saw the time to and from courts as a weak link in the jail system. If one planned to escape, this time was considered to have a better-than-average chance of success. Few escaped, but the perception of vulnerability during transportation time was prevalent among prisoners.

Most of the long bus rides could have been avoided if there had been a central criminal court. There was a tunnel from the jail to the main court building across the street. Sadly, most judges working in outlying courts didn't concern themselves with this. They wanted the prisoners at the time and place they decided. It was nearly impossible to get the presiding judges in the five different jurisdictions to coordinate their starting times, which would have relieved some of the burden on the Bureau. So now, besides managing patrols, I was running the one of the largest bus companies in the county. Like most bus companies, we didn't make a profit.

Horses and Dogs

Sheriffs and horses go together because we conjure up images of the Old West from the television of our youth. Today, sheriffs still have a close affinity with horses. Larger sheriff forces throughout the country invariably have "sheriff's posses." Posses include local residents, usually political contributors to a sheriff's election campaign, who are of a horsy nature. Today, most would be clearly identified as being part of those often hated and tax-avoiding (as liberals would describe them) one-percenters. They're able to afford expensive silver saddles and costly, but garish, uniforms to display when they ride in parades or take part in other ceremonial events. Sheriffs will usually deputize posse members as "special" deputies, but the members have no real police power. However, they have lots of the accoutrements of power such as badges, guns, and big cowboy hats.

Our force hadn't had a posse in many years. From time to time, there would be talk of starting one again, but nothing significant happened. We did have a mounted unit. It differed from a posse in that the riders were all regularly sworn deputy sheriffs with full police powers. When I joined the force in 1966, patrolling on horseback was a distant memory for the department.

This marked the beginning of our modern age mounted patrol unit. Since then the mounted squad had grown, but we only had a few horses and they had been donated to the department. The equipment was poor and not standardized at all. Duty on the mounted squad was ancillary, the training sporadic, and there were never enough volunteers who knew how to ride a horse properly. I had a strong affinity for the mounted squad because of my previous experience as one of the original members on the squad.

Over time, the squad attracted deputies from patrol and the jail who owned their own horses. Reserve deputy sheriffs who owned horses also joined the unit. This helped strengthen the squad not only in numbers, but in expertise as well because all these horse owners brought with them their knowledge and experience. They were all willing to share it with the other members.

Reserve deputy sheriffs, unlike "special" deputies, were required by law to have a specific amount of training directly proportional to the police power they wielded. Some reserve deputies could only exercise power under the direct supervision of a regularly sworn officer. Others could operate on their own once they accumulated the same amount of basic training as any other peace officer.

The most interesting thing about reserve officers was they didn't get paid, yet they willingly subjected themselves to the same abuse other cops received from time to time. I saw a recruitment poster for reserve cops once that stuck in my mind. It showed a darkened alleyway. At the end of the alley were two thugs who looked menacing. They were all tatted up with weightlifter builds. One was carrying a shotgun and looking over his shoulder directly at the camera. The other had a crow bar inserted against a doorjamb and he, too, was looking toward the camera as if he just noticed someone. The caption read something like, "You wouldn't go down that alley for a million bucks, but a reserve officer does it free." It was a powerful message, and it perfectly captured the essence of reserve police officers.

With the help of the reserves and deputies from throughout the department, our mounted unit was used often. They were out patrolling on beaches, in parks, and at events where large crowds were expected. We seldom received complaints about the horses, and the tactical advantage they provided was unsurpassed.

Our biggest complaint came from the captain of our Honor Farm where we housed low-security prisoners. The Honor Farm was, in fact, a farm. It was basically a truck farm that helped offset the cost of feeding inmates throughout the jail system. A barn and corral were built there to house the county-owned horses we had accumulated through donations.

Sometimes, in organizations, the second and third order effects of decisions aren't considered. No one discussed the plan to stable the horses at the farm with the captain. The captain's complaint was the cost of the horses. They were eating up his budget. No one thought about how much it cost to take care of five horses each year. The captain had to cut in other areas to make his budget. He was a friend, but I'm sure he believed I had done him a disservice. Many years later, although he, too, had retired, the subject was a mild annoyance to him.

Police dogs have a checkered history working in law enforcement organizations. During the height of the civil rights marches, police dogs in the South were used against demonstrators. Those of us old enough to remember, can hardly think about civil rights demonstrations without conjuring up the image of vicious-looking police dogs attacking helpless demonstrators. As a consequence, the use of the police dogs was not only more circumspect during demonstrations but, in California, dogs were hardly used at all. By the late 1970s, though, California law enforcement agencies were establishing K-9 units, as they were called in police parlance.

We all knew police dogs had reached a certain level of acceptability in our area when an extremely progressive police force announced they would be using K-9s. The chief of this city was a studious person who, I'm sure, thoroughly researched the issue before deciding to implement the program. He lectured me one day (in a way, I'm sure he would have said he was mentoring) about dogs in police work. He pointed out that the biggest problem with dogs in law enforcement was image, nothing more and nothing less.

He, or his staff, had struck upon the unique idea of using not German shepherd dogs, as was the gold standard among police agencies, but rather Bouvier des Flandres. These dogs look like overgrown poodles with unruly hair and a reputation as calm and gentle animals. They weren't a particularly popular breed in the US. Averaging seventy-five to ninety pounds, these Franco-Belgian beasts were impressive and would certainly catch your eye.

The chief waxed poetic about his new innovative approach for the use of dogs in his modern, community-oriented police force. The chief explained how implementing the program with Bourviers had sold his city council and the residents on the program. The dogs didn't look aggressive, he lectured, but they could do all the things other police dogs could do. They had a gentle appearance the community was more willing to accept.

In a spirit of cooperation, I went to see the new dogs in action. It was true the dogs didn't look aggressive at all. They were big, hairy galoots, and they looked positively non-aggressive and a little disheveled. Unfortunately, the chief had spent so much time on the dogs' image, he must not have given much thought to the officers who would be handling the dogs.

The police dog handlers were dressed in jumpsuits with the trousers bloused into their combat boots. Today, it's not unusual to see police wearing battle dress uniforms such as these, but then it was strange to see an officer assigned to patrol duty wearing such an outfit. Any mitigation the poodles-on-steroids might have gained in the eyes of the public, the officers in their combat-looking gear erased.

By the 1980s, police K-9 units were established in a large number of agencies. It was finally time for our force to implement a K-9 unit as well.

We had the benefit of having a large number of business and community leaders who had formed a not-for-profit organization dedicated to the support of police work. The president of the organization offered to purchase five police dogs for us at his expense.

Within a short time of his offer, deputies were chosen as handlers, patrol cars were retrofitted to accommodate the dogs, dogs were purchased, and the dogs and handlers were trained. The big question was how we should identify these special patrol units. Some agencies use "K-9" written in large letters on the back door of the patrol car, some of the agencies suggested we write "Deputy Dawg," but we settled on the words "Police Dog" on the back doors of the patrol cars. It was plain and simple and worked for many years. I noticed the other day, however, one of our K-9 units had written on the side, "K-9 Detection Unit." I didn't understand what it meant. Was this patrol car out looking for dogs?

Helicopters

Helicopters were expensive. They were expensive to buy, expensive to maintain, and the cost of training was high. It was one of the few functions in law enforcement where personnel costs were out stripped by maintenance costs. But in a populous and sprawling county with a traffic system buckling under the strain of rapid and robust population growth, the value of helicopters was unquestionable.

During most of my career, I heard our bosses vehemently reject the idea of using helicopters. Surprisingly, their objections didn't center on the high cost but rather on the efficacy of helicopters for police operations. The growth of our force never kept pace with the increasing number of residents moving into our jurisdiction. Our patrol units were spread thin and our response times to emergency calls grew dangerously long. It was finally time to look seriously at helicopters.

The turning point came during the 1984 summer Olympics held in Los Angeles. Several Olympic events spread into other counties, and our county provided security for four different sporting competitions. The need for helicopters was painfully obvious since the events would be located in widely separated parts of the county. There was no way, however, we'd be able to purchase helicopters and train personnel before the Olympics started.

Here, the benefit of working for an elected law enforcement official came in handy. The sheriff called upon some of his supporters who owned helicopters to help us. We agreed to reimburse them for fuel and maintenance and they would fly the helicopters with our deputies on board. In the meantime, we began the bureaucratic process of budgeting for helicopters and schmoozing the county supervisors to support a sheriff's helicopter program. The Olympics provided the opportunity to incorporate these useful and proven law enforcement tools into our force. I never believed that the sheriff ever understood that police helicopters had proven their worth long ago.

When the Olympics started, we put our sheriff's decals on the privately owned helicopters and used them throughout the games. At one venue, a county supervisor was present with her husband. She saw one of the private helicopters bearing our logo land and a deputy sheriff emerge from it. I was standing not far from her and heard her say to husband, "Look, the damn sheriff has already gone and bought his helicopters before the board has approved them!" I interjected myself into their conversation and explained that the helicopter was owned by one of the sheriff's supporters and the supporter was volunteering the use of the helicopter for the Olympics. I'm not sure she believed me.

Before the end of the year, our two slightly used McDonald-Douglas 500D helicopters had arrived, deputies had been trained to fly them, and our helicopter program was up and running albeit several years later than it should have been. We held a big ceremony to christen the helicopters and inaugurate the program. I wanted to name the helicopters Trigger and Silver, but we didn't. As the headquarters' patrol commander, I was the master of ceremonies for the event, which drew a crowd of about six hundred people at a large football stadium across the street from our main building. Both helicopters were sitting on the ground in the middle of the stadium. There was a stage at center field filled with dignitaries.

My first order of business was to introduce the people on the stage. I had written them all down and, if I do say so myself, did a commendable job. After introducing the sheriff, I sat down and waited for him to finish his remarks so I could introduce another speaker. I was looking around the stage and happened to glance over at my boss, the assistant sheriff. He didn't look happy. He wasn't on my list. When the sheriff finished speaking, I went to the podium and made a joke about forgetting my boss. I thought by the time the ceremonies ended the incident would have been a distant memory. But nearly everyone who came up at the end of the ceremony mentioned this gaff not only to me, but also to my boss.

We were fortunate to have some deputies who had military helicopter flying experience, so the training time to transition to our helicopters was short. The airships were incredibly effective, but noisy. Desk officers were inundated with noise complaints. We changed the tail rotors to make them quieter, and we changed the minimum ceiling for flying over residential areas. We even avoided flying them early in the morning or late at night. The new tail rotors made a big difference, but the noise complaints continued.

We noticed many of the complaints came from the southern part of the county. There were two military bases in the area and another large military base immediately south of the county line. The military flew big helicopters all over and at all times of the day and night. Often we received noise complaints when our helicopters weren't flying. Some of the people who complained said the helicopters were so loud they rattled the windows in their house. We knew one of our helicopters would have to land on a person's roof for it to rattle windows. It seemed we were bearing the brunt of complaints for the military helicopters. The military was pleased to note a sharp decrease in helicopter noise complaints since the implementation of our law enforcement helicopter program.

I was beginning to like my new assignment. Then the captains were told there was going to be an opening for assistant sheriff. Promotions had come easily for me, but I knew I wasn't going to be promoted to this position. I was the newest, youngest, and least experienced captain on the force. Of course, I would apply anyway.

EIGHT

THE JUNIOR EXECUTIVE

✧ ✧ ✧

He felt his whole life was some kind of dream and he sometimes wondered whose it was and whether they were enjoying it.

– Douglas Adams (1952–2001) *The Hitchhikers Guide To The Galaxy*

How to Get Promoted

All the captains received a phone call one afternoon telling them about a meeting the next morning at a nearby coffee shop. Attendance was mandatory. There was a big buzz among the captains, but no one knew why we were having a meeting or why it was going to be at a restaurant. Rumors flew from office to office and most of my phone calls that afternoon were from other captains inquiring about what I knew of the mysterious meeting. There was speculation, but no hard information. These kinds of things always set people on edge. We were anxious. I don't think any of us expected the announcement we heard the next morning.

The sheriff and his three assistant sheriffs were present, along with all the captains. My assistant sheriff seemed to be in a particularly good mood and I soon discovered why. The sheriff had decided to reinstitute the position of undersheriff. The undersheriff would be the second-in-command. He would be the equivalent of a chief of staff. When the sheriff was first elected, he had eliminated the undersheriff position since he felt it wasn't needed. He opted instead for three chief deputies to handle the three areas of corrections, services, and operations. Later he changed their titles to assistant sheriff.

The new undersheriff would have the overall daily control of the department. Creating an undersheriff would leave an opening for a new assistant sheriff for operations. The sheriff was quick to point out he had consulted all three assistant sheriffs and they agreed my boss was the right choice for the new job. Although he had come from another agency and joined our force when the sheriff was first elected, he and the sheriff had become fast friends. When he had first arrived, my boss wasn't popular with many of the managers, supervisors, and officers and, at best, most people were leery of him. Over time, he worked hard to establish good relationships. Yet, many still saw him as a disciplinarian and an unabashed kiss-ass to the sheriff. He was only cautiously accepted by a few of the troops.

The sheriff told us he wanted every captain to submit a letter to him explaining why he should be chosen as the next assistant sheriff. That was it. That was the whole process. He didn't want the letter to be longer than three pages. He believed he had worked with us long enough to know us and the kind of work we were capable of doing. Written tests and interviews, he felt, would serve no purpose for an important executive management position.

A three-page letter with me as the subject wouldn't take long. I knew lots of stuff about me. I couldn't wait to get out of there and write the letter and be done with it. I knew I didn't have much of chance, but I had other work to do, so I went back to my office and wrote the letter in about thirty minutes.

My letter was simple. I pointed out my strengths and, unlike any of the colleagues (I would later learn), I pointed out my weaknesses. My letter was straightforward, maybe even a little blunt. But since I didn't have anything to lose, as I didn't consider myself a serious contender, I gave it a shot. It's not that I didn't want the job, but it was way too early for me. I knew it, and so did everyone else. I also thought that one of the other assistant sheriffs would move into the operations slot, and the new assistant sheriff would be left with special services or corrections. Neither of those positions was appealing to me. Of course, I wouldn't turn down a promotion if it were offered, regardless of the position. It was always easier to transfer than get promoted.

I kept my letter and didn't turn it in until the day before it was due. During the interim, I checked out how the other captains were coming along with their letters. They were cautious about telling me what they were writing. Since they didn't see me as a serious contender, a few shared their stratagem.

I visited one of the top contenders for the position. His office was across the hall from me. He was working on his letter when I arrived. His desk was covered with papers and files. I asked how it was going and he said he was having a hard time keeping it short. He was on page seven and still hadn't included everything he thought was important for the sheriff to know about him. "Wow," I said, "I thought it wasn't supposed to be more than three pages and I had a hard time writing that much." He told me he believed he had a good chance at the promotion and wanted to craft an exceptionally good letter. He alluded to the fact that I hadn't been a captain long, I was young and kind of immature, and didn't have a lot of experience. He implied I didn't have a chance. I didn't point out that if he were to list his good qualities, he shouldn't include subtlety.

After the letters were submitted, there was nothing to do but wait. Two weeks passed. I had a vacation coming up and would be out of the country for three weeks. I wanted to know who my new boss was going be before I left. One Thursday morning I asked the newly minted undersheriff when they would make the announcement. I told him Friday was my last day before my out-of-country vacation and asked if he'd call me overseas so I'd know who was promoted. He acted surprised about my vacation and said he didn't know when the sheriff would decide, but he'd try and reach me with the news when it happened.

I went back to my office and enlisted a few other people to call me when the news broke. Later in the afternoon, a memo was circulated informing all the captains of a staff meeting scheduled for Friday morning. I wasn't thinking about the promotion when I walked into the administration offices the next morning. I was one of the first to arrive and I could feel a palpable change in the atmosphere. People weren't acting right. I walked back to one of the assistant sheriffs and asked him who was being promoted. He told me to go into the conference room, sit down, be a good sport, and congratulate my colleague when the announcement was made. I knew it wasn't going to be me, but at least I knew they were going to make the announcement at the staff meeting before I left on vacation.

I sat alone in the conference room and as some of the other captains were arriving, the undersheriff stuck his head in the door and said the sheriff needed to see me. The only thing I could think of was that the sheriff was transferring me. Oh, crap. I was enjoying patrol and didn't want to move to another assignment. As I was going out the door, the other captains were coming in and I felt like a fish swimming upstream. I wasn't happy, and my heart was racing thinking about what was going to happen in the next room with the sheriff.

The sheriff's secretary told me the sheriff was on the phone and I'd have to wait. I figured if I was waiting, the others in the conference room were probably waiting as well since I was sure the sheriff would be the one to make the announcement. After about ten minutes, when he was done with his phone conversation, I entered his office. He looked at me and said, "Well, I guess you're going to run operations for us." I told him I thought I was getting transferred, and I may have referred to him as a son of a bitch. Maybe I was testing how executive managers spoke to each other. We talked and I thanked him for his trust in me and for making my career so enjoyable. After a while, the undersheriff came in wearing a big smile followed by the other two assistant sheriffs who were now my new colleagues. By the time I left the office, the captains were gone.

I was returning to my office to clear up a few things before leaving with the sheriff, undersheriff, and my two new colleagues for a luncheon celebration. A narcotics detective with whom I had been a friend for many years saw me walk by and called me into the narcotics office. He and the rest of the crew there congratulated me. My friend told me he made a lot of money with my promotion. The narcs had an office pool on who would be promoted.

My friend went to his desk and pulled out a piece of paper. The others tried to stop him, but he managed to give it to me. Everyone, except my friend, had picked someone else. Jokingly, I told them that even though my friend had stuck by me, they would not have to worry when I promoted him to sergeant over them in narcotics. They were relieved. I pointed out they probably wouldn't be working narcotics once I returned from vacation. We all had a good laugh, and I told them I was as surprised as they were.

I received various phone calls from people congratulating me but none of the other captains called me. The odds-on favorite, and the person whom I thought would be promoted, was surely disappointed. Most of the candidates realized, however, one of the other assistant sheriffs would be retiring in about a year and they would have another opportunity. As it turned out, another young captain with about the same amount of time on the department as me was promoted to the next assistant sheriff spot when the retirement came a year later. The odds-on favorite eventually left the department and became a police chief. Me, I was under forty years old, had been on the force no longer than eighteen years, and was feeling euphoric about my newest promotion. I had reached the apogee of my career.

A Sharp and Painful Learning Curve

Every promotion and change of assignment brought with it a certain amount of anxiety. I had always felt lost whenever I was promoted. I was curious as to how the new job would shake out and worried about whether

I had the necessary skills and experience. Promotion to assistant sheriff was a quantum leap, however, above my other promotions so I was more concerned about my abilities. I had entered the executive ranks. I was part of a class of employees called executive management. This meant my salary was determined differently, there were more liberal rules involving the use of the undercover car I was issued, I was salaried and wasn't required to account for my hours or, for the most part, my comings and goings. My office even had a window.

I settled into the job with the undersheriff coaching and mentoring me during my first few weeks when I returned from vacation. Gradually I felt comfortable with the daily responsibilities of my new assignment. Everything was going smoothly. I thought the job wasn't so tough or demanding. Deputies and staffers paid deference to me wherever I went and I was feeling good.

One day, about a month into the new job, the patrol captain advised me of a fatal shooting involving one of our deputies. The incident started as a traffic stop but turned deadly in the most tragic set of circumstances. Following a short pursuit in a residential neighborhood, the traffic violator sought sanctuary by pulling into his driveway and running into his house.

As the deputy was getting out of his patrol car, the young man who had been driving the car came out of his house with a rifle. The deputy drew his service revolver. The young man and the deputy were yelling at each other. The deputy ordered the suspect to drop the rifle. The suspect hurled epithets at the deputy. Another family member ran out of the house and grabbed hold of the rifle as the suspect lowered the gun and fired it at the deputy. The deputy fired his revolver at precisely the same time the rifle was fired.

The deputy's bullet killed the family member who was trying to get the rifle away from the suspect. How did a routine traffic violation, which usually resulted in the issuance of a traffic citation, result in the death of an innocent person? It was difficult for the public to understand. The deputy was devastated, the family and friends of the victim were devastated, the neighbors were upset such a thing could happen, the community was worried and concerned about whether or not the deputy had truly needed to use deadly force. All these emotions were whipped into frenzy by a voracious news media.

As a public entity accused of wrongdoing, our response had to be measured, accurate, and protect the privacy of everyone involved. This is true for, not only for the police, but also all the various government agencies such as school districts, road departments, water and power, and all the rest. The people who make accusations aren't restrained by convention or, it seems sometimes, by common sense. They're free to say whatever they want, and when preparing a lawsuit against the public entity, the things they say can beprovocative, one sided, and extreme.

As the case unfolded, we found we had made mistakes. We failed to find the bullet fired from the rifle that had lodged in the right, front fender of a motor home parked behind the deputy's patrol car. It was found the next morning by a neighbor who called us. After our crime scene technician left, the family found bullet fragments in the garage door. Two detectives taking witness statements wrote different responses from the same witness. The deputy's baton, which had been taken for evidence was lost. All these things were indications of the poor handling of the crime scene.

In all, after reading the reports, I documented over ten procedural errors, which made us appear blundering. While none of these things changed the deputy's belief that his life was in danger and that he fired at the suspect to protect himself and others, the errors we made weren't helpful in making that point.

The news media clamored for direct access to the sheriff. We scheduled a press conference for the next day. I spent the remainder of the day preparing information for the sheriff to bring him up to speed on the case. He wasn't happy about the mistakes, and he was disgruntled. I briefed him the night before the press conference and left him a large package of information to take home and review.

The press conference was scheduled for mid-morning. Our press information officer came and told me the news media was waiting for the sheriff. There were five television stations represented, six newspapers, and several radio stations. I went to the sheriff's office and told him the press conference was ready to start. He looked at me and said he wasn't going. "You handle it," he directed. I had never done a formal press conference and while I had prepared the material for the sheriff and I knew all about the case, I really wasn't expecting to stand in front of all those cameras and answer questions. I was taken aback. As I left the sheriff's office, he said, "How do you like being an assistant sheriff today?"

"I'll get through it," I answered. What I wanted to say was, "Fuck you!" Instead, I left his office and gently closed the door.

I've watched a National Geographic special where they film sharks attacking a piece of meat hung over the side of a boat. The press conference was something like that with me as the piece of meat. At first, I thought it was going to be professional. The press officer told them I was going to read a statement and would take questions following the statement. I ended my prepared statement something like, "The officer demonstrated great restraint and acted bravely in difficult circumstances."

As soon as the words were out of my mouth, I realized I had given the news media their headlines, and I had apparently pushed their aggression buttons because they all started asking me about the last line I had spoken. The questions were not nice and all were framed in such a way to elicit a bad response from me. For the most part, I didn't fail them in that regard. I was terrible and the press conference seemed to drag on for hours. I became worse by the minute. Finally, the press officer ended my torture. It was only forty-five minutes, but I thought it was hours, and I was wringing wet at the end. As I anticipated, my line about the officer acting bravely received a prominent place in most of the stories.

Well, maybe this assistant sheriff stuff wasn't going to be as easy as I had thought. My lack of skill with the press didn't put us in a good light and didn't help the community understand how this tragedy happened. Eventually, with a lot of help and guidance from many people, I became better when dealing with the press. I discovered my new job was no different from any other job in police work; the routine days were interrupted by unusual events, violent incidents, police misbehavior, acts of valor, and heart-wrenching suffering. All of which required personal oversight by the assistant sheriff in charge of operations.

Thanks to Rodney

How does any boss know if employees are doing what they're supposed to be doing when the boss isn't around? Police bosses wonder the same thing. The exercise of police power by government is a delicate balance between protection of society and protection of individual freedoms. Policies, procedures, value statements, goals, objectives, and mission statements promulgated by law enforcement are the official vision of how an agency ensures the proper balance. But the implementation of those guiding official principles and procedures for doing police work manifest themselves in the behavior of the individual officers. So the critical limiting factor for success of any law enforcement agency rests on the shoulders of officers and their daily contact with the public.

Several things confound direct observation by police supervisors of their officers. Officers disperse throughout their jurisdiction. A supervisor can't appear at every call to monitor the performance of all the officers in his or her command. Naturally, officers perform well when being observed by a supervisor. An officer's behavior under supervision may be different from his performance when not being observed. Complaint reports from citizens about an officer's performance can be inaccurate and biased. It would be helpful if sergeants followed up on calls after the officer has left and ask the people how they thought the officer performed. Few, if any, supervisors do this. In police work, we make judgments about officers' abilities and skills in mostly subjective ways.

A couple of years after being promoted to assistant sheriff, I was shown a story about video cameras mounted on the dashboards of patrol cars. The story, on a TV news show, played some of the actual tape from some of the cameras. It was spellbinding. There were car chases, shootings, wrestling matches with suspects, and drunk drivers. The officers had a wireless microphone that recorded the conversations. Eureka! Someone had discovered a way to put a disinterested third party in every patrol car. These cameras would allow our sergeants to review the performance of deputies. The cameras' footage could be used as evidence in court for drunk driving and other cases. The cameras would also protect the deputies from false allegations of misbehavior and help victims of bad police behavior prove their case.

Several staff members worked on the project to bring video cameras to our organization. They did great work. All that was left was for us to review the actual hardware from the various vendors so we could decide on the best video equipment for our patrol cars and determine the cost. We scheduled vendors for one-hour presentations one right after another. Eight different vendors arrived to show us their stuff.

Driving to work that morning, I heard a couple of short news stories about allegations of a police beating that had taken place in the Lake View Terrace area of Los Angeles. Apparently, a witness had videotaped the officers during a confrontation with a suspected drunk driver from across the street. I guessed it wasn't pretty.

When the vendors arrived, they were all talking about this videotaped confrontation. It was my first introduction to the Rodney King case. The next day we started getting calls from the news media asking if we were installing video cameras in our patrol cars because of the King case. I don't think they believed the timing of the vendor presentation, but it was pure happenstance.

That case didn't prompt us to use video cameras in our patrol cars, but it sure gave our proposal legs. I can't remember any proposal that sailed through the bureaucratic approval process faster than our proposal for video cameras. We became the first large California law enforcement agency to install them in our patrol cars.

They quickly proved their worth and generated some interesting stories.

Smile! You're on Video

We installed the cameras in the patrol cars quickly, before we instituted the four-hour training for the deputies and before we distributed the procedures for handling the cameras. We wanted to wait for the cameras to be installed in all the cars before we started the program. One day, before we were ready to begin, we received a call from the owner of a video rental store. He complained about a deputy who rented a video and returned it damaged. In the middle of the movie, he said, there was a ten-minute scene of a female officer issuing someone a traffic ticket.

On a slow day shift in a small town, a deputy was bored and decided to watch one of her favorite movies on the video equipment we had installed in the patrol car. The video player/recorder was in the trunk, the camera was on the dashboard, and a small screen was mounted on the center console. While comfortably watching her movie on a balmy California spring day, a troublesome traffic violator distracted her attention. Annoyed at having her movie reverie interrupted, she quickly activated her emergency lights, pulled the violator over and issued him a citation. Satisfied she had done her duty, she moved to a shady spot and finished watching her movie.

What she didn't know, because we hadn't done any training yet, was that turning on the patrol car's emergency lights automatically activated the dashboard camera. If there hadn't been a tape in the machine, nothing would have been recorded, but since there was a perfectly good videotape, her entire traffic ticket-writing adventure was caught on the tape for the next person who rented the movie.

One of the first complaints about a deputy after the video system was up and running alleged two deputies stole a pair of handcuffs from a security guard that they stopped one night. The officers thought the driver of the pickup truck was acting suspiciously and followed the truck into the parking lot of a liquor store.

The driver said he was a security officer, but didn't have his driver's license. The passenger in the truck had a driver's license and confirmed the identity of the driver after the two were separated. The two men were searched, and one of the officers discovered a pair of handcuffs in the pocket of the driver. The officers told the driver he couldn't drive without his driver's license, so the passenger and driver exchanged places. The next morning the driver called to complain the officers kept his handcuffs.

When an officer is accused of a crime, the subsequent investigation is detailed and time consuming. In this case, one of the first things the investigators did was review the videotape from the patrol car. The videotape recorded the incident as described by the suspect. However, the tape showed the officer finding the handcuffs and putting them on the lip of the bed of the truck. One of the deputies was heard telling the driver where he placed the handcuffs. The handcuffs were there as the officers drove away from the scene after releasing the two men. We showed the tape to the driver, who realized he forgot the officer put the handcuffs on the edge of the truck bed. When the driver left, the handcuffs must have fallen onto the street or parking lot. Case closed.

Women driving alone at night may feel vulnerable. A deputy spotted a woman sitting in a parking lot next to an ATM late at night. He decided to check on her welfare. By the time the deputy approached the car, the young woman had slid over to the passenger side of her car. The deputy walked to the passenger side and the woman opened the door. After a brief conversation, it was clear nothing was wrong; the woman was going to use the ATM but had a difficult time locating her ATM card. The deputy said goodnight and left.

The woman reported the deputy had opened her passenger door and stood in front of her, pushing his pelvis near her face and making suggestive comments. A review of the tape showed the officer stood behind the opened passenger door and his entire conversation with the woman was professional. It turned out the woman, who was eighteen years old and still in high school, went somewhere after her encounter with the deputy and arrived home late. She made the allegation to explain to her parents why she was late. She told them the deputy had kept her at the ATM for over an hour. The entire time recorded was less than five minutes. Without this video record, the allegation would have cast a shadow over the deputy's entire career.

We hoped deputies would also use the video cameras for self-training and evaluation. We encouraged them to playback traffic stops they made and see how they performed. The video equipment would allow the deputies to playback anything they recorded but they couldn't erase anything or record over existing footage. The next incident made me wonder if deputies did review their performance, would they be smart enough to recognize when their performance was poor?

One of the patrol captains showed me a video of a traffic stop made by a deputy. The female officer had stopped a woman for speeding. The vehicle contained three small children. The roadway on which the mother was stopped was busy and noisy. Both the mother and the deputy had a hard time hearing each other. The deputy sounded angry about the mother's speed with children in the car. The deputy, also a mother with small children, appeared as if she wanted the mother to grovel and recognize the deputy's authority and superiority.

There was a strident verbal confrontation between the two. At one point, the deputy told the mother she could take her to jail and her children to the probation department, which could result in the children being place with a foster family. Eventually the mother signed a speeding citation and, after a few more choice words by the deputy, drove away.

All of this was captured on the dashboard camera. Near the end of the tape, a male officer came into the picture and greeted the deputy in front of her patrol car. The male officer asked if everything was okay. The deputy said she was grateful for the video cameras. She told the male officer she almost had to take the driver to jail as the mother was out of control. The deputy then looked at the camera and said she was glad there were videos in all the patrol cars.

The deputy didn't have a clue about her behavior, or who might have been out of control. When asked if she played back the car stop, she said no. We had a supervisor play the video for her and point out ways in which she could have de-escalated the situation.

Sometimes I thought the deputies didn't believe anyone watched the recorded videos. Of course, some of the sergeants did. It was a great way to see how effective deputies were in handling incidents. Also, it would show when the deputies didn't perform their duties well and were in need of training.

A lieutenant walked into my office one day carrying a video and said, "Boss, you're not going to believe this." A deputy stopped a young man, suspecting him of illegal dope possession. As soon as the man was stopped, the deputy spotted narcotics in the car in plain view. The driver was young and full of piss and vinegar and completely unaware the deputy saw his dope. The officer called for another officer to assist. The video showed the back-up deputy arriving and the suspect standing on the sidewalk next to the right rear fender of the patrol car.

The suspect was heard mouthing off and seen moving around. The back-up deputy was asked to search the suspect while the other deputy retrieved the dope he'd seen when he first approached the vehicle. The back-up deputy handcuffed the suspect and told him to shut up. He bent the handcuffed suspect over the trunk of his partner's patrol car. The deputy yelled at the suspect to be quiet and told the suspect this was his last warning.

The back-up deputy looked up and down the street. He reached for something on the right side of his gun belt and appeared to be shaking a canister. He looked around again, this time in the direction of the camera on the dashboard of his own patrol unit, then with his right hand, put a mace container in front of the suspect's face. I thought, *No, he's not*. But yes, he did. Right there in front of the camera, he maced the handcuffed suspect because he refused to be quiet.

Maybe I was learning more about the behavior of deputies than I wanted to learn. We did see a decrease in the number of complaints about the deputies on patrol. I don't know whether the cameras changed the deputies' behavior or if some people who complained realized there was another set of eyes that maybe wouldn't support their allegations.

I tried to get the district attorney's office to accept the video as evidence in drunken driving cases. My idea was to submit a short crime report and the video. Normally there was a long follow-up report in which the deputy described everything he and the driver did during the encounter. I thought the video would be more telling, more probative, and save time.

The feedback from the DA's office wasn't positive. They said they wouldn't have time to watch the videos. The DA's office was busy and they usually didn't read the officers' reports until minutes before court started. I failed to see the difference between a deputy district attorney not reading the police report, as usual, and not watching the video. My colleagues in the DA's office didn't appreciate my comments.

Community Feedback

When I was a captain, I developed a program to monitor the performance of deputies in the field by providing feedback to supervisors and managers. The video system we installed in the patrol cars was an adjunct to a program entitled Community Feedback. It was the workhorse in helping us get a sense of how we were perceived by the community. While the video program had more sex appeal to the public, our Community Feedback program collected data on a daily basis about our effectiveness.

As an assistant sheriff, I was able to expand the program, which had won several national awards and had been studied by police in the United Kingdom, Panama, and El Salvador. By the time I was promoted, the Community Feedback program had established itself as one of the longest running community/police assessment instruments in the country.

Most police leaders recognize communication as the critical link between effective law enforcement and the community. But few police agencies regularly measured, in a systematic way, their community's perception of how well the police perform their duties.

When we began our program, we wanted to collect citizens' perceptions about our patrol services. Like other police forces, we routinely collected information on personnel complaints, but that information didn't explain in specific behavioral terms the methods by which police/citizen communication techniques could be improved. These data also failed to record a representative sample of our service population since they focused on people who complained about our service in general and the performance of deputies in particular.

I developed an inexpensive survey instrument to randomly solicit thoughts about our performance from victims and people who called us for service. We targeted 10 percent of the calls for service. Questionnaires were mailed to the selected people along with a short letter of explanation from the sheriff.

Each questionnaire was marked as to the type of crime or request for service, the name of the primary officer responsible for handling the call and the area in which the incident occurred. The questionnaires were designed to elicit the respondent's impressions of the officer's friendliness, helpfulness, promptness, and effort, as well as the respondent's perceptions of the telephone contact with the desk officers who answered their call when applicable.

It may be, from the standpoint of formal research methodology, the design I used was flawed. But it didn't matter. The effort wasn't to do scientific research but rather to find out what our service population thought of us as a police agency. The consumers of our service were asked straightforward questions about our effectiveness. A police administrator shouldn't be looking for a research program for the sake of research, but rather for the policy implications of the research results. For me, I thought we could do a better job by knowing whether or not the public, in fact, perceived the things we thought were good as good.

On average, almost seven thousand questionnaires were sent each year at a minimum cost to the department. For a small investment of less than two dollars per questionnaire, we received a fortune of information. Half of all the questionnaires were completed and returned to us. We considered it a fairly impressive rate of response. The rate didn't diminish during the life of the program. Of course, we had a leg up over other survey takers.

The people we contacted via first-class mail had had a recent encounter with an officer, and naturally their attention was drawn to mail arriving in an official sheriff's envelope. The recipients had a vested interest in opening this piece of mail. I would imagine nearly every recipient opened the survey and, even if they didn't complete and return the questionnaire, knew we were interested in what they thought of the work we did for them in handling their incident.

When the responses came in, they were tabulated and routed to the officer through a field supervisor. In this way, the supervisor was privy to an independent view of the officer's performance in the field. The most important destination for the responses was the officer who ultimately received the feedback. In reviewing the responses, the officers, we hoped, would get a sense of how others perceived their behavior. The responses were overwhelmingly positive. Many officers saved their questionnaires. Some officers brought them to promotional interviews as evidence of the positive image citizens held of them.

While the program was an assessment of community perceptions, it was also therapeutic in nature. Knowing their individual performance may be evaluated in this manner, we believed some officers probably chose more appropriate behaviors with victims and informants than they may have in the past. Our fondest hope was that any behavior changes would be generalized to all their field contacts.

I made it my job to make sure the Community Feedback program was kept viable and its importance understood by all our captains. Whenever possible, I would allude to the program or use program statistics to make a point or prove a case. Once, in front of the board of supervisors, I was asked about a small group of people who had complained about receiving poor service from us in their neighborhood.

One of the board members asked if this was indicative of the level of service we provided throughout the county. It was an easy statement to refute. I happily did so by pointing out we had responses, at that time, of about twenty-five thousand people who saw our service as friendly, helpful, prompt, and effective. This program gave us the power to know how we were doing from the public's view.

It was my philosophy that knowing what you are doing wrong and where you are weak makes you strong. Not only did Community Feedback provide for constant "pulse taking" of the community, but also it supplied us with a stream of information about how we could improve our services. Everyone was wining with this program. The deputies received feedback about how others perceived them, sergeants learned about their subordinates' behavior on calls, the public recognized our interest in their input about our performance, and the department got a macro view of service levels and where it needed to improve.

Much to the chagrin of the captains and directors working in corrections and special services, the program was greatly expanded after my promotion to include many new areas of the department. Captains in Operations provided monthly reports, but the reports became routine. I wasn't sure if the captains were reading the responses or doing any analysis of the data.

In speaking with one of the captains, I asked if he had done any analysis of the information. He told me he didn't know what I meant. This was a man with a graduate degree. He wasn't embarrassed to tell me he didn't know how to do such a thing. Like many higher-ranking officers in our force and many other police forces of the day, this captain had received his college education through a life experience program. Life experience programs were basically a way to gainsay the educational system. Instead of attending courses, participating in class discussions, reading books, doing assignments, and passing the course through an examination or the writing of a paper, life experience programs gave college credit for the work a student had previously done.

So, for a captain with five years tenure in rank, the requirement to garner a certain number of college units might be to write a paper explaining all the work he had been involved in over the years. Most of these programs didn't require much more than that. We had many officers who possessed college degrees but who couldn't write at a college level, do even some basic research or analysis, or do any critical problem solving.

On the other hand, we had several captains who had little college education, but who were brilliant. One such captain was an outstanding writer and one of the most cogent speakers I had ever encountered. His abilities to conceptualize a problem and develop alternative solutions were unsurpassed. It was too bad he was unappreciated and under-utilized because of his lack of a college degree.

My Crew

Moving into a new position requires some time for nesting and getting used to the view from my newly acquired rank. I wanted my office to feel comfortable, so I brought personal mementos I collected over the years. I had a big, carved wooden eagle that graced the wall behind my desk. It was a gift from an old girlfriend many years before. I hung the framed results of my MMPI psychological test. It was a gift from my wife. My daughter's third grade, award-winning watercolor of five turtles had been part of my office décor since my time with the tactical staff at the sheriff's academy. Putting all these things together was part of the nesting process.

Dealing with a new crew of former captain colleagues, now my subordinates, was part of the nesting process, too. However, it wasn't as straightforward as getting my new office squared away. There were five captains assigned to me in Operations. During the thirteen years I served as assistant sheriff, I worked with a total of nine different captains as a result of transfers, retirements, and promotions. Every one of my captains was older than I was, but fortunately, a few had less seniority, giving me a slight edge managerial-wise. Some of them were lazy, some were smart, some were difficult, and they ranged in their individual managerial styles from soup to nuts (and for one or two of my captains the emphasis was on the nuts).

One captain had the habit of disappearing at lunchtime for about two hours nearly every day. He would be "out of pocket" starting around 11:30

a.m., and the best I could hope for would be for him to return before two o'clock. One of his former colleagues who had been promoted to assistant sheriff a couple of years after my promotion told me about a lunchtime incident he had with the captain. He was a lieutenant at the time and working for the captain when his pager went off during lunch. The lieutenant instinctively reached for it. The captain directed him not to answer as they were having their lunch. The captain told him he should wait until they finished before answering the page. Remember, this was a captain working in law enforcement where emergencies don't only happen after lunch.

In his yearly evaluation, I remarked about his tendency to be unavailable during prolonged lunch periods. He was offended and pointed out that his secretary always knew where he was and how to reach him. He had forgotten his secretary and her husband were friends with whom my wife and I socialized. His secretary often complained about the captain disappearing in the middle of the day leaving her to try to explain where he'd gone and when he was coming back.

This captain had a strange sense of management. I believed he thought his role was to make sure the ship was going in the right direction, and if a course correction were needed, he would give the order, but never do any of the actual work.

When projects needed to be done, he would assign them to one of his many lieutenants. If a staff report were needed, it would be written from the lieutenant to the captain. The captain's job, it seemed, was to glance at the report and hand it to the secretary to make the important correction (i.e., change the heading so it read, "From the captain to the assistant sheriff"). The poor lieutenant who did all the work was never acknowledged unless I found the report to be inadequate. Then the captain would tell me he had had a lieutenant working on it and he would get the lieutenant and the report squared away.

Another captain couldn't organize his life or his desk. His office was cluttered with reports. The sheriff and the undersheriff disliked him and whenever a case was perceived as having been mishandled, they would blame this captain regardless of the circumstances. He was eventually moved to different assignment outside of my command. He only worked with me for a short time before he was moved to his new job. I liked him and thought he was a hard-working, competent, albeit messy captain. In his new position, I would hear rumors that he was an alcoholic. These were sparked by his friendly nature becoming volatile and unpredictable. It turned out he had a neurological problem that affected his behavior. After medical treatment, he was fine.

I never considered myself to be inordinately bright. In fact, the nuns in my grade school had me convinced I was, at best, middling in the brain department. But, as the years went by, I read a lot, went to graduate school, and was able to find ways to apply my learning to police work. The one thing I knew never to do, even in my dumbest moments (and I had plenty of those), was to tell my boss how to do his job.

One captain in my command apparently couldn't resist pointing out what he thought I was doing wrong. Within a short time of coming to work for me, the captain decided to inform me about all the things he found wrong with my management style, my personality, and he probably didn't like my clothing choices either. He had a difficult time accepting me as his boss. I assumed he didn't like me and probably never had. It must have galled him to have had to report to me, for I was a lesser, undeserving person. He was a close friend of another captain whom most believed should have been selected over me for the assistant sheriff position. Our relationship never blossomed because maybe I really wasn't a good boss.

Whatever the case, he should have known there wasn't anything he could have done about my management style, and confronting me only made matters worse. He was the only person who ever worked for me who blatantly disobeyed a direct order. When he left the force, he became a police chief in a small city and his tenure there ended quickly in bad circumstances. He was heard to say that he never realized how difficult it could be to manage people who didn't do what they were told. Happier times came for him when he took another police chief position in a larger and more stable city from which he eventually retired. I was pleased he learned, as an executive manager, that supervising employees could be taxing, especially if they don't like you and don't do as they are told.

The man who took this captain's place was a sycophant of the highest order. He agreed with everything I said, at least to my face. I was never sure if I liked his behavior better than the behavior of the captain who constantly confronted me. One of the investigators who worked for the captain was a longtime friend of mine. The investigator and I would often meet for coffee. The poor investigator always paid a heavy toll for being my friend. People assumed he was telling me things I shouldn't have known. In reality, we spoke about women, as men are wont to do.

Mostly, though, we talked about our wives and our children and eventfully our grandchildren. In all the years I knew him (and we're still friends today), he never complained to me about his boss or anyone else. He did complain, frequently and vociferously, about the department in general, and particularly about new procedures or requirements I'd promulgated. But his poor captain never understood this and when there was an opportunity to screw over my friend, he would do so.

Two captains who worked for me became assistant sheriffs and worked with me for a good many years before I left the force. One was quiet, diligent, bright, and hard working. The other was perceived as a self-promoter and not as bright as the other, but he was a great public speaker, well meaning, and the community loved him. Both of these men would show their administrative courage by remaining friends during my troubles.

Panama vs. El Salvador

Our department's community programs unit ran an excellent drug awareness program. It was publicly lauded by President George H.W. Bush as one of the best programs in the United States. In 1992, we received a call from a government agency to bring our message to the Central American countries of Panama and El Salvador. Since we served a fair sized population of Spanish speakers, we had produced most of our program's ephemeral material in Spanish as well as English. I figured this would be helpful in explaining our program to our Central American colleagues.

In a short time, I was heading to Panama with armloads of books and pamphlets to help spread our anti-drug program model for school-aged children. A US embassy official picked me up at the airport. On the drive to the hotel, he explained my schedule for the two days I'd be in country. Everything was straightforward.

My hotel was next to the Panamanian Papal Nuncio's residence where a short time before, former President Manual Noriega took refuge from American troops who eventually arrested him on drug trafficking charges. I was told it was safe to walk around the area of the hotel but not at night. With that simple admonishment, I was dropped off at the hotel.

The following day and a half went by quickly, as they were filled with one meeting after another. My time was spent explaining our approach to the drug problems in our jurisdiction. Some of my meetings were with US government officials, a few Panamanian officials, local schoolteachers, and a couple of private organizations that focused on drug use interdiction. The private organizations appeared to be the most interested. I gave them half of the printed material I had brought along. My time was short and, before I realized it, the embassy official was driving me back to the airport for my flight to El Salvador.

There was an appreciable contrast between my reception in San Salvador, the country's capital, and Panama. Someone from the US embassy met me, but that was the extent of the similarities between the two countries.

The airport was more frenetic than the one in Panama. The official hired a local person to deal with the luggage. We followed him to a waiting van. My rapier sharp powers of observation kicked in, and I determined this was going to be a different ballgame. A man in some type of uniform sporting a fully automatic weapon was standing next to the van. He looked serious. The luggage was loaded into the van. The driver was in mufti with a sidearm. The security officer with the rifle sat in the front passenger seat. It looked as if his head was on a swivel. He was alert and ready for action.

As we moved out on our drive to the embassy, I noted the windows in the van were bulletproof. I guessed security in San Salvador was a big issue.

As we approached the embassy, I saw many Salvadorian soldiers scattered completely around the outer wall. We pulled up to the gate where our identifications were checked. The outer gate opened, and the van pulled into a holding area. When the outer gate closed, embassy security guards checked the vehicle's undercarriage with mirrors for explosives. When finished, the inner gate opened and the van rolled into the embassy grounds. US Marine guards checked our identifications before we were allowed to enter the embassy's main building.

In a conference room, I listened to a security briefing. Here are the highlights:

> Don't use public transportation
> Don't exercise outside or run in the street
> Don't go shopping
> Don't take any rides with strangers (fat chance, I thought)
> Stay inside the hotel
> Stay with an embassy person if you go outside
> If you hear an explosion, just follow the audience's reaction

I'm guessing the last little piece of advice was because the audience had some experience and they would take the appropriate action. Okay, I was thoroughly briefed on security issues, so they transported me to the hotel. All and all the hotel wasn't too bad, especially since I saw it as a safe haven from the certain death awaiting me outside. During the first night of my stay at the hotel, I heard a few distant explosions and the electricity went out for an hour.

The next morning the embassy picked me up and took me to another hotel where I was to give a talk to a group of about a hundred and fifty people. It was a much better hotel than the one where I spent the night. Fortunately, I had a bit of experience dealing with other cultures and countries. My development and participation in police exchange programs taught me things that worked well in the United States didn't necessarily work well in another country.

When I started my talk, I explained my purpose was only to tell them about what we were doing in California, not what they should do. I waxed eloquent about how many of our officers taught classes in the schools and how our anti-drug material was printed in two languages and so on.

I took questions at the end of my talk. Many hands shot up. The police weren't trusted in this country, so how could I suggest that the police should be in classrooms? Obviously, that didn't come from a local cop, but rather someone who didn't pay any attention to my caveat about my not telling them how to do things in their own country. Their big problem, they told me, was to keep kids from smelling glue to get high and to get them into school. It was clear our program wouldn't work in El Salvador. They were right. It obviously wouldn't work where police weren't trusted and large numbers of children didn't attend school because they were addicted to glue sniffing.

Before they could tar and feather me, we adjourned to another room for a little soirée. At the reception, everyone was nice and friendly, and most thanked me for my time and effort, although clearly my effort wasn't helpful. The crowd began to dwindle to only a few people. My embassy escort pointed to some people and said they would take me back to the hotel. He had another appointment. Wait, I thought, what about the rule to always be with an embassy person when out of the hotel? I hooked up with the three local people who were to take me back to my hotel. They didn't speak English, and I didn't speak Spanish. Through intricate hand gestures, witty facial expressions, and precise pointing, we managed to communicate.

Pulling out of the hotel parking lot, I was quick to register the fact that the car turned left, not right. I remembered having come from the right and, to my way of thinking, we should have turned right. I sat back and took in the sights as the kidnap vehicle, as I perceived it, tooled around the back streets of San Salvador. I was exposed to the raw underbelly of the city. Eventually, we arrived in front of my hotel. I had cheated death.

The next day I toured a drug rehabilitation program operated by an ex-addict who was the daughter of a prominent Salvadorian. I knew little about the efficacy of drug programs but the young woman diligently showed me around and paid me more deference than I think I was worth. Later at lunch, some of the American officials asked what I thought of the program. I figured it was at least partially funded by some US money, and they wanted a cop's opinion.

Later in the afternoon, I flew back to the States. The agency called several days after I was back to work. The woman said I had done a good job, wished I spoke Spanish because if I did, she had other cool Central and South America stuff she could use me on, but she'd be in touch if my particular expertise was needed. I never heard from them again and within a few years, the agency ceased to exist. I wondered if the agency's demise had anything to do with my performance in Central America.

Sunshine

One of the greatest things that ever happened to me while I was the assistant sheriff was a simple matter of happenstance, nothing more. Whenever I traveled out of the country, whether on business or on vacation, I spread my sheriff's department business card around like confetti. Usually they landed in the hands of international police colleagues who were part of a police exchange program or one whom I would happen to meet during a trip overseas while I was on vacation. One day I received a call from a sergeant with the Ontario Provincial Police (OPP) in Canada. He said he had my business card and was calling to ask for some help.

I didn't remember ever having given the sergeant my card, but he explained he had received the business card from another colleague. He was searching for someone in California who would be willing to assist his force and the Royal Canadian Mounted Police (RCMP) with a program helping physically challenged children.

The Sunshine Foundation of Canada flew children with life-threatening illnesses to Disney World in Florida. Most of the children were from the eastern provinces of Canada. Once in Florida, they would team up with a group of sailors from a nearby naval base. There was one volunteer sailor for each child as they spent the day at Disney World. The children would board a chartered airplane in Ontario early in the morning with a contingent of medical personnel, some OPP and RCMP officers, and a cadre of volunteers from Canada.

Upon landing in Florida, they were greeted by the sailors, escorted to the park, and enjoyed a day of rides, to the extent each child's disability would allow, and fly back to Ontario after closing. It was a full, exciting, and exhausting day for the children and the volunteers.

It was a heartwarming story, but I wasn't sure what the sergeant wanted. He explained there was another chapter of the foundation in British Columbia, and it wanted to replicate what his chapter had been doing in Ontario. Disney World was too far for the children to travel in one day, but Disneyland was a shorter flight. The foundation had the money, the plane, volunteers, and the children. They needed additional volunteers from us to escort the children in Disneyland. He asked if I could assemble seventy-five deputy sheriffs to escort the children. I was a little taken aback. Not because I thought it was a bad idea, but because I wasn't sure there would be many deputies who would want to do it.

I must not have had a clue about the good-hearted nature of our deputy sheriffs. I recruited the assistant sheriff from the jails as a partner. I thought many of the volunteers would come from the jail and, if he was included as my partner, he would support it and it would easier for the deputies working for him to get the day off. It was a good move. He didn't have to do any work, and he put his arms around the program as if he thought of it. By the end of the first day after I put out the word calling for volunteers, we had over a hundred, and we had to close the list. I called the sergeant back and told him we'd be honored to be part of the program.

We needed a special waiver for their airplane to land at our airport, as it violated sound restrictions. The permit was obtained easily. The local transportation authority donated drivers and buses, a local high school sent a band to meet the plane, and the fire department joined us in greeting the children when they landed. It was spectacular. Everyone was there on his or her own time and not being paid.

The children came down the ramp full of excitement. Some had to be carried, and many were in wheelchairs, but all had gigantic smiles. Each excited child was teamed with an equally excited deputy sheriff. Everyone was loaded onto the buses, and we were off for a thrilling day at Disneyland. Disneyland had provided specially discounted tickets, and the children were allowed to by-pass the lines and go right to their favorite rides.

Two RCMP officers came off the plane dressed in full Mounties' regalia. As we walked around Disneyland, many people thought they were part of the park's entertainment. They attracted a nice crowd wherever they ventured. It was a little distracting, but that's what happens when a police organization has fine-looking uniforms. Disneyland eventually dispatched two security officers to walk around with the RCMP officers. It was kind of funny and cool, and Disneyland was particularly cool about the whole situation.

It was amazing to not only watch the children have a great time, but to also see the bonds between the children and their deputy sheriffs develop as the day progressed. By nightfall, everyone was exhausted as we made our way back to the busses for the drive to the airport.

The good-byes at the airport were tearful. Some of the children didn't want to leave or wanted to take their deputy home to Canada. Most of the deputies went onto the plane with the children for a final good-bye, and it was difficult to get the deputies off the plane. Not one deputy left the tarmac until the plane was in the air. It was a moving experience for everyone who participated. The deputies, the bus drivers, the school band members, and the firefighters who were there to see the plane off couldn't wait for the next opportunity to participant in this great program.

Every year we repeated the program. Every year it improved. Sponsors donated hats, tee shirts, and sunblock for the children and the deputies. Today the sheriff's department still participates and volunteer deputies are still plentiful. It has become the preeminent program for the force. I understand there's always a mad scramble to get on the volunteer list.

If anyone cares to search hard enough, they will find my fingerprints on many programs operating in the department today. I played an important part in developing our helicopter program, getting patrol dogs, creating the Community Feedback program, installing dash cams in the patrol cars, monitoring the development of a 800 MHz radio system, contracting law enforcement services in every new city in the county since 1985, starting the "Student And The Law" program and other programs operating today. I was able to do these things because of the hard work and dedication of people who worked in Operations while I was the chief. However, none matches the pride I felt about my part in teaming our force with the Sunshine Foundation of Canada.

NINE

RECALLING BRAVE MEN AND MY FINAL CURTAIN

✷ ✷ ✷

I know the virtue of a fight. Who knows it better than I? For I have fought against beasts and men, the elements, mutinous crews, treachery, and my own ill humor. If wisdom, cunning or a moderate measure of yielding what is mine, cannot preserve me from a fight, then let my enemy look to his guard. Peace bought at the price of cowardice, is too dear.

– *Tros of Samothrace*, Talbot Mundy (1925)

Courage

I'm a sissy, especially when it comes to experiencing pain. Whenever I'm sick, my life is shit. Once I had a herniated disc in my lower back. The pain was so bad one morning it dropped me to the floor. I laid there in agony with tears welling in my eyes.

The pain subsided after I was loaded with Demerol at the local hospital emergency room. As the drugs wore off, the pain returned, although not with the same acute sharpness. Then, a chronic loss of feeling developed in one leg. I was unable to walk more than a hundred feet without experiencing pain in my legs and hips.

During all of my adult life, I had kept physically active by a regimen of weight lifting and running. The lower back injury prevented me from doing even mild physical activity and I was miserable. I was also scared that I would never be my old self again. Fear drove me to a neurosurgeon, who operated on my back and fixed me. Nevertheless, even today, I remember how scared I was waiting in the pre-op room having signed a waiver which stated I had been advised of all the potential unplanned consequences of the surgery, one of which was death.

It wasn't easy to admit to being a sissy and fearful about my physical well-being. As I grew older, I became more fearful. As a child, I was fearful of the dark, perhaps an artifact of an early Catholic school education. I thought the police were supposed to be brave. They'd confront dangerous situations without hesitation. When it came to their own well-being and confronting the innumerable frailties that weaken our physical capacity, I realized most cops weren't much different from me.

Maybe this was a good thing. What really mattered though was how we responded to those injuries, which physically and emotionally damaged us. That was what set some officers apart from others. During my career, some cops stood out from the rest. Their courage, in the face of the most horrendous physical pain, was an inspiration to all law enforcement officers.

In the early 1980s, a sheriff's investigator named Ira Essoe was working with his partner looking for a suspect in a large shopping mall. Both officers were in soft clothes, a police euphemism for casual clothes, not the standard detective suit and tie. They weren't dressed like undercover cops either, but more like what the average person would wear to a shopping mall. Since their job was to track down people with arrest warrants, they tended to dress like everyone else with the hope of blending in.

Driving around the shopping mall parking lot, they spotted some young men who appeared to be up to no good. To the investigators, these guys looked as if they were trying to break into a car to either steal the contents or steal the car itself. None of the three men was the one for whom they had an arrest warrant, but duty dictated they stop to investigate what was going on. Things went wrong quickly. One of the suspects got Ira's partner's weapon. The suspect shot Ira in the back. All three of the suspects made good on their escapes. It turned out they were youthful offender escapees with violent backgrounds. They were eventually captured, tried, and convicted. Two are enjoying their freedom today, having served their time in jail. The third man died after his release from jail.

Ira Essoe, who died in 2010, spent the remainder of his life in a wheelchair. Through years of painful surgeries, some resulting in the amputation of his legs, Ira maintained a stoic composure. His life since the shooting wasn't easy and it certainly was anything but pain free. Yet, whenever Ira spotted a colleague, he'd smile, grab your hand, and nearly pull the person into the wheelchair with him. This man, a former gymnast, while robbed of his physical dexterity, never allowed the circumstances of his life to reduce his enthusiasm for it. He never complained about his plight to any of his fellow officers. For more than twenty-five years, he endured his pain and suffering while maintaining an extended family.

Bravery isn't measured only by how a person reacts in an instance to a set of circumstances. All cops are expected to put themselves in harm's way. Confronting a gunman, wrestling a drug-crazed man out of a car, chasing a burglar into a dark building or any of the other brave acts police officers do in the course of their job is expected. Those brave acts are done without thinking of the potential consequences if the gunman shoots the officer, the drug-crazed suspect badly beats the officer, or the burglar stabs him in that dark building. How one reacts to the unplanned consequences is what determines the depth of one's bravery.

To have lived each day in pain and not complain or blame or whine made Ira Essoe a remarkably courageous person. He was, perhaps, one of the bravest men I ever knew.

Big Bird

Vince was a tall man with a prominent nose, thus the moniker Big Bird. He was six feet five inches and thin as a rail. I knew Vince before he came to work for the sheriff's department. He was dating a girl who was the workmate of my girlfriend. When I first met Vince, he had what I considered a dream job. He worked for a travel company and drove around the western US staying in and rating hotels and motels. He thought I had a dream job since I was a deputy sheriff. He eventually went to work for a police force, and after a few years, transferred to the sheriff's department. His wife, too, became a deputy sheriff. They would both eventually be promoted though the ranks to lieutenant.

Vince was a good, solid cop, but he was also a good, solid person. People naturally liked him. He was easygoing and could always be counted on whenever needed. He was a good athlete, knew everything there was to know about construction, and a good family man. He was everything I was not. I was clumsy and couldn't fix anything.

He was always available to help friends with any ongoing home improvement project. He had a side business constructing patios and swimming pools, but he could do nearly everything. I don't know if Vince demonstrated any particular courageous moment during his police work. He probably took the same risks all patrol officers do, chasing cars, wrestling suspects to the ground, searching buildings for bad guys, and generally protecting the public. I frequently pointed out that we pay the police not for what they do, but for what they may have to do. Vince stood ready for those times when he might have been called upon to risk his life. He survived police work but ended his life fighting cancer for more than eight years.

Those were the years of his greatest bravery. During his illness, I lived with Vince and his wife for more than a year. In all of that time, I never heard him complain about the chemotherapy treatments that would leave him physically exhausted and extremely sick. He took his life, what was left of it, one day at time. He knew if he were to survive, he had to undergo many different treatments and surgeries, and he approached each with determination.

Vince was always at the top of the list of volunteers for the Sunshine Foundation. Vince was undergoing chemotherapy when the Canadian children came on one visit to Disneyland. He had a medical port inserted in this stomach. He was injecting the chemo himself while showing a child with his own life-threatening disease around Disneyland. Every year for the remainder of his way too short of a life, Vince participated in the program. Most people had no idea Vince was battling for his life. To most of the people in the program, he was simply another kind deputy willing to take a day off to help those children have a good time.

Maybe bravery is, in the final analysis, the manner in which we live our lives.

Medal of Valor

During the first twenty-five years of my career, the department recognized outstanding performance, meritorious service, and bravery in a haphazard way. We relied on service organizations. They would contact us and request deputies whom they could acknowledge in yearly police recognition luncheons. A service club from a city would contact us and ask for a deserving officer from their area to whom they could fete with a lunch and whom they would award a plaque.

Some service clubs out did others. One small club hosted a lunch at a yacht club with a great view of the harbor. They would award six deputies with nice plaques, certificates, and would have the county supervisor for the area present an official commendation for the officers from the board of supervisors. The award ceremonies weren't equal and often well deserving deputies were overlooked and not recognized for their contributions.

With the help of a citizen's support group that had worked with the department for many years and was comprised of over six hundred business and community leaders, I developed a program of yearly recognition for employees who distinguished themselves. The idea for a more formal recognition ceremony had been floating around for many years, but for whatever reason it had never come to fruition. Our support group was able to cover the cost associated with the program. They purchased medals for various levels of recognition such as valor, bravery, meritorious service, life saving, and even a Purple Heart medal for those who were injured or killed in the line of duty.

Each year department employees were called upon to nominate their colleagues in the various categories. At the awards luncheon, attended by over five hundred people each year, the deserving employees were hosted at an upscale hotel and provided a gourmet lunch. Giant posters of the awardees were hung around the room and a television personality read the accounts of the circumstances that led to the employees' nominations for recognition. The county supervisors presented official certificates to the awardees and the sheriff presented the medals. It was a formal affair and fitting for the type of performance the employees had demonstrated.

While some of the awardees were recognized for meritorious work, others were at the ceremony because of acts of bravery. A committee of their peers from throughout the department chose the awardees. Any employee could nominate any other employee and the nomination didn't require any formal process. Staff personnel assembled the necessary background information about the nominee, and the committee members made their decisions based on the criteria for each award category.

A few officers, nominated themselves. Some never fully realized the rules of the nomination. We would call for nomination at the start of each year for performance during the preceding year. Yet we frequently received nomination for police performance that occurred years before we started the program.

In one case, a deputy nominated himself for an encounter with an unarmed suspect whom he had shot. The shooting was questionable at best and had taken place several years before the awards ceremony was conceived. Obviously, in his opinion, the department had overlooked his bravery. There was also an effort to recognize an officer who did indeed perform courageously in a dangerous encounter, but the confrontation with the armed suspect happened nearly thirty years before. The officer received appropriate recognition at the time of the encounter, but now some officers believed it was too little. Of course, over a hundred years ago an undersheriff was shot and killed by a bandit. I suppose some officers felt that he, too, should receive a posthumous Medal of Valor.

Once we started an organized ceremony to highlight our employees, everyone wanted to get into the act. The most glaring example of hubris, however, came from someplace I least expected. One day I was called into my boss's office. He spoke at length about the awards ceremony and what a good event it had turned out to be over the years. He hinted that something was missing. People who had done good work over the length of a long career were being overlooked was the gist of the conversation.

As we continued to speak, he subtly began to talk about himself and the contributions he had made to the department. I wasn't quick on the uptake, but eventually I understood he wanted me to nominate him for a special award, the category of which wasn't clear in my mind. I left his office without making any commitments to my boss and erstwhile friend. To my knowledge he was never nominated for an award, and I'm sure he felt slighted by oversight.

Bullets Flying

Working in a patrol car alone, an officer was confronted in a mere fraction of second with terror. In the early evening hours of a summer night, a deputy saw a car off in the distance parked in a wetlands area across the road from a popular beach. It wasn't unusual to see cars there since it had been used for years as a place for couples to steal some intimate moments away from others. Deputies would confront the occupants of such vehicles, check their identification, and send them on their way. On this particular night, the deputy thought the car contained some teenage lovers. His plan was to roust them out of their love nest.

Things weren't as they seemed that night and the officer was better than most people at understanding this. The deputy turned on his emergency lights, hit the high beams of his headlights, and shined his spotlight on the car. As he stepped out of his patrol unit, shots from a semiautomatic weapon sprayed the front of his car. One bullet struck the left side spotlight and fragments from the bullet and spotlight hit the deputy near his eye. The vehicle sped off while someone in the car continued to fire at the deputy, who was crouching down and returning fire with his 9mm pistol. His sidearm wasn't a great weapon against the automatic assault rifle that was now firing hundreds of bullets at him. The suspect vehicle drove in a semi circle around the patrol unit as the deputy crawled under his car to escape the onslaught of deadly fire landing near him.

The car headed out of the wetlands making good its escape along a busy beach road. The deputy called for help on his radio, giving a description of the suspects and the car they were driving along with the direction of travel. The deputy's car was disabled and it was later discovered that over one hundred bullets had struck it. Deputies and police officers who responded to the deputy's call for assistance quickly arrested three suspects. A fourth suspect was found hanged the next morning in the garage of his house not far from the shooting scene. It was never clear why they shot at the deputy but all three of the surviving young men were convicted. The deputy fully recovered from his wound.

Was it the deputy's quick reaction to the gunfire, or was it poor marksmanship on the part of the shooter? Did the shooter wait too long to fire or should he have waited until the deputy was completely out of the patrol car and walking up to the suspects' car? Or was it plain good police work and survivor instincts that saved the deputy's life? Perhaps it was a matter of good luck. Whatever it was that saved this deputy from death or serious injury, it wasn't in the cards for another deputy years later when he also confronted a man with an automatic weapon.

There were two priorities for cops working alone on the midnight shift. One was to learn what's open throughout the night that has coffee and food. The second was finding a place to pee. Of course, on the midnight shift an officer could, in fact, pee anyplace he wanted. Maybe it was a need for coffee or the thought he needed to do a safety check of a business open late at night that prompted one particular deputy to drive to the mini-mart located on one of the main roads in the city he was patrolling.

As he drove into the parking lot of the mini-mart, he saw a man standing outside the store. The man was holding something, and as the deputy drove closer, he was probably surprised to see the man had an automatic weapon. The deputy stopped his patrol car and was reaching for the radio when he was cut down in a hail of bullets. He died instantly sitting in the patrol car. The suspect escaped but was eventually captured, tried, and convicted.

What had made the difference in the outcomes of the actions of these two brave men? In law enforcement, and especially in these two circumstances, the routine can turn deadly in the blink of an eye.

The Softening Lens of Time

My days as assistant sheriff passed quickly. Before it seemed possible, I had been in the position more than thirteen years. The job I held as chief of operations was the kind of job I'd always wanted. I was in charge of one third of our whole force, and it was, in my view, the most exciting part of the sheriff's department. Nearly all of the law enforcement responsibilities of the sheriff fell under my command.

It was relatively easy to do good work and to look good since my area of command was on the front line. My colleagues who worked in the jail weren't so lucky. There weren't a lot of "attaboys" given out because your division saved some money on toilet paper or scored a big hit of free cheese from the federal government to help reduce the cost of the care and feeding of prisoners.

As hard as the jail employees worked and as good a job as they did under difficult circumstances, most people weren't interested in what was happening in a jail, unless of course, a prisoner died. When a jail death occurred, the focus on the jail was laser-sharp. Many different people and agencies investigated every aspect of a jail death.

If the price of food (a major part of any jail budget) skyrocketed, jail funding would come in over budget. There were many opportunities for things to go wrong and not many opportunities for jail staff to significantly impress bosses. I lived in fear that, as my Operation's tenure grew, the chances of someone suggesting that the assistant sheriffs rotate would somehow catch the sheriff's ear.

As a result, I never showed interest in jail operations and tried not to be around during any jail discussions. I don't know why I had this aversion to the jail, but I did, and I didn't spend much time delving into the psychological reasons for my "jailaphopia." I was happy at my job and didn't want to think about doing something else.

Working closely with the administration at the top tier of management, I noticed something that in retrospect wasn't so good. Christoph Tiedemann was a minister without portfolio to the German Chancellor Otto von Bismark in the 1870s. He worked closely with his boss and made the observation; *there is something great to live one's life in and through a great man, to enter into and be absorbed by his thoughts, plans and decisions. In a certain sense to disappear in his personality. One's own individuality runs the risk of being ground down.*

The same could be said of me, I think, as I worked closely with a middling politician who wielded a strong personality and who demonstrated the same propensity for fits of pique as the great German chancellor. It wasn't so much a matter of being ground down, as Tiedemann noted, but rather of taking on certain personality traits of the boss. In my case, two bosses. Always impatient with people, the pressure to produce made me more impatient and intolerant of people who couldn't keep up or who couldn't perform at a level necessary to meet the standards I'd set.

When I look back at my life then, I want to remember only the good times. I'm sure there were bad days, days when things didn't go right or days when other people would set my hair on fire. Some days I would, as was my wont, set my own hair on fire and spend the day trying to put it out. Over time, however, those bad days softened and the good times were enhanced. But my terminal episode, my last day, was burned in my brain like a brand.

I'll Always Be Your Friend

There was nothing more important in a time of personal crisis than friends. When my life was knocked off kilter and I began to spin out of control, it was the support of family and friends that helped me maintain my balance in the world. The crisis I faced twisted and turned me emotionally and physically to a point where I was unable to think clearly or objectively determine a path back to normalcy. Without a strong support group, I would have floundered. I never fully appreciated that until I found myself in crisis mode.

One Friday after work, I received a call from the undersheriff. He said we needed to meet the following Sunday morning. He couldn't tell me what it was about, only that it was important I meet him in his office on Sunday. It wasn't particularly unusual to go into the office during the weekend. Often police administrators have to work on weekends since crime doesn't occur only during regular business hours. At first, I didn't give it much thought. By Saturday afternoon my curiosity was driving me nuts. I couldn't figure out why I would be meeting with the undersheriff or why he couldn't tell me the purpose of the meeting. I didn't sleep much Saturday night and was up early Sunday morning and heading to the office to find out what was going on.

Something was wrong, but I didn't know what. Another assistant sheriff was in his office speaking with a deputy. When I walked into his office, my colleague asked me to wait in my office. I walked down the hall and into the undersheriff's office. He looked solemn. As I took a chair, he informed me that there was a sexual harassment complaint about me. It was a woman who worked in my command. The undersheriff placed me on administrative leave until the investigation of the complaint was completed.

Now I should point out here that all five attorneys I eventually hired during this incident advised me never to talk about the details of what happened. I paid them lots of money, and I fully intend to follow their advice even though the allegations centered on circumstances that occurred many years ago. I've only told my tale of woe in general terms. What I've said was only my perspective of things. I didn't, in my mind, harbor any grudges, but I was disappointed in the behavior of some people toward me during this time. I hoped that despite the disappointment, I took the high ground and didn't demean those fuckers who were less than forthright, mean spirited, disloyal, and in some cases, simply gutless. Well, perhaps I'm still a little scarred by it all, sorry.

When the undersheriff finished explaining the nature of the complaint and the rules involving administrative leave, which were basically similar to placing me under house arrest, he came around the desk and hugged me. As he was hugging me, he said, "Dennis, no matter how this turns out, I'll always be your friend." It's been fifteen years since he said that to me. It was the last time I was to hear from him. What a guy.

I can't remember the drive home. I seemed to have gained consciousness as I approached the off ramp to my house. I have no idea how I got out of the office, down to my car, and twenty miles down the freeway. I was in a panic. My heart was racing and I was fighting to maintain control of my emotions. I kept thinking, *Calm down, calm down*! But I wasn't calm. With almost thirty-two years on the force, I was being placed on administrative leave, usually the first step out the door. Being a cop was all I knew how to do. I had no other marketable skills. It was all I had done my entire adult life. I was a good police administrator based my on yearly evaluations which often rated me at 500 out of 500 points. My average evaluation score for the previous ten years had been 490 points. I knew my craft, but I didn't know anything else.

I thought I knew the worst and I knew what I was facing. Things went from bad to worse. Over the next few weeks, while serving my time basically under house arrest, several other women joined in a chorus of six women making allegations against me. They all worked in the same work unit and they all hired the same attorney. I was eventually told I could leave my house but always had to provide a phone number where I could be reached and available to respond to the department within thirty minutes. My company car was taken away. Some people made an initial and perfunctory call to see how I was doing but none called back and as time went on, only a few truly good friends remained close.

I labored under the mistaken belief that workmates were friends. They were the people with whom I socialized and most of my life involved them in some way or other. But I was sorely mistaken. Of the many people who worked directly for me, three made the effort to call and speak with me. Many business and community leaders called me. After taking several of these calls, they sounded similar, almost as if they were orchestrated. Everyone said the same thing, sounded uncomfortable, and were quick to find an exit out of the conversation.

I was impressed, though, with Michael Wayne. He was John Wayne's oldest son. I'm sad to say Michael is now deceased. I had known him awhile, and he was always kind to me. He ran his own production company, I think, and was the keeper of the John Wayne image for the family. He spoke to me at length, even offering to create some type of job for me within his company so I could make some money. I didn't take him up on his offer, but his kindness found a special place in my heart.

Over a six-month period, the department conducted its investigation, interviewing fifty people. Most, I was shocked to learn, didn't have nice things to say about me. I thought I was a swell guy, but I guess having a good self-image can be wrong headed. I wouldn't recommend going through an internal investigation to get a good sense of what people think, but I can truthfully say it was a painful but helpful technique. Around August, I learned the sheriff intended to fire me. No one called to tell me, I heard about from a TV news story. In October, without exercising all my administrative remedies, I retired. It wasn't over yet, as all the women sued the county and me. I, in turn, sued them and the county.

I had hired an attorney to represent me during the various administrative hearings I attended as part of the internal investigation the department conducted. Then I hired an attorney to represent me during the lawsuits. Additionally, I had a bankruptcy attorney, a financial attorney, and, sadly, a criminal defense attorney.

A Romp through a Sexual History

One woman, out of whole cloth, alleged I had sexually assaulted her. At first, I was told that I was accused of rape, and later it was changed to sexual assault. No one told me the specifics of the case and, after nearly a full year, the district attorney's office held a press conference announcing there was insufficient evidence to try me. I wasn't officially told the reason, but I suspected they finally caught my accuser in her lies. In fact, years later, one of the main investigators on the case told me the woman admitted lying about the incident.

Usually in such cases, detectives will interview all the pertinent parties, collect any physical evidence, and try to corroborate the accuser's story. Depending on the complexity of the case, this takes, at most, a couple of months. This investigation wore on for a year. The detectives spoke to women I had dated twenty-five to thirty years ago. It made no sense. They were looking for someone to say I had assaulted them, I suppose. Each night I would go to sleep and wonder if I had pissed off some old girlfriend evil enough to say bad things about me. Would there be a knock on the door and I'd be hauled off to jail?

I heard that one person in the district attorney's office told one of the women who was suing me that they had me dead to rights and I wouldn't be given the option of surrendering. Rather, in a display of bravado for the plaintiff, the man told her he was personally going to slap the cuffs on me and book me. The woman he told this to wasn't the accuser and why he would be talking to someone not involved in the criminal case about me was a mystery. Nevertheless, these kinds of stories scared the crap out of me. What the hell was happening? Why was there a concerted effort to, not just put me in jail, but also somehow extract a pound of flesh?

In a prelude to the civil litigation, I was deposed over a period of six days. My attorney and I found it interesting that when someone was interviewed about the criminal case, the plaintiffs' attorney would ask me questions about that person. It was obvious somebody in the sheriff's department or the district attorney's office was giving information to the defense attorney.

It was a terrible year. I had the threat of a criminal trial hanging over me, I had to pay for all my attorneys (although I did get some help from my homeowner's insurance), and I was facing six separate civil trials that, if I lost, would leave me financially liable. At this point, the latter worry didn't matter as I had little money left. When the district attorney's office finally decided not to prosecute me, supposedly for lack of sufficient evidence, a great weight was lifted and I could concentrate on the lawsuits. The romp through my sexual history had ended, devious schemes against me abated a little, and while I'm sure some people were disappointed, I can state today as I have always that there was no sexual assault. No one will remember that. They'll remember only that I was accused.

When the lawsuits were first filed, my financial attorney told me they would all settle out of court and within two or three years of the cases settling, I would be financially whole. As it turned out, all the cases did settle out of court with all parties holding each other harmless. In each case, the plaintiffs won various amounts of money, a small part of which I had to pay. I settled my lawsuit with the county. They paid me a small sum of money I guess so I could say I won something.

The cases cost me about $125,000 in attorney fees and damages. Since I was forced to retire three years before I had planned to retire, my retirement check is $30,000 less per year than it would have been. So, in effect, each year I'm fined $30,000. Over the years, I have lost about $420,000 and will continue to have a substantially reduced retirement check for the rest of my life. The longer I live, the more money I lose.

I'm surprised that my first impression of people I'd known for more than thirty years wasn't fully formed until the day I was placed on administrative leave and during the course of the following year. The realization of friendship, fealty, and brotherhood, so readily assumed during one's nascent days in police work, were broken in such a swift, cavalier, and nauseating fashion I was left limp with despair. For the first time, I realized few people cared about me other than what I could do for them.

In the days since then, I've often thought about the fragility of relationships. It changed me and how I view my responsibility to the select few friends I have. I hope the experience has made me a better friend to them. Despite all this, the feeling of loss and unease mingles with the hope that the passage of time will lessen the sense of foreboding that sometimes still creeps into my thoughts.

The Plan

Through the three years of turmoil, I always had a plan in the back of my mind as to what I was going to do when it was all over. A young sergeant I had known in the department had left the force for greener pastures and a promotion in another law enforcement agency. Things turned bad for him and the police chief in short order, as sometimes happens in a police force. He left his new job under bad circumstances resulting from intense political turmoil.

He found work overseas in a United Nations peacekeeping mission in Bosnia and Herzegovina. I would hear from him occasionally and found what he was doing as part of the International Police Task Force (IPTF) in Bosnia especially interesting and adventurous. He moved on from IPTF to another agency where he was primarily involved in training Bosnian police officers.

I had always harbored an interest in working in a foreign country. In my fantasy, I would have a nice apartment right outside of London, purchase a couple of bespoke-suits from Savile Row, and take a train each morning into central London to my office in a nice building near Trafalgar Square. I hadn't thought about the conflict in Bosnia and the difficult to fathom bureaucracy of the United Nations. Nevertheless, a mission to Bosnia seemed the right ticket since there were few options for me in the US.

During the middle of my lawsuits, I applied to the private contractor who handled America's staffing commitments of civilian police to the United Nations' mission in Bosnia and the International Police Task Force that monitored the behavior of the Bosnian police. One of the recruiters told me to re-apply after I was finished with my legal imbroglio. When the lawsuits were done by January of 2000, I did re-apply, and by March, I was in Dallas attending an orientation course with about seventy-five other officers from around the country. Most were being deployed to Kosovo in Serbia, and nine of us would be seconded to the Bosnia Mission.

I was excited when I arrived at the training site in Dallas. The course wasn't difficult and the physical requirements, for me at fifty-five, were easy. On the first day of our physical training, nearly ten younger men and women failed to complete a one-mile run at a slow pace. A six-foot wall was the bugaboo of the truly uncoordinated and physically weak applicants. Although each candidate knew the physical requirements, many obviously hadn't put much effort into their preparation. After various tests involving physical agility, weaponless defense, psychological stability, reading and writing ability, and a demonstration that we could speak clearly, the group was pared down to fewer than fifty.

Maybe it wasn't the best plan I'd ever had, but at least I had one. The challenges were met, my plan was operational, and I found myself on a chartered flight heading to Bosnia. Our small Bosnian group would be dropped off in Sarajevo and the rest would fly on to Kosovo. After seeing the plane, I was glad those of us going to Bosnia had the shorter flight. We loaded onto a Russian jet that was probably rolled off some Siberian assembly line in the mid-sixties.

There was an all-male, Russian flight crew whose sole purpose was to throw inedible food at us, then try to ignore us for the rest of flight. My seat had a seat belt. Many did not. Food trays were broken or completely missing. The carpet in the aisle had come loose from the floor and bunched up under a dirty food cart as it was wheeled, or dragged, up and down the aisle. I had had some experience in Russia during a couple of police exchange programs and was aware of their strange ideas about toilets. I hoped the general Russian approach to toilet cleanliness didn't apply to airplane toilets on an international flight, albeit a charter flight. I was wrong, so wrong. The few restrooms were terrible. The thinking must be, "Why clean toilets? People shit in them."

Normally, I would have been thinking about my life and my future in my new job. Maybe I would find redemption, experience a restoration of my reputation, validate my skill as a cop, replenish my finances, have new friends and not just workmates, and perhaps buy a new Porsche while overseas. But there were no visions of sugarplums dancing in my head; in fact, most of the time I spent trying not to think about having to pee. I didn't want to have many bathroom experiences during the ten-hour flight.

TEN

WARRING FACTIONS AND LANDMINES

✼ ✼ ✼

Politics is war without bloodshed while war is politics with bloodshed

– Mao Tse-Tung (1893–1948)

Welcome

I was awakened from a fitful sleep by a heavily accented voice announcing our approach to Sarajevo. I had nodded off during the flight from Dallas to Sarajevo. I hadn't thought I would sleep during the trip. I was worried about the flight worthiness of the Russian plane, and I wanted to be awake when we plunged to earth after the wings had fallen off. I thought about starting a new life in a new country and wondered about how it would work out for me. Being away from my family and friends who had stood by me during my troubles was going to be difficult. But too I was excited that early morning as we bumped along the runway.

The nine of us assigned to Bosnia stepped onto the stairs from the plane and into the bright sunshine of a chilly spring morning. We were in our dark blue utility uniforms, one of many choices of uniforms we had been issued as part of the American contingent of the International Police Task Force (IPTF). As we ambled down the rickety stairs, we saw a group of men waiting for us near the fence. Some crewmembers threw our large and heavy duffle bags, full of uniforms and police equipment, onto the tarmac along with our personal suitcases loaded with clothes and necessary articles we were allowed to bring with us.

A group of men on the other side of the airfield fence was waiting near what our police instincts determined were UN vehicles. The large UN black letters painted on the sides gave us a clue. Most of the men appeared to be American, but their choices of uniform were different from ours and different from each other. Some officers from other countries were also present in uniform, including some Bosnian officers who checked our passports. I learned I was allowed to wear any of the many uniforms that were issued in any combination I wanted.

We had long-sleeved and short-sleeved blue polo shirts, long-sleeved and short-sleeved white dress shirts, blue polyester dress pants, two types of dark blue utility shirts, utility trousers, two sweaters, turtle neck shirts, winter boots, summer boots, dress shoes, and several types of coats and jackets along with rain gear. Many officers would buy black tennis-type shoes once in country to wear instead of the so-called dress shoes.

The sartorial choices were mind-boggling. The deputy police commissioner (a slot in the mission hierarchy always filled by an American) who greeted us wore a pressed white shirt with dark blue trousers along with a badge. I didn't know there were badges involved. No one told me we had a badge option while I was in training. Another man wore a white shirt but with his utility trousers bloused into his boots, and a third looked as if he were heading to the garage to work on a car in his rumbled utility uniform. This was my first official introduction to some of the American police officers who were part of the IPTF.

Most of us were in a fog from the long, uncomfortable flight. A nice relaxing afternoon in a quiet room on solid ground would be perfect. It didn't happen that way. Our training wouldn't wait and our colleagues drove us to a UN building where training began immediately. We were told that after the training we'd be taken to our hotel.

We started our six-day orientation program designed to put us through various tests and introduce us to the basics of the police mission in Bosnia. One speaker after another came to a podium and spoke about his or her area of expertise. None of the speakers was involved in the police part of the mission. The rest of the day, we listened to non-native English-speakers, and it took awhile in most cases to tune in to what they were saying.

Finally, at five o'clock we boarded a small UN bus and were driven to the Sarji Hotel at the far north end of Sarajevo. It was a refurbished building with a Scandinavian flavor to the design. I was surprised to learn that responsibility for the cost of my room rested with me. They had told us in Dallas to make sure we brought about $300 with us. Fortunately, I had enough money in my pocket. The room for the few days cost almost that entire amount. We wouldn't be reimbursed for the cost of the hotel room, although the next day the UN advanced us part of our per diem pay so we wouldn't be without funds for the first month of our deployment.

Our orientation included a driving test and an English test. The English test was both written and oral. We'd all been driving and speaking English (except for the two Texans in our group, who spoke something similar to English) for a long time, and those tests didn't hold any dread. Later, during my time in the mission I wondered if everyone automatically passed the driving test based on my observations of some driving habits of a few international police colleagues.

As I took the driving test, I thought it required some dexterity in the handling of a four-wheel-drive vehicle. I believed it gave the examiner a fairly good idea about the driving ability of a newly arrived member. Later, seeing some of the driving habits of UN employees, I began to doubt the efficacy of the test.

The official language of the mission was English. To work in a peacekeeping mission, an employee had to have the ability to read, write, and speak the mission language. The UN wanted to be fair and required native English-speakers to go through the same tests as those whose native language was not

English. From time to time, some American officers would have trouble with the reading and writing component of the English test. Our group breezed through the driving test and the first two parts of the English test. Then we had to appear before two examiners who would have a conversation with us in English and evaluate our speaking ability.

A large Ukrainian police colonel and a stern-looking Austrian police captain sat behind a desk in the interview room. As the senior officer, the Ukrainian led the interview. I had difficulty understanding him. His accent was thick and his questions were crazy. I'm not sure what he asked me, but I began to tell him about my work experience. Once I started talking, I didn't want to stop, as I was afraid he'd ask another question I wouldn't understand. When I stopped, they smiled. The Austrian captain thanked me and told me I had passed the test. Whew! My orientation was done, and I was ready to get my new assignment and learn what I'd be doing and where I'd be living for the next year.

Ranking

People in their own country come to more or less accept the policing structures they grow up with over the years. America developed a decentralized policing system, and we feel comfortable not having a national police force. We are different from most countries. They all have a national police force of some type or other. Canada, while it does have a lot of local forces, has the Royal Canadian Mounted Police. Britain has about forty police services that fall under the aegis of the Home Office. British police all wear similar uniforms, have similar recruitment and training standards, receive equal pay, and drive police cars that look pretty much like all the other police cars in England. Eastern European countries have strong national forces, as do most of the developing countries that, it should be noted, often comprise sixty percent or more of the international police forces seconded to UN peacekeeping missions.

When deployed to a peacekeeping mission, the international police officers are referred to as civilian police or CIVPOL. Each country has a rank structure, and the deployment to a mission doesn't change their rank. Although later I would learn that some countries artificially promoted officers only for the duration of the mission. Within mission, the highest-ranking officer in a country's contingent supervises and manages all the other officers in their group. Contingents ranged in size from a few officers to hundreds.

There was also a ranking system in the Bosnian mission, as well as other missions. Although the UN said ranks weren't important, in effect, officers were chosen for the most prestigious and important mission positions based on an officer's rank in his home force.

It was usually the case that police captains or majors were assigned as regional commanders or chiefs of large departments in the mission. Patrol officers were relegated to desk officer positions or monitors or some such, with basic, but frequently mundane duties and responsibilities. In fact, two ranking systems operated at the same time, and were inter-related.

One involved the rank an officer had in his or her police force and that rank was displayed on the uniform. The other was the ranking of the position assigned by the UN and determined largely by the officer's departmental rank. In some cases, a British chief inspector (roughly the equivalent of a senior lieutenant) could hold sway over a police major from Ghana.

Adding to the confusion, the American contingent was unlike others in the mission. Since there is no national police force, our contingent was comprised of officers from the thousands of independent police and sheriff forces from across the country.

Most American police forces have fewer than fifty officers. US CIVPOL officers arrived in Bosnia without any rank. Each officer, regardless of prior rank, experience, or education was equal to any other officer in the American contingent.

CIVPOL officers were at various times referred to as police monitors, police advisors or, in United Nation nomenclature, as "Experts on

Mission." Once seconded to a UN mission, our non-ranked CIVPOL officers discovered a whole set of hierarchical positions and assignments. Since nearly all other CIVPOL officers wore their ranks and Americans didn't, the American contingent was at a disadvantage.

There was a reason for this. In the US, each state establishes its own standards for hiring and training officers. A police sergeant may supervise three officers in one force, but a sergeant in another police agency may command twelve or more officers. To say someone was a police sergeant, lieutenant, captain, or deputy chief was, in some respects, not helpful in understanding the person's knowledge about police work, police supervision, or police management.

The Bosnian multi-national CIVPOL mission was staffed by national police forces or military police units such Spain's *la Guardia Civil*, France's *Gendarmerie,* or Italy's *Carabinieri*. The contingent's top-ranked officer was designated as the contingent commander. A US contingent commander could be of any rank and, in the early years of our police deployment to Bosnia, they were chosen through the vicissitudes of civilians.

An officer's rank didn't help IPTF administrators determine the best candidate for a position because of the way American police forces assigned rank. Throughout the US, police agencies established ranks in a wide variety of ways.

The rank of commander had different meanings in different forces. Many small law enforcement agencies whose budgets didn't support captains' positions changed the rank of lieutenant to commander. The commander's position had the same pay, same duties with a different more important sounding title. In some forces, the rank of commander was one rank higher than captain. Still other agencies replaced the title of captain with commander. A large-force commander might command several different divisions with hundreds of personnel.

Some forces used major as the first rank above captain similar to the military rank structure. A police inspector in the US could be a detective (below the rank of sergeant) or a rank above captain. There were police agencies in which the title of colonel was used to designate a police chief.

A colonel would wear silver eagles as their rank designation. Other chiefs might wear gold or silver stars, sometimes one but occasionally as many as five stars.

All of this was confusing to our international colleagues. Rather than develop a system with the American contingents deployed to peacekeeping missions that would create a more standardize system, the solution was not to recognize any prior police rank. The American officers on mission were on unequal footing with the foreign police officers with whom they worked side by side.

Cops Behaving Badly

Most of the Americans in the mission had garnered their police experience in relatively small police forces in the Midwest and South. Only a few comfortably spoke a foreign language and the majority hadn't traveled outside the United States. They were significantly different from the officers from the forty or more other countries serving in Bosnia. These circumstances sometimes led to trouble.

I never knew exactly how many American officers got in trouble during a mission overseas. It appeared that the actual percentage was low when compared to the thousands of Americans who participated in CIVPOL missions around the world. But there seemed to be a sense of unease about our officers. Some believed our officers were over represented in the cohort of officers from all the nations who had been repatriated, by the United Nations, for misbehavior.

Reports of misconduct become worse in the telling as the distance becomes greater. By the time a simple act of misconduct arrived at the US Department of State, the agency under which the management of US CIVPOL forces fell, it had traveled a circuitous route. The story changed with the many iterations of the event. The political environment in which an inappropriate act occurred also affected its perceived magnitude. The media could add to the problem by pursuing their own agenda. Getting the facts in these cases was difficult and there was often a swirl of emotion that didn't bode well for judicious problem solving.

An officer in a foreign county with an organization that practiced management with a multi-national flavor made the problems of managing police behavior more problematic. Many people in the UN believed the road to progress rested on understanding the primacy of *laissez faire* management. There was a pervasive sense that managers should let officers perform their duties with minimal oversight. Doing nothing was seen as the best course of action.

This wasn't an ideal atmosphere for American police officers. US officers thrived on structure and enjoyed making decisions quickly in their home force. However, an overly flexible, casual, and confusing organization, such as they encountered in the mission, was stressful.

Arriving in a foreign country for the first time, an officer loses most of the behavioral anchors and guideposts of his former life. The structure of the US CIVPOL contingent was also confusing for newly arrived officers who jockeyed for positions to their liking. A UN mission in a foreign country was a wilderness each officer had to negotiate. An officer's aggressiveness may have helped in a police career. In a mission, it was construed as typical, hollow American bravado by others.

Police are boundary testers. They push the limits, and it can be a good thing under the right circumstances. But it can be a disaster when the boundaries are not clearly marked or not consistently enforced. Police on mission were known to do things they would never do in their own country. American officers were no exception, and I frequently heard of some extraordinary events of misconduct while I was in Bosnia.

In part, what I saw as the American proclivity for misbehavior on mission was caused by the lack of a clear chain of command, confusing reporting authorities within the UN, and weak management practices in general.

Dennis LaDucer

A Trooper in Novi Grad

When the nine of us completed our training in Sarajevo, we were told where there were openings for Americans in the country. I learned quickly how important one's nationality was and how the UN thought it necessary to spread all nationalities around the country as evenly as possible. Later I learned that that wasn't always the case. There were no openings in Sarajevo, probably because it was a nice, exciting city with lots of things to do. Sarajevo had many restaurants with varying degrees of edibility, a movie theater, stores, and the corporate headquarters for the UN mission in Bosnia. Nearly everyone wanted to be deployed in Sarajevo.

Since we didn't know the country, it was difficult to choose an opening. All the positions would be about the same. Except for a few special people with some hard-to-find expertise, we'd be basic police monitors. It was where everyone started. I thought that maybe I'd get a cushy job by mentioning my police administrative experience. After thinking about it for a while and contemplating why I had come to Bosnia, I decided I only wanted to be one of the troops. After all, I had been a boss most of my law enforcement career.

I was in the mission to let some time pass, heal my emotional wounds, and spend an exciting year doing an international police job while earning some pretty good money. One of the police monitors in Sarajevo told me the Bihac Region was a nice assignment. It was far away from UN HQ, close to Zagreb, Croatia and, the theory went, out of sight-out of mind. I raised my hand along with two others when they asked who wanted to go to Bihac. Luckily, there were three openings. A Haitian American from the NY Housing Authority Police, a middle-aged woman from a Pacific Northwest police force, and I got the gig in the far north of Bosnia right on the border with Croatia.

We were told we would leave the next morning with some CIVPOL officers who were already driving to Sarajevo from Bihac. We were scheduled to leave with them the next morning for the seven-hour drive north. I assumed we would be meeting fellow Americans. The three of us waited in the hotel's dining room after breakfast. We were packed and ready to head out. Soon four officers walked in, one from Romania, two from Egypt, and another from Indonesia. To assure there was sufficient room for all our gear, they had brought two UN vehicles. The vehicles were older SUVs built for rough roads, and it was clear they'd seen better days. It was good they had thought ahead since the three of us could barely fit all our gear in the back of the two vehicles.

There was lots of talk in three different accents, make that four, as our Haitian-American officer had a pretty good accent himself. The officers from Bihac were anxious to get going, reminding us of the long drive ahead. We headed across Sarajevo toward the airport. The SUVs stopped across the street from the airport. Our new colleagues had some shopping to do for themselves and other officers at their station. They entered the French PX where they purchased booze, cigarettes, and various sundry items. When we finished, we stopped by an Italian PX for more shopping, then a local market. The SUVs were bulging with supplies.

I asked why they had to shop here and not in Bihac. They explained that we weren't going to the city of Bihac, but to Novi Grad, a small city about fifty kilometers south of Bihac. It was part of the Bihac Region, which actually had seven IPTF stations in various locations. We would be replacement troops for the station in Novi Grad, a city of about ten thousand people. There was a long drive ahead of us so I had plenty of time to take this all in. Although the officers had picked us up at the hotel early in the morning, we didn't leave Sarajevo until mid-morning when all their shopping was completed.

Around one o'clock our two-car caravan stopped high in the mountains for lunch. But I think we really stopped so the officers could enjoy cigarettes and coffee. We piddled around at the restaurant for a good hour before we were off again on our northern journey along a one-lane mountain road that was twisty, narrow, and poorly maintained. I was told this particular road was one of the better ones in Bosnia. Short distances in this country did not mean a quick trip. Every trip of any distance was an adventure because of road conditions and the amount of heavy truck traffic using them. The trucks and cars I saw were old and appeared to be in terrible condition. There weren't many stretches of this highway where speeds over fifty miles per hour could be reached. Under those circumstances, we arrived in Novi Grad, my new home for the next year, at dusk.

In Novi Grad, in the waning daylight, I saw a war-torn small town, and my first thought was about finding a place to stay. The only hotel in town was a bombed-out shell of a building. Part of the fourth floor of the building served as the IPTF station. Most of the other floors were empty and the war had made the hotel's business moribund. We met our deputy station commander (another Indonesian) who welcomed us and told us they had chosen some accommodations for us. Accommodation was the UN word for housing. I didn't like someone else deciding where I was going to live.

The three of us were shown a one-bedroom apartment on the second floor of a fairly nice house on a hill. The apartment had a living room, dining room, bedroom, and a newly redecorated bathroom. Once I saw the bathroom, I said I'd take it. I figured it was every man for himself. The deputy commander said the owners were asking too much money because we were Americans. The cost was almost $200 a month, an outrageous amount he thought. I struck a deal with the owner who lived downstairs. It didn't matter at this point; I wanted to settle in. It worked out perfectly as my two colleagues liked the other two places, one across the street from me and the other right behind me. So we became the Americans living in Beverly Hills, as the other officers called the area because of the price of the apartments and, of course, it was on a hill overlooking Novi Grad.

The Lay of the Land

Our first day at work involved basic job orientation and meeting our workmates. The station commander was a young Polish police lieutenant. His deputy was an older Indonesian police officer of undetermined rank whom we had met the night before. There were twenty-five other officers from various countries including Romania, Egypt, Hungary, Russia, Indonesia, Italy, and Malaysia performing a variety of specific jobs. There was a clear pecking order. The Eastern Europeans were on top of the pile, probably because of personalities more so than nationalities.

Some work was preferable to other assignments. Day shift work was better than night work. Driving around and monitoring the local police was better than being restricted to desk duties. Working on human rights issues such as investigating the illegal confiscation of people's property during the war to help them get their homes back was more interesting than taking complaints about the local police.

My two fellow Americans and I were assigned to desk duty. Everyone started as a desk officer we were told. We were given a tour of the city and some of the outlying local police stations. All in all, this didn't appear to be a bad assignment. I had no real responsibilities, there were a few unadorned but nice restaurants in town, there was a small gym, and the location was perfect for several reasons. Novi Grad was located on the juncture of two rivers. One was the Sana, (a tributary of the Sava River) which formed the border between Croatia and Bosnia in this area making its way to the Danube and eventually the Black Sea. The other was the Una, which flowed south toward Banja Luka, the capital of the Bosnian Serb territory.

A temporary military bridge had been laid across the Sana. As an international police officer I could walk across the bridge in five minutes and be in Croatia. The little town across the river, unlike Novi Grad, had reliable phone service, a post office that was credible, and a number of stores stocked with more and better produce and products. The UN provided bus service five days a week from Banja Luka to Zagreb, the capital of Croatia. The bus stopped at the bridge and picked up UN employees and whisked them away in air-conditioned comfort to Zagreb in a mere ninety minutes. Zagreb was a whole different way of life. It was like a siren's call on a day off with nothing much to do. Thirty minutes away from Novi Grad was a NATO military base where members of the IPTF could shop at the various post exchanges and purchase western style products.

Just out of sheer luck, I had raised my hand for assignment in the Bihac Region and was deployed to this small, heavily bombed, barely hanging on yet friendly town in the northwest corner of Bosnia. On my first day off, I caught the UN bus to Zagreb. I walked around, shopped, and generally enjoyed my day off in the flourishing capital of a former Yugoslavia Republic. Before my next days off arrived, the station received a memo from UN headquarters in Sarajevo advising that the bus service was discontinued effective the day before my next holiday. Crap!

But there was still the opportunity to walk across the bridge into Croatia or drive the thirty minutes south to Banja Luka where I could get chips and salsa, Reese's Peanut Butter Cups, and the other items of life-giving manna necessary for an American's survival in the wilderness of Bosnia.

Crossing the bridge soon became of paramount importance. The NATO facility in Banja Luka closed its doors to UN personnel, including the IPTF. Apparently, this was the result of some thefts from the various exchanges, and civilians were suspected. Now, I had only the small Croatian town across the river.

While I could score food in Novi Grad, it took time and effort to stop by many different stores and search their small shelves stocked with meager amounts of the bare necessities. Live chickens and eggs were readily available on the two market days each week in Novi Grad. The women who sold the live chickens would kill them for you but the plucking was left to the buyer. I didn't know what to do with a dead chicken with the feathers attached, and I didn't want to learn; it was a skill I could live without.

A month into my tour, the final insult came. It started as a rumor. A detachment of Hungarian Army engineers was coming to disassemble the temporary bridge across the Sana River. It couldn't be true. No bridge across the Sana at Novi Grad meant people going to Croatia from Bosnia would have to drive forty-five minutes east and north to reach the closest crossing point or drive north to Bihac and cross the border there. This was just plain wrong. A few weeks later the bridge was gone, and I was, pretty much, stuck in Novi Grad and had to make do with what I could find there.

As summer approached, I was the only IPTF officer on duty in the city. I worked from ten o'clock in the evening until eight o'clock the next morning. My duties were simple; I was to make sure the UN generator that provided the only electricity to the building kept running throughout the night, check to see none of the UN vehicles was stolen, keep a sharp eye out for fire in the building and spread the alarm if there was a fire, send out faxes that had been prepared during the day, log in any faxes received, and, in the morning, call the NATO base in Banja Luka to make sure we had good radio contact on the off chance something untoward should happen.

I don't remember the precise time, but it seemed as if it was just before sunrise as I wrote in the log about the faxes received during the evening. There I was, ten thousand miles from home, thirty-two years as a cop, a graduate degree, and substantial work toward a doctorate in public administration. Yet, I was confined to a bombed out hotel, logging in faxes, and basically performing duties a trained monkey could do. I was disappointed, sad, yet somehow strangely inspired. At eight o'clock I made a call to the deputy police commissioner during which I retracted my earlier comments about not wanting to be a boss. I told him I truly and fervently wanted to be a boss and wanted him to set me free from this incredibly boring job.

A short time later, orders came in from Sarajevo instructing me to meet with the deputy police commissioner. The Novi Grad IPTF station was abuzz, and everyone questioned me as to why I was summoned to Sarajevo. Feigning ignorance, not a stretch for me, I left the station to pack for my overnight trip.

My Little Russian Friend

A few weeks before the bridge across the Sana River was removed and before I left to meet the deputy police commissioner in Sarajevo, a Russian police officer was deployed to our station as a replacement for one who had left. He was a thirty-something, quiet man of diminutive stature who, it must be said, always wore a clean uniform and didn't smell. The Russians had crappy militia (as the Russians called their police) uniforms. During my two Russian police exchange programs, I had an opportunity to see how they worked in their communities. Bathing was not a high priority for them and the uniforms were often in poor condition.

This I'm sure was because of the low pay. They could ill afford frequent uniform maintenance. The uniform itself was made of cheap material, and the uniform shirt was styled after a 1950s calypso shirt worn outside the trousers. The shirts hung at various lengths below the waist. It wasn't a good look.

This officer, who held a rank equivalent to lieutenant, looked pretty good, all things considered. One day I was assigned to show him around our area of responsibility. He had the vehicle keys in his hand. As we walked toward the vehicle, he tried handing them to me. He said it would be better if I drove. That was unusual as most of the officers from Eastern Europe and former Soviet countries loved to drive big powerful vehicles such as the UN's patrol SUVs. Even though our vehicles were old and had spent time in another mission in Africa, they were nice vehicles compared to the Russian-built Lada patrol vehicles the militia drove. I wouldn't take the keys and he landed in the driver's seat staring at the instrument panel.

When I asked him about his driving skills, he said he had driven a patrol car in Russia for ten years. He continued to look vacantly at the instrument panel. I assumed newly deployed officers knew how to drive and had passed the UN driving test during their orientation days in Sarajevo. In a short time, that assumption was put uncomfortably to rest.

He was visibly nervous, which made me nervous, but he insisted he knew how to drive. After a few false starts, we were off patrolling the streets of Novi Grad to the amazement of the residents as this large UN vehicle came bouncing along, gears grinding, engine bucking, and passenger officer crying in fear. As time passed, he settled down and got the hang of gear shifting, but his steering ability was below par. He would wander across the centerline and make right-hand turns by first moving way to the left before turning right, something most drivers in Bosnia did routinely. Maybe he had some Bosnian DNA. I wanted to show him the town across the Sana in Croatia thinking he might be interested since it was their market day.

We managed the bridge crossing without killing anyone. What followed could've been partially my fault. As we were driving around the town, during a particularly busy market day, I saw a stall selling fresh mushrooms. I needed fresh mushrooms. I shouted at him, at the last minute I'll admit, to turn left. He almost made the turn safely, but in negotiating the turn, we clipped the table of a vegetable and egg stall, upending it and spilling the contents on the roadway.

At this point, I wondered about the legality of being in Croatia with a UN vehicle in the first place. I knew it wasn't legal to run into people's property and smash their things. I didn't buy any mushrooms, but together we purchased about three-dozen broken eggs at a premium price in US dollars. There was no other damage, and the old woman vendor was pleased to have sold all her eggs. She dusted off the veggies scattered on the ground and placed them back on the table we righted for her. Having some hard currency in their pockets made most people in the Balkans smile, and the vendor was no exception. She was also happy, I'm sure, to see our totally embarrassed butts heading across the bridge back to Bosnia with me in the driver's seat.

When I became deputy police commissioner for the mission, I should've realized my little Russian friend was a driving disaster waiting to happen. He became a regular driver, but never a safe driver, and he remained a long way from skilled. One day, driving along a long, straight road, he swerved right and struck a young boy standing by the roadside. The officer was in a personal vehicle he had purchased. He wasn't driving a big heavy UN vehicle. The boy's injuries weren't life threatening, although he did spend a few weeks in the hospital. To his credit, the officer paid all the hospital bills, probably gave the family some money as well, and throughout his tenure in the mission, he kept in close touch with the boy and his family. To my knowledge, he didn't have any more accidents.

A Police General

I learned that most of the military police forces working in the mission had military ranks, including the rank of general. I liked the whole idea of being a general. Italy, France, Spain, and Chile all had national police forces structured along military lines and often with military duties and responsibilities beside their police duties. I never quite understood how they differentiated their police functions from the military ones.

The *Carabiniere* from Italy, for example, worked as part of the IPTF, but also had members assigned to NATO as soldiers in the Stability Force (SFOR), which handled the military aspect of the mission in Bosnia. The *Carabiniere* appeared, to me, based on my experience in Bosnia and my observations and discussions with them during many visits to Italy, to be primarily a police force with specific specialized police duties and some military responsibilities.

La Guardia Civil were, at one time, the national police force of Spain. Over time their duties were circumscribed, and they now perform highway patrol duties in some, but not all, parts of Spain. In Bosnia, *La Guardia Civil* officers were assigned to SFOR as part of a rapid response team, but there were none in the IPTF. *Carabineros de Chile* is the only police force in their country. They perform a variety of duties, including acting as justices of the peace in rural communities. I was never sure why they were referred to as military police types as they only performed police duties in Bosnia.

The French *Gendarmerie* was another force that appeared mostly military but performed police duties in Bosnia. The commissioner and his many countrymen who surrounded him as *chefs de cabinet,* drivers, aides, and other French officers did nothing in the fourteen months during which I worked closely with he and his staff to disabuse me of the many, admittedly, stereotypical impressions I held about the French.

At the risk of sounding more biased against the French, and maybe casting some dispersion on my sexual orientation, there was something else about them that seemed plain weird to me: their pants were too tight. Every single one of them sported trousers that looked as if they were tailored for a woman trying to get a man's attention. They had a certain swagger to their gait and, combined with the tight pants, was off-putting bordering on disturbing. Perhaps I've said too much.

The *Gendarmerie* is mostly a military force with some police responsibilities. In France, they work in rural areas and in small towns while the

French National Police take responsibility for the large urban centers. The *Gendarmerie* had a large presence as part of IPTF, but a larger contingent of officers in SFOR.

A police commissioner, a high-ranking police official from some European country, always led the IPTF. The deputy police commissioner was always an American, usually a retired police chief or deputy chief from a mid to large force. During my tenure in the mission, the police commissioner was a brigadier general from the *Gendarmerie*. He was short and rotund with a middling command of English. He spoke brusquely. He possessed all the pomposity Americans associate with French people when we are painting with a broad brush.

The Commissioner and Me

When I arrived in Sarajevo from Novi Grad, I met with the deputy police commissioner. His charge was to run the day-to-day operations. This required him to keep track of the two thousand officers from forty different countries working in the IPTF. Those international officers monitored, mentored, and advised the forty thousand local police in the Cantons of the Croate/Bosnian Federation and the *Republika Srpska* held by the Bosnian Serbs.

The deputy police commissioner was a retired deputy chief from a force in the western US. He was a congenial, plain speaking, and insightful man with excellent police experience. He not only knew his police craft, but also had been a quick study as to the strange ways of the United Nations. He was able to provide a roadmap through the vagaries of the mission with cogent, timely, and helpful advice. I liked him immediately and we've remained colleagues to this day, working together in another mission in Central Asia and for a Department of Defense (DOD) contractor involved in training civilian personnel deploying to the Middle East.

The deputy commissioner said there were three job openings into which he could place an American, me. One was the position of advisor to the police chief of Sarajevo, another was the chief of operations for the mission, and the third was the soon-to-be-vacant job of regional commander of Sarajevo. He didn't suggest one job over another, but took the time to explain the duties and responsibilities of each. He suggested I speak with a young Foreign Service officer at the US embassy to see if the embassy had a preference. I duly set up a meeting over coffee at the embassy in the afternoon. The young officer had a lot to say, but wasn't particularly helpful. Next, I met with the commissioner.

The commissioner asked what job interested me. Since I had been the chief of Operations, I suggested it would be a fitting position for me in Bosnia. I had decided the advisor to the police chief wasn't for me. The commissioner told me he was planning to give Operations to a colleague from Senegal who was arriving in the mission soon.

By default, Sarajevo regional commander was the only job left. I didn't receive a commitment from the commissioner then and was soon heading back to Novi Grad. I was anxious because nothing was settled, and I wasn't sure I could find my way back by myself. I had time to think on the drive back. Had I made a good impression? Would I have the regional commander position or would some other job open? The Sarajevo regional commander, a man from Bangladesh, wasn't scheduled to leave the mission for over a month. What would happen in between? Would it be more logging of faxes in and faxes out?

I found my way back to Novi Grad without any problems. The next day I returned to work on the day shift at the station. Immediately, during roll call, I noticed a sea change in the way others were interacting with me. They were curious about my trip and my meetings with the commissioner and the deputy commissioner. They assumed I was a man of standing in the mission and had the ear of the senior-most bosses. The station commander told me I'd be working day shift. Our sole woman who had come to Novi Grad with me had, on her own, finagled a transfer to a station close to Sarajevo where she would be working on human rights issues. I was going to take her place on the day shift.

A week went by and there was no word from HQ. My duties took some colleagues and me to the city of Bihac. There were many Americans assigned there, and I wanted to meet them. When I walked into one of the offices, I introduced myself to several of them. They said they had received a message that I was going to be the new regional commander in Sarajevo. They knew, but I didn't. I spoke to the deputy commissioner on the phone from Bihac and he confirmed my assignment. Better yet, he was having me transferred to Sarajevo as soon as possible so I could train under the current Bangladeshi who occupied the commander's position.

ELEVEN

BALKAN STORIES

✯ ✯ ✯

We Americans have no commission from God to police the world.

– Benjamin Harrison, 23rd President of the United States

The War in Bosnia

The war in Bosnia was confusing and difficult to explain. It started in 1992 following the passage of a Bosnian referendum for independence. It was a terrible war and speaking about it in laymen's terms was no easy task. The Socialist Federal Republic of Yugoslavia was comprised of six separate republics. They were Bosnia and Herzegovina, Serbia (which included the two autonomous provinces of Kosovo and Vojvodina), Croatia, Macedonia, Montenegro, and Slovenia. The sway of communism diminished when the Cold War ended in 1989. The various republics of Yugoslavia wanted to go their separate ways and establish independent countries. When Bosnia did this through an independence referendum, the initiative was opposed and rejected by the Serbs living in Bosnia. With the support of the Yugoslav People's Army, the Bosnian Serbs declared war. From April 1992 until the end of 1995, bitter fighting, indiscriminate shelling of cities and towns that held no strategic military value, ethnic cleansing, systematic mass rape, and genocide raged throughout the country. It was estimated that Bosnian Serbs perpetrated 90 percent of the war crimes, according to some sources.

It was a territorial conflict between Bosnian Serbs on one side and Bosniacs and Bosnian Croats on the other. But the Bosnian Croats were also fighting to secure part of Bosnia in the central cantons (similar to a county in the US) for themselves. Bosnia's residents were divided among the Bosniacs (44 percent) who were mostly Muslim, ethnic Catholic Croats (17 percent), and the ethnic Serbs (31 percent) whose main religion was Christian Orthodox. People assumed this was a religious war, but the Bosniacs, while declaring themselves Muslim, appeared to be more secular than religious.

True, there were many mosques in Bosnia, but my landlord's father, who lived on the ground floor of my accommodation, was typical and makes the point. I'd see him sitting in the front yard drinking homemade wine. Whenever he heard the prayer call for Friday evening prayers at the main mosque a short distance from our house, he'd put the wine down and walk over to pray. He'd be back after prayers drinking again in the front yard during the late summer evenings. Few Bosniac women wore any form of head covering or traditional dress.

Historians have said that the different ethnicities in Bosnia were all southern Slavs, whether Bosniac, Croat, or Serb. In many cases, the family history of a Bosniac reveals incidences during the Ottoman rule of the Balkans where a Catholic or Orthodox Christian converted to Islam to make life simpler. Conversions weren't necessarily because of a fervent belief in the value of Islam over other religions. Under Ottoman rule in Bosnia, life was economically better for a Muslim than a non-Muslim. People of different ethnicities and religions intermarried and peacefully co-existed before the conflict.

In early 1995, NATO entered the fray, and negotiations for peace among the different factions began. These efforts ended in the Dayton

Peace Accord in December of the same year. The Accord stopped the fighting and held the parties to the various portions of the territories they held at the time of the signing. Alas, the Accord was too late for the seven thousand men and boys massacred at Srebrenica by the Bosnian Serb army.

The Accord set the boundaries for the soft partitioning of Bosnia. Where the Bosnian Serb army had stopped became the territory of the *Repubilka Srpska*. Where the Bosniacs and Bosnian Croats stopped became the basis for the Federation of Bosnia and Herzegovina, a collaboration of the two parties. Yet Bosnia is one country. The UN would never say it was a partitioned country. Each section of the country, the Federation or *Srpska*, governed their areas in their own style pursuing their particular self-interests. Those were the political circumstances when I joined the UN Mission in Bosnia in April 2000.

There were tender feelings, raw emotions, and provocative prejudices among the people of Bosnia when I arrived in the mission. It was nearly five years since the cessation of hostilities, but the façade of peaceful coexistence was still fragile. Despite the plethora of organizations scattered throughout the country, such as the Organization for Security and Cooperation in Europe (OSCE), the Office of the High Representative (OHR), the International Organization for Migration (IOM), the International Red Cross (IRC), the United States Agency for International Development (USAID), and Non-Governmental Agencies (NGOs), acts of resistance to the forced co-mingling of Bosnians were common. Nearly every European country and NGOs from those countries were present in Bosnia either monitoring the peace or helping people who had been displaced, injured, or whose property had been stolen.

A joke making its way through the various international organizations at the time sums up the feeling. A Serb, a Croat, and a Bosniac were walking along the Drina River in Sarajevo earnestly trying to resolve political differences in light of the Dayton Peace Accord. In a flash, a genie appeared and said they were honest men. As such, he had the authority to grant each one a wish. He cautioned them that once spoken, the wish couldn't be rescinded. The Serb explained, "We are peaceful people. Life would be much easier if the Croat were dead. I wish him dead."

The Croat countered the argument saying, "The Serbs have made life miserable and if you kill this Serb, peace will prevail in all of Bosnia. Kill the Serb."

The Bosniac asked, "Are you going to grant them their wishes?" The genie confirmed he would and the two would be dead by nightfall. The genie asked the Bosniac for his wish. The Bosniac said, "Then I'll have a cappuccino."

Managing a United Nations Police Mission

The United Nations Mission in Bosnia and Herzegovina (UNMIBH) was the lead agency in the effort to bring stability to the country. Or was it the lead agency? There was also the Office of the High Representative (OHR) who had a similar brief from the UN, but had a different reporting relationship. Confused? Me too. I remained confused about the different responsibilities, duties, and goals of all the different agencies throughout my eighteen months in the mission. There wasn't any clear direction or progress toward the nebulous objectives of these organizations. The objectives were written in diplomatic language and said a lot while saying nothing. It was, in my opinion, impossible to measure progress in the short term.

UNMIBH was led by what I will call a special envoy to the country. The envoy was an American with the title of ambassador, and he represented the secretary-general of the United Nations. This mission was divided into a Civil Affairs section and the IPTF. Civil Affairs dealt with the political aspects of implementing the Dayton Peace Accord, promulgating policy, and assuring the compliance of Bosnian politicians with the principles of democracy. The Civil Affairs section of UNMIBH was staffed with three thousand UN career employees.

IPTF was responsible for monitoring the local police and to ensure they carried out their duties within the parameters of democratic policing. There were two thousand international police officers in IPTF and, unlike the career employees, they were seconded to the UN from their home forces.

The envoy was tall, overweight bordering on obese, jowly, garrulous, profane, and at least one standard deviation beyond self-absorbed. He was a retired general officer, having spent his part-time military career in the reserves. But he lacked any military bearing even on those infrequent occasions when he chose to wear his old uniform. He would answer to "ambassador" (I think he liked that best), "general," or "sir." His time in diplomatic service had honed a certain child-like charm in him, and in both social and business settings, he was always the consummate raconteur. At least he was while he kept his temper in check. He had a short fuse, and a visitor never quite knew when he would explode with a string of profanity.

Next in command of the mission was the deputy envoy who was the complete opposite of his boss. The deputy was a career foreign service officer who appeared to be British. But he was born in Africa to British parents, I think, and schooled in the UK. There was some talk about him having a passport from a Caribbean country. I would jokingly ask him, given his background, if he worked from MI5, MI6, or some other part of British Intelligence. He was a charming and competent administrator with a treasure trove of experience, training, and knowledge he willingly shared with colleagues seeking guidance. He, too, was tall and overweight, but unlike the envoy, the deputy had a perfect command of his temper. In every circumstance, he acted professionally. Problem was, though, the envoy didn't appear to like him, and as a consequence, failed to share information with his deputy or seek his opinion on matters of policy or action.

The next in line was the Chief Administrative Officer (CAO). The deputy was frequently bypassed while the CAO and Envoy would plan, plot, eat, and booze as they wiled away hours developing stratagems to save Bosnia from itself. The CAO was from a near-east country, but I wasn't sure exactly what country. He was in his mid-fifties, soft, and talkative but often in an evasive way that bordered on mendacity. I don't mean to be unkind, but he was an ugly man. He appeared to have been assembled with non-fitting parts. I was always uncomfortable interacting with him. He just wasn't an easy person for me to like, and shame on me for not having tried harder.

The dynamics of the UN administration were made more difficult by the fact that the Envoy was frequently at odds with the high representative. The high representative was the head of the OHR. OHR had the authority to enact rules and regulations in the country that had the power of law. The envoy didn't have that kind of power. The high representative didn't report directly to the secretary-general of the UN, but rather to a committee from various countries appointed by the secretary-general to oversee the development of Bosnia under the peace agreement.

Still confused? So was I, and I was there. The fun part, however, was the fact that the envoy appeared to hate the high commissioner. I'm sure both would deny it, but there was friction. The envoy felt he was the supreme leader and the high representative was an interloper.

Coordination between UNMIBH and OHR manifested itself in a "Principles' meeting" held the first of the week during which all the major players in the mission were present. It was chaired by the high representative and held at OHR. He was a European who had a good command of English, dressed impeccably, acted arrogantly, and would always be ten or more minutes late to his own meetings.

This was the administrative milieu in which the IPTF operated.

My Big Job Interviews

I shouldn't be so harsh since, as the regional commander and then the deputy police commissioner, I was part of that administrative camarilla. I learned how to be a regional commander from a Bangladeshi police superintendent whose place I would take when he left the mission about a month after I arrived in Sarajevo. I don't know what I was expecting, but

I was pretty sure there wasn't much he was going to be able to teach me about police work. I had actual field experience as a police monitor and he didn't. I was more than likely way ahead of him. Add to that all my police management experience in the US. Surely there wasn't much he was going to teach me.

The superintendent was tall, enthusiastic, hard working, and spoke in that singsong kind of flowery voice Indians, Pakistanis, and Bangladeshis use. I had no idea how internally political the UN could be, but through his good suggestions and advice, I learned when to keep my head down. Everyone in the UN, especially the regular UN employees and to some extent the IPTF officers, thought of themselves as a boss, or chief, or head of this or that. No one thought of himself or herself as a worker. Everyone was important, even if they weren't so important. The superintendent taught me how to deal with so many important people.

A case in point involved getting an extra set of keys for my UN vehicle. It was easy to accidently lock the SUV with the keys still in it. I wanted to avoid such a mishap, so I spoke to a man in the motor pool. He said they didn't have key-making facilities, but I could go into town, have some made, keep the receipt, and they would reimburse me the cost. It was a simple enough solution, so the next day I did as my friend in the motor pool suggested. The next day I went to see him with my five-dollar receipt in hand. He directed me to another building where another man would pay me the five dollars. When I handed this man the receipt he asked what I had bought. Then the trouble began.

I explained I needed a second set of keys. In a gruff voice, he informed me he had not authorized me to have additional car keys. I think my response was something like, "Are you kidding me? I'm the regional commander, and if I want a second set of keys, I can have them. I don't need your authorization."

He took the keys and the receipt from the counter and put them on his desk. He told me I couldn't have the extra set of keys, and I wasn't going to be reimbursed. I swear I would have maced him if I had had any. Instead, I reached over the counter, retrieved my new second set of keys and receipt, and stormed out of the building. When I told my Bangladeshi mentor about the incident, he explained it was a battle I'd lose, why I'd lose, and the nature of UN employees on mission.

Apparently, regardless of the loftiness of the position held in the mission, it was necessary to respect each person's bailiwick. Failing to do this made life more difficult, if not, at times, impossible. I wondered if I could claim the cost as an unreimbursed business expense on my taxes the following year.

The superintendent's approach to people in the mission was soft and gentle. It was a successful approach even during some tense discussions with UN colleagues from Civil Affairs. He taught me, by example, how to handle my job as the regional commander, and how to get things done in the mission. I missed him when he left, but have remained in contact with him as he deployed to other missions, became the inspector general of his force, and for a short period led his entire national police force during a transitional period in Bangladesh.

Within a few months of having the regional commander's helm on my own, the deputy police commissioner decided not to renew his contract. I was asked if I was interested in the job. I said yes but failed to check things out at home. My original contract was for one year, and I was halfway through it. To become the new deputy commissioner, I had to sign another contract, which meant I'd finish my mission in November instead of earlier in March. Basically, it was a six-month extension. I didn't think it was a big deal but my wife did. It was a marriage kerfuffle that calmed over time.

Before being knighted into the august position of deputy commissioner, I went through a series of interviews unlike any I had experienced previously. Remember, I was only a candidate. No one said I could have the job. My first interview was with our French police general who headed the IPTF. He wanted to know my rank, why I didn't wear any rank insignia, and how many people were in my command. I told him my rank was assistant sheriff, had two stars on my uniform, but didn't wear rank in mission because that was the policy of the US DOS, and approximately one thousand officers were under my command in my home force. I added that

I would wear the two stars on my collar, just as he did as a police general, if I were chosen.

The only other question he asked was about my plans for the Christmas holiday. He was going to France to spend Christmas. We both couldn't leave the country at the same time, and he was going home for Christmas. I'd have to stay in the country over the holidays. That was fine with me. That was it. No penetrating, thought-provoking, or insightful queries, just what was my status in my home force and what were my Christmas plans. On to the next interview.

Naturally I had to be interviewed by the envoy the next day. While the commissioner's interview was lacking, the envoy's interview was weird. I was ushered into his office to find the envoy and the CAO sitting in chairs, smoking Cuban cigars. They had me sit on the couch as they leaned back in the easy chairs on each end of the couch, inhaled large volumes of cigar smoke, closed their eyes, and blew cigar smoke in my general direction. Although I've never smoked and cigarette smoke does annoy me, I kind of enjoy the smell of a cigar, especially a good expensive cigar. In front of me on the coffee table was a large container of M&Ms. My thought was, since they were enjoying their cigars, I should enjoy my favorite candy treat. So without asking, I dipped into the M&Ms and started munching.

They looked at each other, but didn't say anything about my forwardness. The envoy asked how I got along with the commissioner. Before I could answer, the CAO spoke up about concerns he had with the commissioner. When he was done I started to take a breath to answer the envoy's question, but the CAO's comments prompted the Envoy into a diatribe about the previous commissioner, a former ambassador, and a host of others. None of them appeared to measure up to the envoy's standards.

He told me some funny stories, and then changed the topic to local politics. During this conversation, he and the CAO went back and forth basically failing to find any redeeming value in most of the politicians in the country. It was as if they were having a private conversation and I was there to observe. Occasionally I would grunt affirmation about a point one or the other made, but never added any substance to the conversation since

I was at a complete loss. I had no idea about the people or situations they were discussing.

I must have done fine during both the interviews because a short time later I was given the nod and moved into the position of deputy police commissioner.

Breakfast at Darlene's

There were many lazy, stupid people working for the United Nations. There were also some smart, hard-working men and women who quite willingly gave up a comfortable life for the more arduous mission life hoping their contribution would play a small part in making the world better. I was fortunate during my time in Bosnia to meet a woman who had spent most of her adult life working to make life better for other people. Darlene (not her real name) graduated with a PhD from one of America's most prestigious universities. Whether trying to help in a refugee camp in Cambodia or Vietnam or helping migrants in Bosnia while at the same time raising a family, she was a person of strong will, unbending convictions, humility, and charm.

A short time after my promotion, I met Darlene and we became friends. She was working for an organization affiliated with the UN and it was housed in our headquarters building. We would speak often as her responsibility involved women who were the victims of human traffickers, a particularly troublesome crime that the local police seemed not to have the political will to investigate.

I went to Darlene's apartment one Saturday morning to have breakfast and see the new apartment she'd been raving about for some time. It was a nice place near the center of town. When I arrived, I noticed there was a large outer door opening into a small courtyard. She kept an ugly dog in there. It was a mongrel dog she had rescued in Vietnam. I subsequently referred to it as her Viet Cong dog. I hadn't seen anything quite like it.

Referring to it as a hybrid dog really did a disservice to normal looking hybrids everywhere. The dog's head was too large for the odd shaped body that carried it. It had mangy-orange dog hair covering its body, but it wasn't distributed evenly, giving the appearance of a dog that had been clipped by an unlicensed and clinically insane dog groomer. The short legs were disproportional for the dog's size.

Darlene met me at the outer door and, when I stepped into the courtyard, the dog started jumping on me and running around. She ignored the dog's behavior and led me to an interior door and steps that wound up to the apartment. When we were at the top of the stairs, she saw the dog had followed us and said to the dog, "How did you get in?"

She took the dog down the stairs, but became stuck at the lower door, as she couldn't find the key to open the door to let the dog back out into the courtyard. She searched her pockets and, after several false starts, found the key and put the dog out. When she came back upstairs, she asked what I wanted for breakfast. "Just coffee and a roll would be fine," I said.

"Well, we'll have to go out to get some things first," she responded. Down the stairs we went and at the bottom she began searching her pockets for the key so we could go out. We discovered she had left the key on the dining room table. When she arrived at the door with the key in hand, she wondered if she needed a hat. I had said it was cold outside. Then the search was on for her hat. While she was upstairs looking for her hat, I waited at the door hoping I wasn't a prisoner since I had an important staff meeting later in the morning.

She returned with her hat in hand and said we had to take the dog with us because the dog had to poop. She damn near had to wrestle the dog to the ground to get the leash on the motley beast. When the task was done, we headed for the outer door in the courtyard en route to the dog-poop park and the stores so we could buy supplies for the breakfast to which she had invited me.

We stopped in front of the outer door, but I didn't see her produce a key. The key was finally located in the same pocket she had searched many times. By now, the dog had wrapped himself and the leash around her legs, and she couldn't move without falling over.

I untangled her from the dog and when we were on the sidewalk, I took the key from her and locked the door. I kept the key with me so it wouldn't go missing again. Then we were on a forced march to several different shops for bread, eggs, milk, juice, butter, coffee, and a poop in the park (for the mutt, not us). Seriously, she invited me for breakfast, but had nothing with which to make breakfast. Darlene only went off-task a few times during our shopping spree and, all things considered, we were back in the apartment in relatively short order.

The apartment had a small bathroom on the first floor, a bedroom one flight up, a tiny, one-person-at-a-time kitchen, and a big, bright living/dining room. I offered to help with the breakfast, but the kitchen was so small there was no room for two people at the same time. So I stood in the living room and talked with her as she prepared breakfast. She started the coffee grinder, but had forgotten to put the lid on. There was coffee everywhere, including her hair. When she got that all sorted, the next thing I heard was, "Oh crap! What's that?" She had put cheese in the frying pan thinking it was butter. She started over and within a half hour, breakfast was served.

She turned over a wicker basket near the dining room table and set the hot frying pan on it. She put the hot coffee pot directly on the table. She couldn't find any napkins. When she opened the milk, she spilled it. She did the same with the orange juice. We ate and chatted. She was extremely bright, and it was always enjoyable having a professional conversation with her about the mission in Bosnia and the problems she was confronting when dealing with human trafficking.

When I told her I was pressed for time because of a pending staff meeting due to start shortly, she asked me for a ride to UN headquarters. That wasn't a problem, but she decided to wash the dishes first. While washing the dishes, she broke the glass coffee pot. Later she discovered the hot coffee pot had burned the tabletop and the hot frying pan burned the wicker basket she had used. When the dishes were done and the damage surveyed, she said she had to change before leaving for work.

She changed clothes much faster than I thought she would and as she entered the living room, she discovered a large burn in the carpet. She examined it for a minute or so, wondering out loud how it had happened. I didn't do it. It was a cigarette burn, and I don't smoke. It was obvious the burn had been there for some time. It was a mystery she wanted to ponder, but my meeting time was drawing close. I told her we had to leave if she wanted a ride with me.

Before leaving, she decided she needed her heavy coat, which she found after a short frenetic search. This time the keys were readily available because I never let them out of my sight. Our exit from the apartment was smooth and uneventful. Even the dog cooperated by staying in the courtyard. Nothing was forgotten as we made our way to the car. Certainly, I won't forget my breakfast with Darlene. They don't just give those PhDs away.

Hand Shaking

Americans shake hands when they meet someone for the first time or after a prolonged absence. In Bosnia, people shook hands incessantly. Whenever I saw someone for the first time during the workday, I had to remember to shake hands. It took me a long to feel comfortable with the frequency with which my European colleagues shook hand.

There was a French officer whom I passed each morning while he was sitting at his desk. At first, I forgot about shaking hands and would simply say good morning and walk on by. He wanted more. He demanded a handshake. He'd follow me, close on my heels, to my office asking if I were angry or upset about something he had done. I explained that daily handshaking wasn't something Americans generally did in the workplace.

Secretly, it was my plan to stop this silly custom. I couldn't see the point. It was germy. Bosnia was full of germs and there weren't many hospitals. In fact, there were no hospitals that came close to Western world standards. Hospitals had few drugs and lacked well-trained doctors. I kept a large bottle of hand sanitizer close by in my office as well as travel-size baby wipes in my pocket. Maybe, by my example of not shaking hands, I could change the behavior of the nearly five thousand UN employees and all the people living in Bosnia.

That didn't happen. I made sure I stopped and frittered away precious time so I could shake hands with my French colleague and every Tom, Ivan, and Jorge coming down the hall. Entering the UN cafeteria was a nightmare. There would be people in there that I had seen the day before, but I hadn't seen them this day. A smile, a nod from across the room seemed sufficient in my worldview, but no, a stroll across the cafeteria was required followed by a handshake.

This was a place to eat and before I could order food, my hands were full of germs. I'd try to discreetly use a baby wipe before starting my meal. Halfway through a meal someone else would come in whom I hadn't yet seen that day, and the freaking germs would be all over me again. During some mealtimes, I'd go through five or more baby wipes. I developed a technique in which I would quickly scan the cafeteria and locate everyone I knew and engage in the ritual handshaking. That way I was sure to use fewer baby wipes, as I would wait until I was done before cleaning my hands. Then I would keep my head down and try not to make eye contact while I was eating.

I didn't know what to do the first time a Middle Eastern colleague greeted me with a hug and a kiss on the cheek. Rubbing my cheek with a disinfectant wasn't going to make me any friends. The more it happened, the more I accepted it. There weren't many Middle Eastern colleagues who felt comfortable, given my rank at the time, hugging and kissing me.

Sometimes a line needs to be drawn. A contingent commander who wanted to speak with me about a personnel problem with two of his troops greeted me in this traditional Middle Eastern style. He wanted to speak privately. We went outside and, as we walked around the parking lot discussing his concerns about members of his contingent, he held my hand. Fortunately, during our orientation training in Dallas, we were briefed about this custom, and I managed to hold hands while we walked around the parking lot talking. After the handholding incident, shaking hands didn't seem so bad. But I still kept my hand sanitizers close by.

Dressing Up and Other Bosnian Moments

The Bosnian culture was different and I advised visitors and new employees to be mindful about how people in different countries behave, dress, drive, speak, and eat. At first blush, Bosnia wasn't so different from other countries. Of course, everything about their way of life had been affected by the war and how they responded to the depredations inflicted on them during the turmoil.

Many Bosnian people fled to other countries. Hundreds of thousands were displaced and lived in temporary housing. At least one million people had their houses confiscated or destroyed. Flying over Bosnia in the UN helicopter, I was amazed to see small farms high on a hillside completely bombed out. It was clear the farms held no strategic military value. Artillery shells couldn't have reached most of these locations, so soldiers had to march over many hilly miles to reach these farms and blow them up.

It was a poor country before the conflict and much poorer after. Five years after the hostilities ended, the infrastructure was still in disrepair. Roads were strewn with potholes and road markings were practically non-existent. The few remaining road signs in the Serbian part of Bosnia were written in Cyrillic so, for the international crowd, these signs weren't helpful.

The vehicles using the roads were wrecks held together by the determination of the drivers to keep them running, a large market of used car parts, and the expertise of weekend mechanics that performed maintenance miracles for little money. The commercial vehicles traveling the roadways were scary. They appeared overloaded and would belch thick black smoke as they struggled along narrow mountain roads. There were many mountains in Bosnia. Except for a few roads in and around Sarajevo, the roads were narrow two-lane affairs. Long driving times belied the relatively short distances between towns.

From time to time, a colleague would point out, mostly in an effort to stop my grousing, how beautiful the country was. In some respects it was a beautiful country but not when I was there. Through squinted eyes, a vision of what Sarajevo had been during its Olympic heyday in 1984 might be possible, but it would require effort.

Admittedly, it was almost magical flying over the country in the autumn with its beautiful display of fall foliage. At a height of twelve hundred feet, the entire country was spectacular. What a great place for a hike one would think. But it wasn't a great place for a hike because there were over one million unexploded land minds in those mountains and along roadways. We didn't know all the locations of minds that were planted during the war. There was an ongoing demining effort underway by the international community, but it was slow going, so hiking wasn't on the itinerary.

There were many beautiful rivers, but they were swollen with various pieces of plastic, mostly bags, than water. What must have been at one time pristine rivers were now clogged with debris, and their banks were covered in plastic trash deposited by the river at its last high water mark. Streets were dirty. People routinely dropped cigarettes, wrappers, half-eaten food, and beer bottles. The smell of urine was strong in most out of the way corners and alleyways. It didn't take long to figure out why my trouser cuffs became so dirty whenever my duties involved walking in the city.

One summer evening in Sarajevo, a colleague and I enjoyed a dinner on the outside patio of a popular Italian restaurant. He was waxing poetically about the ambiance of the country and how he would like to live permanently in Sarajevo. I disagreed. He told me to look at the beautiful mountains (which were replete with land minds) and the lovely rivers like the one we were overlooking (which was polluted). It was, he said, the Balkan way of life that had captured his heart. The Balkan way of life was a daily struggle for most Bosnians, so I was never able to see his vision. I think he'd gone round the twist.

Whether at the movies, in a restaurant, or taking an afternoon *paseo* along the market streets of old town, the younger local women, regardless of ethnicity, liked to dress up. Their fashion choices must have come from television or movie magazines because they dressed to the nines. Some wore the shortest skirts I've ever seen in public. The men, not to be outdone, wore the finest tracksuits money could buy. Dressing up for them meant new jogging gear, complete with clean, white running shoes, although I never saw anyone running in the streets of Sarajevo except a one-off American or Brit. I had run in the street when I was stationed in Novi Grad. People gaped as I huffed and puffed along in my finest tracksuit.

Driving was full of surprises for the uninitiated. Not only were the local vehicles decrepit, the drivers would do things a Western driver couldn't anticipate. It wasn't unusual for a car to stop in the middle of a two-lane road to chat with a friend on the sidewalk. The driver would roll down the window and a leisurely conversation with the pedestrian would ensue. If it were a busy street, it would be difficult to drive around because of oncoming traffic. Other local drivers would queue up behind the stopped vehicle and patiently wait for the car to move on. This happened frequently. I thought about how it would play out in California. I'm sure there'd be gunfire.

Some roads had sidewalks, but most did not. It didn't matter because few people used the sidewalks. They seemed to like walking in the street with their backs to oncoming traffic. The locals on foot believed, it appeared, they had equal rights to the road and didn't feel a compulsion to stay close to the curb. My accommodation in Sarajevo was a short distance from UN HQ and most of my route had wide sidewalks, which was unusual for any place in the country.

Each morning I'd pass a woman in the same location near my apartment pushing her child in a baby carriage. She would have her back to me, and while there was a perfectly good sidewalk, she walked in the street three to four feet off the curb. This required me to swerve around her. This went on for months during my tour of duty, and then she was no longer there each morning. Either she had a different routine, moved, or was plowed down by a local driver.

Local driving schools used the streets around my accommodation for driver training. This required constant vigilance to avoid the bonehead vehicular moves the student drivers would make. They drove slowly. They did crazy things at the behest of their driving instructor, who would sometimes reach over from the passenger seat and grab the wheel, taking the car in a totally unexpected direction. Right hand turns didn't start close to the curb. The drivers swung wide to the left, usually across the centerline, and then negotiated the right turn with half the car facing oncoming traffic on the new street.

Training for U-turns took place at small, narrow T intersections. Although the trainees would be close to the centerline, as they approached the intersection they'd swing wide to the right and start their U-turn. But the intersections they trained on were too small for a novice driver to complete the turn successfully. The car would nose into the curb, back up, start the turn again, back up, and make yet another attempt at the U-turn. This resulted in major traffic jams, as the driving instructor was busy gesticulating frantically and trying to steer the car himself.

There were no signs on driving school cars to warn other drivers. A cautious driver had to look for clues such as a slow moving car, a passenger sitting too close to the driver, or a fearful look on the driver's face, which matched the fearful look on the drivers who had the misfortune to be in the proximity of a driving instructor and a trainee. Bob Newhart could've had a field day writing about these driving instructors.

The Apartment

When I arrived in Sarajevo to become the regional commander, there were a number of Americans who gave me advice about where to live. I was staying at a hotel that charged pretty close to Western rates, so I wanted to rent my own place quickly. I spent half a day with a young American cop from the South. He showed me lots of places that could be all mine for about the same price I had been paying in Novi Grad.

The $200 a month I paid in Novi Grad didn't purchase the same quality of accommodation in Sarajevo. The places we saw were terrible. I had the impression my guide was worried about how much money I should spend rather than the quality of place I would live in for a year. Most of the places were far from the regional headquarters, where I was originally assigned to work, and the UN HQ. The winter prior to my arrival had been brutal, and I thought it best to live close to where I was going to work.

I changed guides the next day and was taken to several different apartments and houses closer to central Sarajevo. Alas, these, too, were creepy, even though they were a little more expensive than the others. When I returned to the regional station in the afternoon, one of the local UN workers told me she knew of a nice, but expensive place I might like. The cost of my hotel room exceeded my per diem allowance and I was running out of money. I didn't hold out much hope because I thought, as a Bosnian, she wouldn't have an appreciation of what I needed. The two Americans hadn't understood what I wanted, so she probably wouldn't either.

By the next morning, she had arranged an inspection for us with the landlady. The location of the apartment was five minutes from work, but my heart sank as we approached. There were blocks of high-rise apartment buildings all heavily scarred with bullet and shell holes from the siege of Sarajevo. They weren't nice.

A few more turns found us driving down what I would call an alley but what passed as a narrow road. On the left were the backs of houses facing another street, and on the right were small apartments and houses. At the corner, I saw a fairly nice-looking building, then a two-story house, then a bombed-out residence, then (TAH DAH!) a relatively newly built three-story house. It had a front yard and off street parking for two cars behind a white metal fence.

The building was owned by a Bosniac living in Croatia who had built it after the war as an investment and a place for his parents to live. His mother was the landlord. She was in her seventies, didn't speak English, and dressed in traditional clothing. She took us to the top floor, and I entered what would become my home for a year. It had two bedrooms, living room, dining room, two balconies (front and back), bathroom with a washing machine in it, and a small but functional kitchen. The furniture was new; there was a television with cable hookup, a place to park my UN vehicle behind a locked gate, and it was located in a generally secure, trouble-free area.

The cost was $400 a month, including all the utilities. I didn't blink an eye about the cost. I moved in the next day. The woman who found the apartment for me arranged for a weekly housekeeper. The housekeeper came one day each week and spent nearly the entire day cleaning the apartment, doing my laundry and ironing. The local woman had a better sense of what I was looking for in an accommodation than my two American police colleagues. Go figure.

Cars and Drivers

The only nice cars I saw in Bosnia were those driven by the UN employees, other international players, local politicians, and high-ranking local police officials. The majority of people drove eight-plus-year-old cars. Better roads and better cars were commonplace the farther north I drove. Once across the border into Croatia the change was striking. If I drove to Slovenia, it was like being in any other part of Europe.

Bosnia was different in the quality of its roads, its cars, the drivers, and, as I mentioned above, the skill of the drivers. The cars put me in mind of a trip to Russia. I met with a Russian police friend at his apartment in St. Petersburg (then still called Leningrad). It was typical of the kinds of high-rise buildings the Soviets loved to build. We planned to meet other police friends, but my buddy didn't have a car. A neighbor was going to drive us.

When we met the driver at the elevator, he was holding two windshield wipers, a distributor cap, and a car radio. I suggested that if he had to assemble the car, it would be faster and easier to hitch a ride. These, he explained, were the items most commonly stolen from cars left unattended, so he wanted to make sure he wasn't a victim. He said he couldn't afford replacement parts.

The car was an old Lada. Half of the floorboard on the passenger side where I was sitting was missing. I could look down and see the roadway whizzing (as much as a Lada could whiz) past as we chugged toward our destination. This Lada was a prized possession for the neighbor.

The Bosnian cars were similar, and they, too, were considered prized possessions, even those in the sorriest state of repair. Many IPTF officers wanted the freedom a personal car could provide. They'd negotiate with local people at large open-air car markets found on weekends in town centers. Officers searched for the best car from a sorry but large inventory. Car costs ranged between two and three thousand dollars for an IPTF officer. They were substantially less expensive if sold from one local to another. The local population was mindful of the money the IPTF officers made and they were savvy business people. The more expensive the car, the better it was.

Better, though, was a difficult concept to determine. These cars had been on the road for a long time, and most had turned 150,000 kilometers. What had been done to keep them running was anyone's guess. The cost was substantial for many of the officers from developing nations whose primary pay was low and who were living off the UN per diem. Most planned to sell the car to a newly arriving IPTF officer when their tour of duty ended. This was what usually happened. For a few, the cars they purchased didn't last through their time in Bosnia and the car was abandoned. I suspect some enterprising Bosnian probably came along, fixed the car, and sold it at a car market to another unsuspecting IPTF officer.

IPTF officers were intrepid when it came to driving these cars all over the Balkans and throughout Europe. I was a passenger in one heading to Verona, Italy. We made it without a hiccup in an early '80s Toyota. As a favor to another officer, I delivered a car to Sarajevo from Banja Luka and was surprised how nicely the mid-1980s Audi drove. I didn't need a car once I became the deputy police commissioner as I had a new Toyota SUV assigned to me along with a driver.

I needed to choose a driver. I spent hours looking through a list of people who had applied for the job. My predecessor had given up his driver, so when I came into the office there wasn't one assigned to me. A high-ranking Turkish officer asked me, as a favor, to select a particular officer from his contingent. Since the officer was leaving the mission in a few weeks and had agreed to host me and another American in Istanbul, I figured I had better do him the favor.

There was some thought about using one of the American officers who had applied, but even though they initially wanted the job, I felt they would come to resent the mildly demeaning position. The candidate officer went through a series of tests to make sure he was the right person. We interviewed him, tested his English reading and writing skills, and received good reports about his work so far in the mission.

He was assigned as my driver. His first mission was driving me to Banja Luka. It was a three- to four-hour drive over rough roads, especially if using a summer time short cut through the mountains on a curvy dirt road. To my horror I realized once we left the paved highway onto the dirt mountain road, we never checked his actual driving ability. It could best be described as inexperienced bordering on terrible. I took the wheel on the way back, trying to give him a fast lesson in police pursuit driving. He spent the next few months washing and gassing the vehicle, doing minor office duties, but not driving me. We found a spot for him in the mission he liked. I didn't fire him as my driver until my colleague and I returned from our weeklong holiday in Istanbul hosted by the high-ranking Turkish officer.

Satellite Phones

On a lonely road in Western Bosnia, a deputy station commander en route to his accommodation after work happened to notice an IPTF vehicle high on a hill with two officers walking back and forth in front of their SUV. He took the dirt trail to the top of the hill. He thought the officers needed assistance with their vehicle and couldn't reach anyone on the mobile phone one was holding. The deputy station commander noticed the mobile phone appeared to have some batteries strapped with duct tape to the outside of the phone. The two officers from Africa told him they had just purchased the mobile phone from another IPTF officer. The officer had converted their mobile phone to a satellite phone at a cost of a hundred and fifty dollars. They were trying to reach home with this admittedly jury-rigged phone.

The cell phone system in Bosnia was marginal, but owning a mobile was still nice to have. No one I knew had a satellite phone except these two officers who were delighted to be the proud owners. The seller told them they'd have to go to a high location for it to work properly.

The day they were spotted on the hill was their first attempt to call their families. The seller claimed he didn't tell them it was a satellite phone, only that it was as powerful as a satellite phone because of the extra batteries. The problem was the batteries weren't wired into the phone, just duct taped to the phone's outer shell. The seller returned the officers' money and his contingent sent him home. I don't know if his country punished him when he returned but I was happy he wasn't an American.

When I first came to Sarajevo as the regional commander, I wanted a mobile. The other six regional commanders had them, but not me because I was close to UN HQ and the theory was that I didn't need one. I did everything I could think of to get a mobile. I begged, pleaded, cajoled, sucked up, lied, and finally accepted the fact a mobile phone was not in the cards for me. What was cool about having one was that personal calls were allowed as long as you paid the UN for them. Maybe if I had met the seller of the satellite phone before he was caught he would have had another customer. I finally was issued a phone when I became the deputy police commissioner.

TWELVE

TROUBLING TIMES

✡ ✡ ✡

I generally avoid temptation unless I can't resist it.

– Mae West (1892–1980)

Alcohol

Alcohol was the bane of the mission experience for a few officers. Some used it as a way to pass what they considered a lonely time away from home. Others were heavy drinkers before they arrived in mission and continued the behavior during their tenure in Bosnia. Most, surprisingly, made it through the mission without mishap. A few had trouble because of it. If one of the few was an American, it was bigger trouble.

An American IPTF officer assigned to a substation was returning to his accommodation from some type of party on a snowy winter's night. His UN vehicle skidded into oncoming traffic at a curve in the road and collided with a taxi. The taxi driver was killed. The local police responded to the scene and the IPTF officer reported the incident to us. The local police Breathalyzer wasn't working, and the police didn't conduct a field balance and coordination test on the officer, so there was no determination as to whether his driving was impaired. There were no skid marks. The local police estimated the UN vehicle was traveling too fast for the weather and road conditions at the time.

Think about this situation as if it happened in the US, two vehicles collide during inclement weather. The police arrive and don't give the surviving driver a chemical test to determine his blood-alcohol level. They fail to give him a balance and coordination test (often called a sobriety test) to measure the level of impairment. There are no marks on the roadway. This case wouldn't go to court. The estate of the descendant might sue the surviving driver in a wrongful death civil action, but without any evidence of driving under the influence of alcohol, a criminal prosecution wouldn't prevail.

By the time word of this incident reached the hallowed grounds of Washington, DC, and the US embassy in Sarajevo, they repudiated the officer's basic rights, in my opinion. They were searching for a way to prosecute the officer in the US. An embassy officials said they would waive his immunity.

Every UN employee in the mission had immunity granted by the UN, not individual countries. The UN was protective of its immunity and had never waived it. The embassy held no authority over the immunity involving IPTF officers and UN employees. It was wholly the prerogative of the UN, and they weren't inclined to waive immunity in this case.

A UN doctor decided she could, even after a time lapse of thirty-six hours, determine what the blood-alcohol of the driver had been at the time of the accident. The officer willingly submitted to a blood test. A short time later the doctor, who had no expertise in doing these types of analyses, opined that the driver's blood-alcohol had been over the legal limit. Since she had no experience in this area, she wouldn't have been a credible witness and wouldn't have been able to establish her bona fides in the field thus wouldn't have been able to express an opinion in an American court of law.

The accident was a terrible tragedy because the taxi driver had a family and was working hard to provide for them. Maybe the officer's driving was affected by alcohol, and he was the proximate cause of the death. But no one thought to do any post mortem toxicology examination on the decedent to determine if his driving ability was impaired by alcohol. Perhaps he contributed to the accident. The second tragedy was the manner in which the officer's own country wanted to extract what I'm sure they saw as justice, but in a manner that was less than judicious.

The matter resolved itself since the officer was at the end of his contract and returned to the States. Washington learned that, absent some type of agreement to pursue prosecutions in the United States for crimes committed in another country, they had no authority to prosecute the officer in this case.

Trafficking Raids

As I was preparing to move into the deputy police commissioner slot, a major public relations brouhaha developed for my predecessor. It would eventually devolve to me. The incident involved a raid on a bar well known as a place of prostitution. In Bosnia, as in many countries around the world, the women working in this bar had been smuggled from other countries to work in the sex trade industry.

Many of the women traveled from other countries through a trafficking network operated by criminals who preyed on them. Often the women thought they were going to the other country to work as maids, waitresses, nannies, and the like. In some documented incidents, the women were sold into the network by their parents. This happened in some of the poorest and most poorly educated areas of the world. In other cases, women who simply wanted to make a better life applied for what they thought was legitimate work in a foreign country. Others may have been aware they would be sex workers and willingly but unwittingly placed themselves in the hands of the smugglers.

Arriving in Bosnia meant the women's passports were taken, the "owners" or their cohorts often raped them, and they were told they had to pay off the expenses the bar owner had incurred before they would make any money for themselves. In these circumstances, there was no option of there being consensual sex between a woman and a paying customer. The woman had to have sex with any customer or face severe consequences from the bar owner.

There were, of course, prostitutes who hadn't been trafficked, which made the matter of trying to reach out and help trafficked women difficult for a number of reasons. 1) There didn't appear to be any local political will to stop the influx of trafficked women into Bosnia. 2) When asked if they needed help, most of the women would say no either because they were scared or for some reason they didn't want to return to their country of origin. 3) The court system in Bosnia was dysfunctional, alleged to be corrupt, and didn't exercise any judicial vigor to work with the local police or the international community to prosecute the traffickers. 4) The women were treated as criminals by the local jurisdictions. 5) The focus and the blame for the flourishing sex trade was placed on the large number of UN and other international workers in the country.

Estimates by a keen observer of all of this told me, however, that 70 percent of sex patrons were local men. Focusing only on international patrons to solve this problem was wrongheaded and ineffective. There was more concern about the international workers who might be patronizing the brothels. Little was done about the traffickers. The majority of patrons were local men, but the police didn't arrest them. Programs to help women caught in the sex trade criminal conspiracy were weak.

Some observers called for the complete legalization of prostitution in the country. They pointed to the Netherlands, where prostitution was legal, but heavily regulated. The Dutch government was also confronting the issue of sex trafficking despite the sex trade's legality.

IPTF was flummoxed. In a country where police services were marginal and under the control of a nascent government facing major challenges, helping trafficked women wasn't a priority. Nor was it a priority, at first, of the UN. IPTF had a few officers assigned to the problem, but IPTF had no executive authority in the country. In other words, they didn't have the power to arrest anyone. They held authority over the local police who they monitored. IPTF could, after various due process steps, remove a local officer from the force, but couldn't do anything else. To intervene in a crime, an IPTF officer had to involve the local police.

Therein was part of the problem with the trafficking raid, the blowback from which landed in the office of the deputy police commissioner shortly before I took over the job. Americans were involved, I'm sad to say, because at first blush I thought their intentions were good and honorable, but they managed to prove me wrong.

An American officer commanded an IPTF station in a medium-sized town in the Serb part of Bosnia. There were several other Americans assigned to the station. The commander was an energetic man in his thirties with a decidedly evangelical Christian bent, I was told.

Another American who became the protagonist in this lurid tale had been visiting the bar supposedly to collect evidence of trafficking. On a couple of occasions, this necessitated a private conversation with one of the women in a small bedroom. He was a nice looking young man with minimal police experience. Over a period of time, other officers from the station, at the behest or with the approval of the station commander, visited the bar and spoke with women.

At some point in time, the commander decided the bar should be raided and the women rescued. The commander and a group of IPTF officers went to the local police station, recruited a few local officers, and within minutes, they raided the bar. Under the direction of the IPTF officers, the police took all of the women into custody, along with the bartender. The women were in the country illegally, but none claimed to have been working under duress or force. The local police made plans to have them deported.

The bar owner was unapologetic and made scurrilous claims against the UN throughout the Bosnian news media the next morning. Naturally he was out his investment in the women and was angry the local

IPTF station had the temerity to interfere in his business. The bar owner was like a bulldog, and every day he made more claims against the UN in general and IPTF in particular. He appeared on television and made a good appearance. To the uninitiated, he was a legitimate businessman upon whom IPTF had preyed.

The story made its way to the States. Washington became involved, the embassy became involved, the envoy became involved, and it was thrust upon the deputy commissioner to sort it all out. There were seven international police officers involved in the raid on the bar. They were interviewed, and basically they told the same story. There was lots of weeping and wailing with everyone trying to put a good spin on the part they played in the unfolding drama.

They were all repatriated to their countries, including the Americans. There may have been a relationship between one of the Americans and one of the women. The raid itself was the result of what I believed were good intentions on the part of the station commander, who may have felt a moral obligation to act in the manner he did. However, the road to hell, in this case back to the US, was paved with good intentions executed in a bad way.

A Rabid French Poodle

One day, an old French woman sashayed her way into the mission. She was short, embarrassingly profane, loud, full of a false bravado, and completely lacking in law enforcement experience. Our understanding was she had worked in the French news media, but how or why she worked for the UN in New York or why she was now in Bosnia we never learned. She was to be assigned to the Human Rights section of the UN.

A story circulated that the human rights team had rejected her because she didn't have sufficient training or experience. Supposedly she'd been sent by the UN headquarters in New York to work on the issue of human trafficking. This was wholly in the human rights area of responsibility.

Since she couldn't be assigned there she was assigned as a special assistant to the Envoy, who promptly dumped her onto the IPTF, but she kept her direct line of reporting to the Envoy. She was injected into the middle of a police mission and quickly demonstrated her stupidity about police work and working in a law enforcement structure.

She was unabashedly self-assured and, without fully understanding the depth of her shortfalls, she plunged into her work at full speed recruiting officers to work with her, developing ill-conceived strategies, and generally pissing off most of the supervisory and management staff. It was amazing to watch someone so ill prepared and so ignorant about a field of work proceed with such self-confidence. Now the UN could say the issue of human trafficking had a special place in the mission and that they were devoting precious resources to it.

I tried to work with her, I really did. It was frustrating to speak with her because a conversation would focus solely on her, what she was doing, and what she knew (never what she thought) was the best way to approach a problem.

She'd eat lunch in the UN cafeteria with the envoy, the CAO, or the commissioner. On occasion I would join them, and she would spew forth her four-letter guttural invectives in a surprisingly strong voice for such a small person. I once told her saying fuck in every other sentence was off-putting and many English-speaking people thought it offensive. She just pooh-poohed my comments, probably thinking that saying fuck with a French accent and coming from a woman was cute. It wasn't cute, at least not coming from this overly made up woman in those circumstances.

She worked in the program for quite a while after I left. I heard later there were as many victims of trafficking despite this woman's harebrained schemes. The sex trade business continued to expand in Bosnia and throughout the world. Self-proclaimed successes by the UN in Bosnia were well-crafted statements, but denied the reality of the data. One thing was certain, there was no efficacy to be found in turning loose a wild, unknowledgeable, French harridan on a group of international police officers, and having her direct their efforts in mitigating a complex, culturally sensitive, and pervasive problem.

Simply put, she was a pest with which we all had to deal. She spoke frequently about her conversations with the UN secretary-general as if she were a good close personal friend. She could have been for all I know, but it didn't make her any smarter or judicious in her approach to solving human trafficking problems or in dealing with colleagues.

I think in her mind she saw herself as the star of a reality show, and whenever she spoke, the cameras were rolling, requiring her to speak and act flamboyantly. Gossip and self-promotion were her stock in trade, demanding intervention by senior staff. In her we had a worker who came to solve a problem, but created more problems. Surprisingly she wasn't the only UN worker to do so.

Not By the Book

The overall supervision of IPTF officers, while I was in the mission, was unremarkable. The international officers from the forty or so countries comprising the IPTF had varying levels of experience, training, and enthusiasm for the work. IPTF staffing hovered around two thousand officers, and there were two thousand different reasons they came to a peacekeeping mission and two thousand opinions about the best practices to rebuild the nation's law enforcement. These officers were indoctrinated into the mission when they first arrived, and given assignments. They participated in on-the-job training, and then were left on their own to do the job assigned to them.

Unlike officers from all of the other countries, a US Department of State (DOS) contractor hired American officers. DOS oversaw the private contractor, but it was the contractor's job to recruit, hire, and train officers from throughout the United States. Some of the officers who took the job were on leaves of absence from their force, some quit their stateside police jobs to work for the contractor, and some were recently retired officers.

In this situation, we were private employees working for a DOS contractor and seconded to a UN peacekeeping mission. It was difficult to define exactly what we were other than American cops working in a foreign country kind of falling under the aegis of the US government. Our pay, however, came from a private company and our daily cost of living stipend came from the United Nations. It was the UN that exercised operational control over us.

Administrative control of the American officers fell to the in-country program manager who was an employee of the contractor. He walked a fine line diligently maintaining working relationships among the US embassy, the UN, the American contingent of officers, and the contractor. It was important for him to keep his finger on the pulse of the two hundred American officers spread throughout Bosnia. The program manager was a tall, well-spoken, fully engaged man who took his job seriously, and he conscientiously watched over the welfare of the officers in his charge.

The contractor paid the officers well, and I'm sure the company was paid well by DOS for the work they did. In most cases, the officers received a higher salary from the contractor than they had been receiving in their former police forces. Their compensation was enhanced because their pay was mostly tax free if they met a few IRS criteria, which most did. In addition to their salary, each was paid $75 per day by the UN to offset the cost of living in a foreign country. This was paid every month and substantially exceeded the actual costs of living in Bosnia.

Many of the officers shared accommodations, which seldom cost more than $400 a month. As an example, my apartment cost that amount, so I was left with slightly under $2,000 a month to live in an inexpensive country. Most of the officers were banking their company pay and living on the UN per diem. In some cases, the per diem alone was more than an officer made in his home force. At that time, there were officers who had been making less than $25,000 a year in their former police agency. A UN peacekeeping mission held a strong financial attraction for officers working in low paying police positions.

To receive these benefits an American officer had to show up for work and complete a time sheet for the contractor. There is nothing unusual about this. Most law enforcement agencies required officers to complete time sheets. It was a standard practice for most jobs around the world. There was an agreement, either written or implied, come to work, do your job, and the company will pay you the agreed upon wage. Simple stuff. Maybe this wasn't so simple in a multinational peacekeeping effort.

There was a difference, however, in the mission. In the daily supervision of an officer's work, the chances were that a fellow countryman didn't supervise an American. Rather, an international colleague probably held sway over the American at some level. It could have been the subordinate American officer held a former higher rank at home than the supervisor in the mission. But the vagaries of police rank structures in the US and the policy of coming into a peacekeeping mission un-ranked made the subordinate-supervisor relationship sensitive for Americans.

In a sense, this relationship was problematic. The quality of the relationship depended on how the officer felt about the stature of his prior rank compared to how he perceived the rank of the foreign supervisor and that supervisor's police experience and knowledge. In fact, this was the case in nearly every subordinate-supervisor relationship in which one or the other was of a different nationality.

I believe the managers and supervisors in the mission were culturally sensitive to the possibility of inadvertently offending a subordinate. Their approach to their managerial and supervisory responsibilities was probably less rigorous and more benevolent. They assumed workers showed up for work when scheduled and performed their work properly. Overall, the supervisors were gentler than they may have been working in their own country. In the mission, the style was more collegial. Collegiality was often not the best approach to managing police officers, regardless of their country of origin. For those who wanted to abuse the system, this kind of work environment was fertile ground.

Whenever I would accumulate six or more days off, I would take my holidays out of the country traveling in Europe. Returning back from one of these excursions, the American contingent commander informed me the contractor had fired an American officer. There were allegations of irregularity in her time sheets and unauthorized absences from work.

I had no authority over the woman in terms of her employment. I could recommend to any contingent commander that an officer no longer be part of the mission if, after an investigation, misbehavior was determined. In this case the contractor was her boss and my boss, too. I didn't have the authority to make employment decisions for the contractor. Those decisions were the discretion of the program manager who represented the contractor in Bosnia.

I was surprised the officer was terminated. I'd heard she had a problematic work history. She had been transferred from a position involving human trafficking to a position at an IPTF station in Sarajevo doing routine police monitoring duties. The transfer resulted from the wide circulation of a memo others described as a screed against the lack of mitigation efforts to reduce the plight of trafficked women. This happened when I first came to Sarajevo, but before I was the deputy police commissioner. It was most likely the case that my predecessor felt her human trafficking duties had stressed her, and she needed a different, less demanding workload.

I wasn't on the distribution list so I didn't read the memo at the time of her transfer, but I did read it later. I didn't think it was so bad in and of itself. It was written in an immature style, and screed is probably the best word to describe it. Too, I understood it was born of frustration. What was more troubling was its distribution far outside her chain of command. It may have provided the author a sense of catharsis, but it served no practical purpose other than to bring her trouble. In the law enforcement agencies with which I'm familiar a similar act would probably result in a transfer of duties at a minimum or days off without pay.

I felt the actions of the deputy police commissioner were appropriate. The transfer to another assignment stirred the emotions of a few UN civilian employees who expressed their opinions. They felt the corrective action was too severe and inappropriate. They made their voices heard, but appeared to be more the noise of a claque organized by the woman herself and not the concerns of those with a legitimate voice in the issue. Her transfer didn't result in a loss of pay. She was still a police monitor, whether assigned to human trafficking or a duty station in Sarajevo. Yet, there were people who felt she was done wrong.

Those feelings still existed when the contractor fired her. The group of sycophantic followers renewed their cries of foul dealing by the program manager, the American contingent commander, and me. Although I had nothing to do with it, wasn't in the decision-making loop, was never consulted about it, was out of the country when it happened, and wasn't informed about it until after the termination, I somehow seemed to have carried some of the blame.

The woman came to see me a few days before she left the mission. She had a Dutch police officer in tow as her witness. Basically, she wanted to know why she was terminated. She asked what I knew. She was miffed when I told her the program manager hadn't briefed me. I explained I had no authority to speak for the program manager or the contractor. In this situation, we were both employees, and the program manager was my boss in regard to employment. She was dissatisfied and acted incredulous that I wasn't fully informed about her situation. She left my office in a huff, dragging her Dutch witness along with her.

Later, she sued the contractor in civil court in the United Kingdom for what I assumed she believed was unlawful termination. Surprisingly, she prevailed against the contractor and was awarded money damages. There were only good intentions by the former deputy commissioner in changing her assignment and the program manager in believing she had violated the terms of her contract. Nevertheless, they were judged to be wrong. There was a sense that on appeal, the company would prevail, but the company was in the process of being purchased by another company. The new company decided to take the loss since in the big scheme of things, it didn't appear to be a big deal financially.

No Sadder Tale of Woe

Like Sam Magee, he was from Tennessee, but in this case, I knew why he left his home. It was a matter of mounting debt, low police pay, and dreams of owning a bar in a rural community. He was in his forties, short, stocky, and always smiling. I suspected he was a heavy drinker, but he never appeared intoxicated when I would see him. He was quiet, but could be induced to tell funny stories, and he seemed to have quite a few tucked away in his brain.

He had a penchant for working night shifts at the regional headquarters station in Sarajevo. No one would say he was particularly bright, and the duties of working as a night desk officer seemed to fit him. I certainly understood, from my experience doing the same type of job in Novi Grad, that a Phi Beta Kappa key wasn't needed to satisfactorily perform desk duties.

Our Tennessean didn't cause any trouble and more or less went along with the program. The longer he stayed in the mission, the more money he made and the closer he came be to his dream of bar ownership. When he talked about his future bar, I'd picture him in a coonskin cap behind a bar in a ramshackle building. Although I didn't know him well, the few times we spoke he was pleasant enough. I liked the fact he seemed happy to be in the mission making money. There were plenty of officers there who didn't appear happy, so he was a step ahead of them in my book.

Mission life can be lonely for some, and our Tennessean started visiting local bars. The bars were the kind where sex slaves plied their trade. These bars could be the end of the line for women who had been trafficked from other countries to work in the sex trade against their will. Smugglers bought these women and sold them to bar owners, who would put them to work as prostitutes.

There was a ready clientele of local men who patronized the bars and the women. With so many international workers in Bosnia to help rebuild a nation devastated by war, it wasn't surprising that some foreigners, too, found their way to these bars. In effect, some of the people who came to

Bosnia to help make it better were contributing to the country's problems by patronizing these kinds of places.

Our officer felt comfortable in one particular bar, and we later learned he was a regular customer. Sex could readily be had in the rooms above the bar after choosing one of the women on offer in the bar where they would meet their customers. It appeared our officer's gaze fell upon one particular woman. It wasn't clear how often he met with the woman or the nature of their relationship beyond sex for money.

Looking at it after the fact, not knowing the conversations they had (her with limited English language skills, he with a heavy Southern accent), it appeared to be an unusual business relationship. I hesitate to use the term business relationship. There were those who said such a relationship wasn't possible because the woman was, in fact, a sex slave. He paid her money for sex and some make the argument that she wasn't capable of refusing the deal.

The story takes an unusual turn here. I'm not aware of it happening anywhere else in the mission when I was there. The officer must have felt something for this woman. Was it lust? Was it love? Was it sorrow for her lot in life? I didn't know the officer's motivations for doing what he did. Many people opined that it was pure lust. The officer told a different story.

After visiting the bar and having sex with the woman a number of times, the officer approached the bar owner and offered to buy the woman. Actually, the officer spun the story a little differently, saying he wanted to buy the woman's freedom. He recognized there was a huge difference between buying a human being and freeing a human being. In any event, the deal was struck, and the woman moved into the officer's accommodation.

Did marital bliss follow? No. When the officer would go to work on his night shift, the woman would return to the bar to work. It wasn't clear why. It could have been that the deal between the bar owner and the officer was for a long-term lease of the woman. Maybe the woman was still under the control of the bar owner and was ordered to return to the bar when the officer was working. We were never able to clarify the nature of all these relationships.

One night, local police, under the watchful eye of IPTF officers, raided the bar and took several women into custody. One of the women arrested was the woman living with our officer. She told the police about living with an IPTF officer and the whole sad, lascivious tale unfolded. During his interview with IPTF internal affairs, the officer said he loved the woman and wanted her free of the traffickers. He couldn't explain why she returned to the bar whenever he was working. I'm not sure he'd known she still worked at the bar while she was living with him. The bottom line was he bought a human being. Maybe he was well intentioned. Maybe lust clouded his judgment and threw him into the kind of trouble that would destroy his dream of paying off his debts and buying a bar.

He did a stupid thing, and it prompted people to say he was a stupid man who was manipulated by the bar owner and the woman. Those who believed that made the officer the victim and the woman complicit in his ruin. It's true the bar owner out-smarted him, but that didn't make the officer a victim. Was this a case of good intentions resulting in a bad outcome? I didn't believe so. The contractor terminated the officer and he was repatriated to Tennessee. The woman was released from police custody. I don't know if she went back to work at the bar. I don't know if our Tennessean saved enough money to buy his bar. He probably wished he had the money he paid the bar owner back. I wondered if he was longing for the woman he left behind in Bosnia.

A Sampling of Needling Problems

One day a delegation of IPTF officers from an African country came to my office to plead for my intervention in a case involving one of their officers and the UN doctor. Their officer was diagnosed with high blood pressure. I learned that in the case of contingents from some countries, arriving officers had to pass a medical examination by the UN doctor. This hadn't happened before to my knowledge. It was my understanding arriving officers had to have passed a medical examination in their own country.

The UN doctor had decided officers arriving from less developed countries, where she believed the medical facilities were inadequate, had to submit to her examination. Remember, IPTF officers were seconded to the UN and weren't UN employees. Why the doctor chose one developing country over another for the new medical examination wasn't clear. The delegation said the doctor wouldn't allow their officer to stay in the country with his medical condition. They asked me to speak with the doctor.

I didn't want to speak to her. I didn't want to be responsible for this officer if something physically untoward happened while he was in the mission. The doctor was aggressive, medicine was way out of my field, and I was convinced nothing I said would change her mind. On the other hand, I didn't want to disappoint the delegation, which included the country's contingent commander. It was a trouble-free contingent filled with cops who were always willing to follow the rules. With a little trepidation, I said I would speak to the doctor. I reminded them that I couldn't overrule a medical decision.

When I met with the doctor, I told her I had promised the contingent I would speak to her about the officer. Further, I said I was filling my promise to speak with her and understood she had the final word in the matter. The doctor was quite nice about the whole incident. She pointed out many of the developing countries that sent officers to the mission failed to conduct any physical examinations. She also told me medicine was hard to find in Bosnia. The officer had a better chance of chemically controlling his blood pressure in his own country. It made sense to me.

The next day I told the contingent commander I didn't dissuade the doctor from repatriating his officer. A few hours later, the delegation came into my office carrying a large gift. They were effusive over the fact I had acted in their behalf. They presented me with a large African mask.

My next encounter with this African contingent happened when a police captain came into the mission with a new rotation of officers from his country. He was deployed outside of Sarajevo along with one of his sergeants. While I was visiting their station, the sergeant asked to be transferred somewhere away from the captain. The sergeant said he was required to cook and clean for the captain in addition to his regular IPTF work. He also described the captain as "nuts," not a technical term, but the sergeant managed to make his point.

Later, I spoke with the captain about moving the sergeant to another location. He started crying; we're talking big serious tears. The captain also said some strange things during our interview. He wasn't all there, as far as I could tell. It didn't take much to persuade the contingent commander to send the captain home. The potential for trouble was thwarted.

Once, I was thoroughly chastised by an officer from a North African country because of US foreign policy. Apparently, according to the officer, we gave less money in foreign aid to his country than we gave to Israel. In his mind, I was a government official, and maybe he thought I could make a phone call and up the ante. I tried to explain why Israel was a friend of the US and his country, well, not so much.

A few months later, his contingent was rotating out of the mission, and I saw this same officer standing by a shipping container near a UN storage facility. The doors to the container were open. It was nearly full with washing machines, televisions, stereo equipment, and boxes containing who knows what. My curiosity got the best of me. I walked over and inquired about what he was doing.

These were items not easily found in his country, he explained, so his government paid for the container and the shipping. This allowed the officers to buy these items on the local Bosnian economy with the money they saved from their UN per diem. These officers were good at saving money, often living four or more to an apartment, cooking modest dishes at home, and since they were Muslim, not drinking alcohol. Their frugality left them with money for a big spending spree at the end of their mission.

He confided that many of the officers planned to sell the items at home for a sizeable profit. Some officers had been commissioned by politicians and other official to purchase specific things for which they would receive a fee and the gratitude of their country's important people. I wanted to ask if the container and shipping costs were paid with foreign aid money we had given them, but I didn't.

There were also Near East and Middle East countries participating in the peacekeeping mission. Many of the officers from these countries practiced Islam. Officers coming into the mission were deployed to the areas where they were needed. This allowed us to keep a balanced mixed of officers. They weren't deployed based on their religious practices.

We didn't want all the American and British officers in Sarajevo, all the Russian officers in Banja Luka or all Muslim officers assigned only to areas where Bosniacs were dominant. We wanted the IPTF to be representative of the entire international community, so we tried to spread our officers throughout the country without regard to the officers' ethnicity, religion, race, or gender. Although we tried to evaluate our officers' abilities and experience, we often deployed them without fully knowing their capabilities and foibles.

On one occasion, we sent three Muslim officers to an IPTF station in a predominately Serb town south of Sarajevo. During the war, many Bosniacs were killed in this town, their houses confiscated and later occupied by Serbs. The Muslim officers weren't happy about being deployed to this town. In the past, other Muslim officers had served there without incident. In this case, the officers verbalized their displeasure to their contingent commander and to the station commander upon their arrival.

Inside of one week, the three officers came to Sarajevo with a note they found on the door to their accommodation. The note physically threatened them, but made no demands. The wording of the note, the syntax, the timing, and other clues led us to suspect the officers planted the note. Nevertheless, we weren't sure and didn't want to take the chance of them being injured. Years before, there had been an incident of violence during which a crowd of Serbs tried to burn the IPTF station there. The violence then was aimed at IPTF and the UN not at any religious group. Anything was possible though, so we wanted everyone to be safe.

The station to which they had been assigned was under an hour's drive from Sarajevo, and many officers liked the convenience of being close to the capital. We transferred the officers. They had made a big deal about being Muslims, and the inappropriateness of a deployment to a predominantly Serb town. Despite their anguish about working in a non-Muslim area, we moved them to another IPTF station wholly inside Repubilka Srpska. Their new station was much farther from Sarajevo, but they worked there without incident for the remainder of their tours of duty.

A small Pacific island nation contributed to the mission in Bosnia by sending five police officers. It was a small country with a population of fewer than 120,000 people. Their contingent was the smallest in IPTF. They arrived full of excitement and ready to work. In short order, they deployed to various stations throughout the country. It lasted about a month before the contingent commander complained of loneliness. All five, he thought, should be deployed to the same place. His point was that there were no other Pacific Islanders in Bosnia. His officers missed the cultural opportunities such as speaking their native language and cooking traditional foods. Well, for some officers it was a harder mission than for others, but we didn't and couldn't keep all the same nationalities together.

Every few months various contingents would hold a medal parade. After six months of duty in the mission, each officer was awarded a UN peacekeeping medal. When it came time for the Pacific Islanders' medal parade, they had settled into the routine of the mission, appeared less homesick, and appreciated the fact we had moved them closer to each other, but not all to the same station.

The medal parade was a big deal. The national police chief came to Sarajevo along with several other dignitaries. I had an opportunity to give a talk during which I pointed out their country was making a larger per capita contribution in police officers than either France or the United States. The chief of police wanted to know if he could send more officers to the mission. I directed the chief to the peacekeeping section of the UN in New York. I guess crime was down on his islands.

It was our responsibility in IPTF to teach the police in Bosnia to operate within the principles of a democratic society. Many of the countries that sent officers to the IPTF were themselves fledgling democracies. We would ask officers about the principles of democratic policing in promotional interviews. Few could answer with any degree of understanding.

In a broad sense, the police operated democratically when: 1) they were held accountable to the rule of law, 2) the police answered to democratic government structures and the community, 3) they were transparent, and 4) the top priority was to protect the safety and rights of people. This last meant they protected human rights, provided professional services, and were representative of the community they served.

In Bosnia, the police didn't represent the community they served. In the Serb parts of Bosnia, even though there were Bosniacs living in the communities, the police force was exclusively Serb. There were mitigation strategies the UN employed to change those circumstances, such as aggressively recruiting Bosniacs to work in the Serb police force, offering enhancement to Bosniac or Bosnian Serb officers who transferred to forces in which they would be a minority, and making the recruitment of women a high priority. This latter strategy was fairly successful, while the two former ones were failures.

IPTF officers, to the extent they understood the principles of democratic policing, monitored the local police for aberrant behavior. They may not have been able to give a good definition of democratic policing, but they did know what didn't fall under its guise. They could recognize bad police practices and what shouldn't be tolerated in a democracy, as they understood democracy based on their experiences in their home countries.

When ten Chinese police officers arrived in mission to join IPTF, I thought our goals and objectives of our mission had changed. Surely, these ten officers from a communist country wouldn't be here to monitor the behavior of the local police forces' compliance with democratic policing principles. I pointed out the obvious to the commissioner and many others who seemed to think my demonstrative concern was misplaced.

A position in IPTF was found into which they fitted nicely, I was told. No one had sought my opinion. Their inclusion in our mission was decided in the diplomatic hallways of the UN's Department of Peacekeeping Operations in New York.

They were all placed as advisors to the Bosnian Border Police and they worked at the airport. At the time, many Chinese were arriving in Bosnia with varying degrees of suspicious travel documents. Chinese police officers could help sort through the documents and help the local border police. They did so, and we didn't encounter any problems with their performance during the mission.

Rumors were a constant source of irritation. New or clarifying information never eliminated the rumors, but rather, it changed the rumors a little to fit the newly divulged information. When I first arrived, I heard the rumor about a group of Eastern European IPTF officers running a brothel in a large town north of Sarajevo. This couldn't be true. Other people in the IPTF administration told me it wasn't true. I later heard another version of the rumor. In this version, one of the officers had his wife come to Bosnia to take over the operation of the brothel. Seriously, this couldn't be true either. I was told repeatedly the rumor had no basis in fact.

After several months in my job, the deputy envoy asked why I hadn't done anything about the "knocking shop," as he called it. He said he'd made several inquiries, but had never received an answer. I told him I would investigate and tell him what I found.

Immediately I knew whom I would send. She was a former New York City police sergeant with lots of mission experience, substantial investigatory ability, and someone who would report back honestly regardless of the consequences. She was forthright, diligent, and knew the politics of Bosnia and the culture of the UN better than anyone else I knew. It was an easy investigation for her. The rumors were based on some observations that would draw most people to believe the rumors. But, in fact, there was a simple explanation caused by poor decision-making by the officers living in the house.

Early on in the mission, a group of IPTF officers from an Eastern European country had rented a house together. Over the years, it became kind of an official house for the contingent. They used it for contingent meetings, and the occupancy of the house was passed along from one group of officers to another. They saw it as their house. It was a nice house and I understood why they had hung on to the house as their contingent cadre changed over time.

Here was the problem. The house was located directly behind a brothel. Anyone driving by could see the brothel and three or more UN vehicles parked behind it. Many drivers, including fellow officers and other UN employees, thought officers were patronizing the brothel. After several sightings of the same thing, a rumor spread claiming IPTF officers were operating a brothel.

The story about a woman coming to run the brothel developed after one of the officer's wives visited. She stayed with her husband at the house behind the brothel for a week. She returned home at the end of her visit. All of the officers denied patronizing the brothel. The bar owner confirmed that no IPTF officers from the house had been in the bar. It was possible the bar owner lied, but it was my experience most bar owners wouldn't lie to protect someone in IPTF. I think the bar owner liked having the officers living directly behind his bar. The local police had never raided the place. This may have been the result of the UN vehicles parked next to his business. He claimed he didn't have any trafficked women working in his bar.

When I spoke to the contingent commander about why it wasn't a good practice to live next door to a brothel, it was eye opening. He couldn't or wouldn't understand how the appearance of impropriety was creating a problem. None of his officers used the brothel he claimed, so what was the concern? Our conversation went round and round until I told him the officers had one month to find another accommodation. He wasn't happy, and after much grumbling, the officers moved out.

A new rumor spread. In this rumor, the brothel had been closed and the officers caught, but nothing was done with the officers and they were allowed to finish their tour of duty. It was true they finished their tour of duty.

The deputy envoy was pleased with our report, but felt maybe something else was going on. It wasn't. I wondered why no one checked out the rumor in the first place. It only took one trusted officer one day to obtain the facts of the case.

THIRTEEN

TRUTH AND JUSTICE

✦ ✦ ✦

It is the spirit and not the form of law that keeps justice alive.

– Earl Warren (1891–1974)

Photo Identification

Despite the fact IPTF represented a small number of internationals in Bosnia, and the internationals represented a small percentage of brothel patrons, the focus on IPTF was laser-like. The internal affairs section of IPTF came up with, what they thought, was a brilliant idea. They randomly selected about three hundred of the two thousand international officers, copied colored pictures taken for their UN identification cards, and made black-and-white copies of them for a book of photographs. In police parlance it was a voluminous photo lineup, but without any of the safeguards normally employed to assure accurate identification.

When a trafficked woman was rescued, she was shown the book and asked to identify any officers who she may have recognized as a brothel patron. No one thought this was unfair, even though only the same three hundred officers were exposed to these perusals and potential allegations. Nor did anyone note the poor quality of the photograph copies. As pages of the book were copied many times, the quality of the photographs was seriously downgraded.

Whenever a woman identified someone in these circumstances, she would sign her name on the picture. The officer would then be called in for an interview and asked to defend himself. If he couldn't provide some type of defense tending to prove he didn't visit a brothel, he was usually repatriated to his home country. Although I heard it said that a repatriated officer wouldn't be able to work in another UN peacekeeping mission, I believe they did.

A young American IPTF officer was identified from one of these photo identifications. He was adamant in his denial. I heard his denials second-hand and, the truth be told, I didn't believe him. Since the accusing women often didn't provide a specific time frame as to when the accused officers visited, it was difficult for any officer to mount an effective defense.

Since these were administrative actions, only a preponderance of evidence was needed. We didn't have to prove the accusation beyond a reasonable doubt. Thinking back on some of these cases, we sometimes made our decisions based on how the officer behaved during the interview, the proximity of the officer's duty station to the brothel, and how much aggravation we were receiving about our treatment of trafficked women.

In most cases, it came down to "he said/she said." In the majority of the cases, we acted against the accused officer unless there was some extraordinary circumstances. The most we could do was have the contractor repatriate the officer if he were an American or request the officer's country repatriate him in the case of other countries. I didn't know for sure, but thought the American officers received the worst of it. Many other countries didn't find as much horror in the fact one of their officers visited a brothel while serving in a mission away from home. Bosnia was a country where prostitution laws were liberal, not fully formed, and not generally enforced. There was little local political effort in the country to stop prostitution.

After the officer's interview, while waiting for the elevator in the UN HQ, unbeknownst to him, his accuser and her IPTF escort joined the queue for the same elevator. They all rode together and, after the accused officer departed, the escorting officer asked the woman if she recognized the man who had gotten off the elevator. She didn't. Later they showed her the picture she had identified and told her it was the same officer who was on the elevator. She said they didn't look alike at all and insisted the officer pictured in the book had patronized the brothel but she didn't recognize the officer in the elevator. The interviewer reminded the woman the picture was that of the officer she had just seen. She stuck to her story.

Later, I looked at the picture. I knew the officer, but if I hadn't known him, I don't think I would have been able to pick him out of lineup after having been shown his picture. I should have tried to improve the photo identification practice because this and a few other cases questioned not only the efficacy, but also the fairness of proceeding with poor quality pictures of a supposedly random but small static sample of IPTF officers.

Why were we working so hard to shoot ourselves in the foot in such a prejudicial way? If IPTF were part of the demand problem that fostered the use of women in the sex trade, it was a small part of the problem. Most clients of trafficked women were locals. The international community contributed to the problem to the extent they patronized brothels, but IPTF, with barely two thousand officers, was a tiny fraction of the internationals in the country. IPTF bore the blame disproportionately because of its aggressiveness in ferreting out IPTF officers who patronized brothels and its transparency in the manner in which the cases were handled.

No Photo Needed

In Banja Luka, the deputy station commander was walking into the building as some of her officers were returning from a raid during which a trafficked woman had asked for help. As the woman was walking from the UN vehicle toward the building, she happened to spot someone she described as a regular. She said he was an IPTF officer. The deputy station commander knew the man wasn't an officer, but rather a UN civilian employee. IPTF, of course, had no authority over the civilian employees, but the deputy was more than a little pissy that the accused employee may have portrayed himself as an IPTF officer.

There was no photo book of a few hundred UN civilian employees shown to trafficked women, just the three hundred IPTF officers. There were more civilian employees than IPTF officers in the mission, and I was sure more than this one UN employee was using the brothels. Considering all the international organizations in Bosnia at the time, if the international presence was helping to grow the sex trade in the country by using these women, then it appeared IPTF was a small fish in the whole sorry situation. I was never told about any effort by any other international organization to identify employees engaging in this type of inappropriate behavior.

After the employee was identified, all the proper internal reports were written and forwarded through administrative channels. The civilian side of the mission operated in coordination with IPTF, but we had no supervisory control over it. All we could do was present the reports. No one on the civilian side seemed excited about any of this. A few days later when the news became common knowledge, an attorney working for the UN spoke at the department heads staff meeting that was held each morning.

The situation was discussed, and the attorney thought if the UN decided to punish the accused, the UN would be punishing someone for exercising a human right. He was quite elegant in his argument. It was his opinion the man wasn't violating the law and it wasn't the man's responsibility to determine if the woman was being held against her will; ergo, he had a right to engage in a sexual business transaction.

This drove people in the human rights section of the mission crazy. They had a good point about women who were the victims of human traffickers having so few choices in their lives that it would be impossible for them to exercise any free will. Many believed women living and working under these conditions couldn't engage in consensual sexual liaison in a brothel and, if this were the case, then any sexual act was rape. I didn't know if the argument would prevail in a court. It focused on the customer and not the human trafficker whose evil design created the environment in which the theoretical rape happened. Thinking about it this way, though, emphasized the plight of the women, who existed in a world of degradation and exploitation.

Not every woman working in the sex business was a trafficked woman, and trafficked women frequently wouldn't ask for or seek help because they feared their bosses. For every woman in the business, there was (more than likely) a different story.

Some were transported to Bosnia knowing what lay ahead and thought sex work would pay well. Others had no idea sex work was involved and believed they would be domestic workers or waitresses. It was difficult to surmise how many were in the latter group. Interviewing women who were rescued by IPTF officers didn't shed sufficient light on the issue. Sometimes women who came to Bosnia specifically as sex workers would claim they were trafficked so they could be transported home without cost to them.

Some women knew they would be working in the sex trade in Bosnia. But they didn't know that their passports would be taken by the smugglers or bar owners thus preventing them from leaving the country on their own. Their subsequent situation was no better than any trafficked women. Regardless of the motivation or circumstance of the women working in the Bosnian sex trade, their freedom was restricted. The anecdotal evidence from many of the trafficked women didn't paint a detailed picture of human trafficking as it played out in Bosnia following the 1995 Dayton Peace Accord.

There was no denying the existence of human trafficking or its terrible consequences on women in Bosnia and around the world. But clearly we needed a better understanding of how human traffickers worked so successfully and with seeming impunity. Human trafficking was a complex and difficult law enforcement, economic, migratory, and social problem. We hadn't done a good job in eradicating the sale of humans for sex, mitigating the plight of the victims, or addressing (perhaps not even understanding) the causes.

Around the time of the millennium, large numbers of Asian women were smuggled into the United States. Most came as sex workers. We consider ourselves to have a sophisticated, although decentralized, law enforcement system yet we appeared as powerless as Bosnia in addressing this problem.

As IPTF's knowledge about human trafficking grew, the sophistication of the traffickers' increased and challenged the limited resources of local police. Maybe it was the confluence of two driving forces that set the stage for human trafficking to flourish. In Bosnia, as elsewhere, the primary cause of migration was economic. People wanted to make a better life for themselves and their family. A lack of marketable skills for some women in poor countries made them vulnerable to human smugglers who plied poor countries with clever advertisements.

Unskilled women were attracted to these advertisements and induced to apply for what appeared to be well paying work.

The growth of the sex industry was driven also by demand. Men could use these services with few if any negative consequences. To meet the demand, women whose economic migratory dreams were in full bloom, were victimized. I could have been wrong, I really didn't know, but that was the way I saw it from my position as the deputy commissioner.

I had several long discussions with a woman whose business was helping trafficked women. She suggested legalizing prostitution was the answer. In the 1980s, I spent two months on a study tour of the Dutch legal system. I lived in Rotterdam, but traveled each day to different cities. Whenever I arrived in a city, an official would meet my train. Inevitably, the first order of business was to tour their red light district. I wasn't sure what reaction they were expecting, so I adopted a blasé demeanor to be on the safe side. After several of these encounters, I started asking questions about how prostitution worked for them. Legal wasn't a good word to describe prostitution in The Netherlands. Prostitution there was regulated. Actually, it was heavily regulated.

Prostitutes working in The Netherlands registered with the police, underwent periodic medical examinations, and complied with a host of legal requirements involving health and safety issues in their work places, and legal proscriptions of their behavior.

There was a cadre of public sector employees to assure compliance in every city. One city didn't have a red light district *per se*, but the city regulated streetwalkers to a certain location at prescribed times. Enforcement of the Dutch prostitution laws was vigorous and often resulted in civil citations for violations. The upside of the system was the tax revenue generated by prostitute earnings.

It sounded like a perfect solution, but The Netherlands too had to confront the issue of trafficked women entering their country as sex workers. In these cases, the women bypassed the regulatory dictates and worked in the business, undercutting the prices of the legalized prostitutes. The migrant sex workers didn't pay Dutch taxes, disregarded health and safety requirements, and confounded law enforcement. In the example of this one country, it appeared that the regularization of prostitution didn't eliminate the influx of trafficked women.

This was a long way around to our unfortunate civilian UN employee identified as a client by a rescued trafficked woman. Unlike IPTF officers, the civilian employee wasn't repatriated and continued to work in the mission. If there was any punishment for the employee, it wasn't made known to me. In fact, the civilian side of the mission appeared somewhat put out by IPTF's disclosure of the bad behavior by the employee.

Days Off

Odd is the best way to describe how the UN regulated the time off for its officers. During half the time I spent in the mission, there was one type of schedule. The latter half of my mission life involved another. The former schedule was, at first blush, easy to understand. An officer would work five days, followed by two days off. Not every officer had the weekend off because we needed officers to monitor the local police around the clock and throughout the week. Nevertheless, most IPTF officers were off-duty on the weekend. The others, like me when I was in Novi Grad and who had no real status, had days off in the middle of the week. As an officer worked, he also accumulated compensatory time off for holidays plus two weeks of vacation.

I didn't understand exactly how these days were calculated, but in a short time, I was eligible for six consecutive days off. I took a trip to Salzburg with a Malaysian officer who worked with me in Novi Grad. He was a big *Sound of Music* fan and I was a big fan of Salzburg, having visited there a few times in the past. To my way of thinking, the schedule the UN was using, while not completely comprehensible, was beneficial so I didn't have any complaints.

Shortly after becoming the deputy police commissioner, the schedule changed for IPTF. The change wasn't the result of discussions with our senior leadership. It was a mandate. The UN mission in Kosovo and the international police officers there worked thirty days in a row followed by six days off. Someone, somewhere obviously with some authority, convinced UN HQ in New York that the schedule for all international police officers in peacekeeping missions around the world should be the same. So it came to pass and we began working a thirty-day schedule.

Vacation and holiday time continued to accumulate at a similar rate as it did in the five-day schedule. Most of the officers working in the headquarters building were assigned as advisors and monitors of higher-ranking local police officers. Those local police officials were off on the weekend, but now, despite this glaring misconnection, we had a full staff of police monitors and advisors trying to appear busy during the weekends.

The civilian UN employees and the local Bosnian UN employees were off on the weekend, so the building was fairly empty. As I wandered around the building during these times, I'd see officers playing on their computers, reading novels, and generally screwing off. My office looked down on the front of the building, and I saw many officers arriving late for work on the weekends. When confronted, they said they'd been at meetings first thing and came to the office when done.

I recognized the futility of having the officers come to work on days when there was little work to be done. Nevertheless, we wanted the officers to be at work on time. There was a new edict, no more meetings before work for officers in the Sarajevo region. Most didn't object as they could start playing their computer games earlier.

Only officers working in HQ were under the gun to arrive on time during the weekend. In outlying stations and other regions, regional commanders and station commanders didn't feel a burning need for weekend punctuality for themselves or their officers. If this had happened in my home force, I would have taken on the issue and made sure workers were on time for their shifts. But I wasn't in my home force; I was in a foreign country with mostly foreign police officers. Many didn't share my view about work, and others had a different concept of time and punctuality. For my own mental health, I stopped worrying about it.

I understood the complex nature of a peacekeeping mission, where everyone saw themselves as a boss with their particular expertise occupying the central position in the mission. It dawned on me how little influence I had regardless of my position. As an assistant sheriff, if I told a deputy to do something, there was a good chance it would be done. As the deputy police commissioner, if I told an international officer to do something, it might not be done, especially if the officer disagreed with my command, was busy doing other things, was preparing to leave on holiday, or any number of other reasons.

The commissioner and deputy commissioner positions weren't titular since we had both authority and discretion we could exercise. It was the collegial nature of the management practices I had to adopt that made it difficult to accomplish tasks through subordinates. I was left feeling managerially impotent. I learned to be adaptive and more easy-going. The alternative would have created unnecessary stress and trouble for myself. Unfortunately, knowing and understanding this didn't always keep me sane.

As my time in the mission was ending, I realized I had many unused holidays. There were strict procedures with precise time frames for scheduling days off and holidays. Although I had a little more than three months left in the mission, I had to take my holidays soon or I would lose them. I made a schedule and submitted it to the commissioner. It was important to coordinate our time off since we both couldn't be out of the country at the same time. Nearly all the days I wanted off conflicted with his schedule.

He made some suggestions to de-conflict our schedules. It didn't matter to me. I had no special plans. I wanted to take the time off and travel. The way the commissioner revised the schedule didn't comply with the procedures and time frames regulating time off schedules. As the commissioner noted, he could make whatever exceptions to the procedures he wanted whenever he wanted. Good point. I went with it. I submitted my time-off request to the civilian personnel office of the mission.

The next day, my request was denied. The denial was either sarcastically worded, or the secretary who wrote it didn't have a good understanding of the import of her words. Attached to my denied time-off request form was a copy of a memo to the head of personnel. In the memo, the secretary kept referring to me as "this monitor" and in so many words asked the head of personnel who the heck I thought I was to flagrantly ignore their procedures. The bitch! It took me awhile to calm down after reading it. My executive officer came in he asked what was wrong. I read him the memo. He laughed.

Looking for a more sympathetic response, I went to the commissioner's office and read the memo to him. Apparently, he couldn't make exceptions whenever he wanted. The commissioner was indignant as only a French person can be and blustered about the procedures being for IPTF, and he was in charge of IPTF, so he could change them. I had revised by schedule only to allow the commissioner to take his time off. Now I was in jeopardy of losing time I had earned. Together we decided I needed to speak with the personnel director.

I knew the personnel director. He was an older Swiss man nearing retirement, and I imagined this was his last overseas mission. He'd been with the UN for a long time. I pled my case, but it took a while for him to comprehend my fast-talking English explanation of why the request didn't conform to the procedures. He promised to look at it and make a decision.

The next day someone from his office came with my request form which still had "denied" written in the margins to tell me it was okay to take the time off. There followed a long discussion during which I told the young man this wasn't good enough. The personnel director had to write "approved" on my request. If I left the mission without an approved request, I wouldn't get paid, I'd be accused of abandoning my position, or who knows what would happen.

A few days later, the request made its way down to my office with the word "approved" on it, but no signature. I gave up. This was the best I was going to get. I had won, and the curt "approved" was a grudging admission of having won. Over the course of the next three months, I took my days off and holidays according to the controversial schedule. They went off without a hitch, my pay wasn't docked, I was none the worse for wear, and the commissioner was able to take his time off.

Blood on the Walls

A few of the Americans in the mission decided to go home after the September 11th attacks. Some spoke about going home to rejoin their police forces. Others had a nebulous sense of wanting to do something, but couldn't be specific about what they could do. I think some wanted the comfort of home. In the end, fewer than ten Americans left the mission. In the final analysis, most officers realized there wasn't much they would be able to do once in the United States.

I was sure, in some cases, the families pressured the officers to come home because they felt the officer would be safer closer to home. The emotion and sense of helplessness overshadowed any logical thinking when it came to a family's safety. I understood and the officers who left did so without anyone thinking less of them.

It was hard to watch the attacks on television ten thousand miles from home. Everyone was on the phone to loved ones trying to figure out exactly what was happening. There was a stream of international colleagues in and out of my office expressing their sympathy. Some of the first were Muslim officers who said such acts were abhorrent to Islam. Emotions ran high throughout the day as the story of the terror attacks unfolded. I discerned a definite sea change in the manner with which our international friends, including officers, civilians, and local workers, interacted with us during the remainder of my time in Bosnia. On that day, everyone was quiet, subdued, and encountered their American colleagues in a gentle and guarded way.

The next day at our senior leaders' staff meeting I read a short prepared statement, and the Envoy requested a minute of silence for the victims. After that, as the days ground on, the mission operated as it always had in its sort of jerky, start-stop fashion. We continued to rush headlong from one minor crisis to another. Now, though, there was more talk about terrorists among us, secret SFOR operations, and old stories about the mujahedeen organizing and training in unspecific locations in Bosnia for terrorist attacks on unspecific targets at unspecific times.

A few weeks after September 11th, a hotel manager reported that a group of heavily armed men, in the middle of the night, burst into one of his hotel rooms and took away two men. The hotel was in a suburb of Sarajevo close to the SFOR HQ base. The room was ransacked, and the manager said there was blood on the walls. IPTF officers confirmed there was blood on the walls. There were no personal items left in the room. Eventually we were told by the military to relax. I figured that was military-speak for "back off." The commissioner told me the soldiers conducting the operation were Americans. He knew this because his *chef de cabinet* frequently liaised with the part of the French *Gendarmerie* assigned to the NATO forces comprising SFOR.

The French IPTF officers were part of the French *Gendarmerie*, a military police force. Other *Gendarmerie* officers were assigned to the military force, SFOR, whose job was to protect civilians, keep the formerly warring factions separated, and enforce the 1995 peace accord. The commissioner and I had long discussions about his force during which he seemed obsessed to engender in me the understanding that the *Gendarmerie* was every bit as real a police force as my sheriff's department.

I pointed out none of my deputies wore paratrooper wings as he and many of his officers sported, nor were we prohibited as he and his officers were, from conducting police work out of uniform. His close ties to the French military gave him access to information about what was happening from their perspective.

While I enjoyed a professional relationship with a couple of American generals and their senior staffs, I didn't have the kind of open relationship the commissioner had with his generals. He was a general and they were generals in, basically, the same force, doing different jobs. Although I held the equivalent of a general officer's rank within the UN, no one on the American military side recognized it. True, some were curious about why I had a two-star rank insignia, but that was about it.

I was mildly surprised to receive a call one day from a person at the US embassy asking me to meet with an American military officer at the SFOR base in Sarajevo as soon as I finished work. I was asked not to tell anyone. I arrived on the base, asked for the officer, and waited about twenty minutes. When the officer arrived, he said he had been at chow. There was no apology for keeping me waiting.

We sat in a conference room, and he asked why I was wearing two stars. I explained it designated my rank in my home force and the rank I currently held in the mission. I saw a slight smirk on his face, so I asked if he found this unusual or funny. He said he didn't. Apparently, I didn't look like general material to him.

We were unimpressed with each other. He explained diplomatically yet circuitously how the American military posture had of necessity changed since the terrorist attacks. Not everything was going to be done by the book, even if it meant stepping on some toes regardless of whose toes they were. I appreciated this information, but I wasn't sure why he was telling me this. I assumed it had to do with the hotel raid a few days prior.

When I asked why he was telling me these things, he said I should know so I could pass this information along to my UN colleagues should something happen that they may not understand. Really. He thought I should explain American military actions if they violated local laws and procedures by claiming some kind of September 11th exemption from the rule of law. While I may have supported those kinds of actions in the wake of the attacks, I wasn't about to say so to my international colleagues. I told him I appreciated the briefing, but I probably wouldn't spend time trying to explain American or SFOR military operations. We left it at that. Fortunately, during the short time I had left in the mission, I wasn't aware of any similar incident like the hotel raid. Maybe SFOR developed more stealth and cunning.

That's Him!

That pesky book with the poorly copied pictures of the unlucky three hundred IPTF officers shown to rescued women came back to haunt, annoy, and embarrass me in early fall. The commissioner had come hurriedly into my office, closed the door, and in a serious tone explained that three American officers had been identified as having used the services of a woman who had worked in a bar in Doboj, a city an hour and a half north of Sarajevo. The commissioner opened the book and thumbed through it pointing out two different Americans. Under each name the woman had placed her signature. He then turned to a picture of an old man. It took a while to realize it was a picture of me, but there was no signature under my name.

My first thought was why I was in the book in the first place. I had appeared on local television several times and my picture was often in the local newspapers when I attended openings of new police stations, police graduation ceremonies throughout the country, and other newsworthy functions. Any investigator worth his/her salt would know that such exposure would prejudice a photo identification of this sort. Nevertheless, there was the commissioner pointing to my picture.

He explained the woman hadn't accused me of using her services, but had simply seen me in the bar one afternoon. Apparently, so the story went, I arrived, had a drink, didn't speak to anyone, and left within fifteen minutes. They would have had me dead to rights if 1) I had ever been to Doboj except once with a large group of people, 2) I hadn't been a teetotaler my entire life, and 3) I had only frequented one bar in Sarajevo and then only to attend going-away functions. I've never liked the atmosphere in the bars. They are too noisy and way, way too smoky for me, as I have never smoked. There were no non-smoking bars in Bosnia. Entering a bar there usually meant a hearing loss because of the noise. That's assuming one's head didn't explode first.

The commissioner asked what he should do. I told him he had to investigate the allegations, but he needed to do so quickly because I only had a few months left in the mission. I informed the program manager and assured him I hadn't been in Doboj, let alone in a bar there, and hadn't been with a prostitute. To be clear, I told him the allegation involved me being in the bar, not being with a prostitute. The bar was a notorious brothel and was declared off-limits for IPTF personnel.

I provided the investigators with my personal journal so they could see my activities during the month of July when I was supposed to have been seen in the bar/brothel. I suggested they check my automated car log for the month. I explained I was only in the country about fifteen days during July. The rest of the time I was in Hong Kong on holiday with my wife.

All UN vehicles had a car log, which automatically recorded the time, speed, and distance the car traveled. Giving them these two pieces of information and the narrow time frame of when the incident could have happened, I thought it would be a quick investigation.

As my time in the mission drew to a close, there was no resolution. I was the acting commissioner during the final week of my contract because the commissioner was out of the country. There I was, ready to finish my work, but that damn, stupid investigation hung over my head.

I completed my contract, was paid a bonus for completion, and flew to London to meet my wife and visit friends in Scotland before flying home.

Several weeks later I was informed that the investigation was completed. I was found to have violated UN rules about being in a prohibited bar. What! I appealed the finding.

Early the next summer I flew to Sarajevo and hand-delivered a copy of a polygraph examination I took at my own expense to the new investigators considering my appeal. The polygraph showed I had 1) never visited a night bar (the local term for brothel), 2) never been to Doboj except on one occasion with a group of IPTF officers, 3) never drink alcohol, and 4) never visited any night bar anywhere in Bosnia. My appeal was upheld and the allegation against me was not sustained.

Do wonders never cease? The woman who sued the contractor and won some monetary damages mentioned me during her court case. I never read a transcript, but was told the allegation about my visiting the bar in Doboj had morphed into the allegation that the deputy police commissioner frequented (frequented!) one of the most notorious brothels in Bosnia. That made the news even in Washington, DC. Later, I heard the contractor fired me because I frequented this brothel.

I hired a DC attorney to get a copy of the report IPTF had prepared. After eight months of back and forth and lots of disingenuous statements by various people in the UN, they said no report existed. I gave up. It seemed I proved I wasn't in Doboj and wasn't fired. In the passing years, I learned to roll with the punches. If people were seriously interested or concerned, I'd give them a copy of my polygraph.

None of this impinged on the work I've done since. I've worked for many different government contractors and the old rumor didn't concern them.

Used To Be

As I grow older, the list of things I used to be grows longer. All of us used to be thinner, faster, stronger, and, for many of us, hairier. But I mean the positions we used to hold and the experiences we used to have.

There was never any doubt about my hair thinning or reaching my sixtieth birthday or my physical vigor diminishing over time. What surprises me is how fast it happens. Shouldn't you feel as if sixty years have passed when you reach that milestone? Well, it doesn't. You look back over your life and think thirty or maybe forty years, at the most, has gone by, yet there you are, a sixty-year-old.

One of the telling hallmarks of my aging has been my increase in the use of the phrase *used to be*. I say it all the time now. "What did you do?" I *used to be* a cop. I *used to be* the deputy police commissioner in Bosnia. I *used to be* a graduate student. I'm no longer what I used be. But I work as a law enforcement consultant today because of the things I used to do. I get jobs because of the things I used to be, and as time passes, I get better at doing what I used to do, at least in my mind and in the telling. Maybe it's good our memories are flawed and we remember, and perhaps enhance, the good parts. Maybe it's a salve for our aging and aching psyche.

When I left police work, I wanted to do something different and get away from the turmoil surrounding my life. Bosnia provided a solution for me, and even though I thought I was finished being a boss, I realized my particular make up didn't make me a good subordinate. I hated taking orders from people whom I thought weren't up to snuff irrespective of all the cultural considerations. Being in charge was my cup of tea. The circumstances and timing in Bosnia were perfect for me to be catapulted to a senior position with the accompanying accouterments of a car, driver, executive officer, translator, secretary, nice office, and a certain sense of self-worth and importance.

Leaving Bosnia, like leaving the sheriff's department, was done in turmoil. I guessed it was the end of my working career. Since I had an excellent retirement, my only worry was how to keep from being bored.

I was invited to give talks in the US while I was in Bosnia. The first time I spoke on the East Coast to a mixed group of military personnel from several countries. The second time was on the West Coast at a school where I spoke to US Army personnel who were transitioning into Bosnia as part of SFOR. They were junior and senior leaders who knew little about

Bosnia and practically nothing about IPTF and the CIVPOL officers who staffed it.

I thought I had done a good job. Following my talk, a retired general officer spoke to me. He introduced me to a man who represented a defense contractor. The company provided training assistance for military personnel deploying to Bosnia. He told the contractor I should be part of the training, and my new job as an independent law enforcement contractor began.

FOURTEEN

BOTTOM FEEDERS

✯ ✯ ✯

The chief business of the American people is business.

– Calvin Coolidge, Speech in Washington, DC, January 17, 1925

I find it rather easy to portray a businessman. Being bland, rather cruel and incompetent comes naturally to me.

– John Cleese (1956–)

Contracting

Since the Afghanistan and Iraq wars began, government contractors have received a tremendous amount of bad press. There have been congressional inquiries, investigative journalists' reports, government agency investigations, and even civil litigation and criminal trials. I don't have the inside scoop on any of this, but I've worked for eight different government contractors out of the thousands of companies providing expertise, equipment, and manpower to our government.

When I thought about them, I divided them into three general categories. One was research and development; this included all the big companies working on weapons systems, space, and science exploration. The second was a general infrastructure category wherein the companies provided food, maintenance, and housekeeping services. The final one was security/protection. Companies providing the staffing for American CIVPOL officers deploying to UN peacekeeping missions, police trainers in various international settings, and protection officers for dignitaries and VIPs in volatile overseas locations I grouped into this last category. CIVPOL was the generic UN term used to describe international police officers working in peacekeeping missions as opposed to military police units.

I often heard about allegations of overcharging the government, outright fraud, or abusive use of power by contractors. I only knew what I read in the newspapers or heard on television. There would be big headlines in the newspapers or leadoff stories on the nightly news, then a few irate opinion pieces. In short order, I'd stop hearing stories on the news and wondered what happened. Were the allegations proved, was it all a simple misunderstanding, was it political posturing, or were the contractors greedy bastards out to screw the government and taxpayers? I can say, however, the companies I worked for as an independent contractor were seriously concerned about providing quality service to the government agency that hired them.

I worked for two different State Department (DOS) contractors that provided American CIVPOL officers for peacekeeping missions in Bosnia, Haiti, and Kosovo. In Bosnia, where I was the deputy police commissioner, I worked for DynCorp. DynCorp has undergone several different name changes as ownership has changed over the years since I worked for them. It has many different divisions and provides many services in a number of venues. When I worked for them, they were pretty much the only show in town as far as American CIVPOL officers were concerned. They supplied American officers for the UN peacekeeping missions in Bosnia and Kosovo.

My experience with DynCorp occurred when they were relatively new in the CIVPOL game. They trained me, supplied me with bottled water when the Bosnian water was suspect, delivered my mail and packages from home, checked on my general health through a company nurse, provided for my welfare, organized a Thanksgiving meal for the American officers, paid me well, and did everything they said they were going to do when I hired on. As an employee, I couldn't ask for more. In every interaction with them, it was my belief they were vigorously trying to improve their service so they would hire only the best people who would represent the US well in the missions.

Much time has passed since I worked for them. They have been involved with police training in the Middle East in addition to other work around the world. Obviously I can't make a judgment about the quality of the company's work in those countries, as I have no independent knowledge of the situation there or even the exact nature of the policing work involved. Based on my experience with them in Bosnia, though, and the knowledge that it was a company dedicated to improving its product, the government was getting a good bang for its buck.

Over time, DOS spread the CIVPOL lucre to other companies. One of the companies trying to get into the game was PAE Government Services. Out of the blue, I received a call from them, met with a representative, and was asked to help them prepare a contract for US CIVPOL officers for Haiti. I worked in their Los Angeles office for about one week. Again I noted the employees were dedicated to the mission of providing the government with a quality product at a fair price. The former was, of course, a natural requirement of the competitive bidding process.

PAE was concerned about the safety and comfort of the officers deployed to Haiti. They developed the pay scale for the officers based on the rates other officers were being paid in Bosnia and Kosovo. DynCorp, my former employer, was also bidding on the CIVPOL contract for Haiti. PAE won the contract and deployed officers to the UN peacekeeping mission in Haiti for many years.

Later PAE asked me to work with them on another contract involving police training in Afghanistan. I spent two or three days in Los Angeles providing some limited input for them. They didn't win the contract for Afghanistan. I believe the contract was given to DynCorp. I was impressed with PAE's professional approach to the development of the contract. I didn't have the benefit of seeing how DynCorp wrote their contracts but I assume they did so in a similar manner.

The most consistent work I did for contractors was with companies responsible for training US Army troops deploying to UN peacekeeping missions in Bosnia and Kosovo. The contractors often changed, and it wasn't unusual to work for a different company each year. They were large companies with hands in the aerospace industry as well as in the training field. My usual title was subject matter expert (SME). I would provide general guidance to command staff and task force commanders about their interactions with police and CIVPOL role players during training exercises. From time to time, I would play the role of deputy police commissioner, not a stretch.

After two or three training exercises, the need for me to help with the Bosnia training evaporated. Fortunately the company I had been working for had the contract for training the troops deploying to Kosovo, so I continued working for them. It was interesting to see that as the various contractors took over the job of training the US troops heading for Kosovo, the SMEs remain the same. The cadre of SMEs was fairly steady and we worked well together.

As happened in Bosnia, The European Union assumed command of the mission in Kosovo, and American CIVPOL officers and American military officers drew down reducing my workload. There was always work of some nature for an independent law enforcement consultant. The military approach in Iraq and Afghanistan was changing. One approach involved the use of social scientists as advisors to Brigade Combat Teams (BCTs). The scientists would provide commanders with a deeper cultural perspective. The scientists were integrated into a new team structure, trained on military decision-making, and how a military brigade functioned.

A small wounded-vet owned company was hired to develop practical application scenarios to enhance the classroom instruction the teams received. Two of the principals in the company were SMEs with whom I had worked on the training for the military deploying to Bosnia and Kosovo. Although I played a small role in the training process, I was enthused about the mostly retired Army officers I worked alongside. It was a group of about twenty-five former Army officers who used their expertise to train the social scientists in the Army way of doing things. The retired Army officers provided the scientists understanding about how they would fit into the process when deployed.

Presidential Decision Directive 71

Known by their initials, PDDs are a type of executive order from the president of the United States, with the consent of the National Security Council. PDD 71 was issued in February 2000, a month before I entered CIVPOL training in Texas. The intent of the directive, as I understood it, was to train a ready cadre of police officers for deployment to peacekeeping missions around the world. DOS headed the effort with a $10 million budget.

At the time it was issued, there were about seven hundred American police officers serving in missions primarily in Bosnia, Kosovo, and East Timor. PDD 71 called for two thousand law enforcement officers to be trained ahead of time for rapid deployment to future peacekeeping missions.

The directive established wide parameters and within those parameters, many different scenarios for a pre-trained peacekeeping force of police officers could be envisaged. Overtime, not much happened. DOS hired a couple of former cops to coordinate the effort. The officers proved to be limited, not only in experience, but in vision and energy. My observations of the efforts to establish any type of peacekeeping force led me to believe it was something that wouldn't happen.

There were government agencies that took umbrage with the idea of DOS leading the effort. There was a general disappointment by government officials about the performance of CIVPOL. Some politicians took a contrary view of our country's involvement in peacekeeping missions and the costs associated with our deployment to those missions. The ex-cop functionaries who were tapped to do the yeomen's work of implementation didn't possess the wherewithal for success. There were a number of reasons. It simply didn't appear as if there was sufficient political will to accomplish much.

The former cops' approach was to attempt to negotiate a buy-in by police chiefs and sheriffs. The approach was doomed to fail. The majority of police forces were small local agencies (small meaning fewer than fifty sworn officers).

It would have been difficult for the head of a small police agency to release an officer to a peacekeeping mission for a year. Often it wasn't possible to keep a job open until the officer returned from his peacekeeping mission. It wasn't unusual for the mission life to seep into a deployed officer's blood. The good pay prompted many officers to seek additional time away from their home force.

Law enforcement agencies without a robust turnover rate, regardless of the size of the force, faced problems placing a returning officer because of the vicissitudes of civil service rules. These issues resulted in a disinclination by chiefs and sheriffs to grant leaves of absence for their officers. As a result, some the officers quit their positions at home to join a CIVPOL mission and hope they'd be rehired upon return. If not, there were other agencies to which they could apply. I attended a few meetings with police chiefs who were being wooed to support PDD 71. The only concern I heard expressed was money. Most wanted to be reimbursed if an officer left for a peacekeeping mission.

I believed we needed a police peacekeeping corps of two to three thousand peace officers who would enjoy the same job protections as members of the National Guard and US military reservists. The Rand Corporation prepared a report (2009) for the US Army about a Stability Police Force

(SPF), which follows along the same general theme. Members of a peacekeeping corps would train one weekend every month and attend a two-week summer training exercise. Their police jobs would be protected. The US would have a ready cadre of trained officers to deploy as needed. There are still many questions to be answered, among them what the cost would be and under whose aegis it would fall. Any change would be better than our current method.

Central Asia

I called them the "Stans" because I couldn't remember all of them: Kazakhstan, Uzbekistan, Turkmenistan, Tajikistan, and Kyrgyzstan. They lie between China and the oil-rich Caspian Sea. The latter provides a clue about US interest in them. They were all part of the USSR until the breakup of the Soviet Union, but Russia, along with China, were keenly interested in all the Central Asian countries. Strategically, they're important to the US not only for the potential oil under the Caspian Sea, but also their proximity to Afghanistan. It wasn't a place I would have expected to spend any time.

In early summer a few years ago, I received a call from the man who was the deputy police commissioner in Bosnia before me. He was working in Kyrgyzstan at the US embassy. A Kyrgyz law enforcement agency, which the US created and heavily subvented, had run into some internal problems. In fact, the agency had run into a large number of problems. My former colleague had an American on board for a while to help sort out the problems, but medical issues arose and he had to return home.

With that phone call, I entered the picture for the rest of the summer in beautiful (read irony here) and hot Bishkek, the country's capital. I was told it was an easy mission, and as compared to my time it Bosnia, it was.

When the Kyrgyz agency was created, potential officers were given polygraph examinations. Unfortunately, these examinations didn't start until after the officers were hired. Some of the officers hadn't done well on the polygraph, and it was the opinion of the examiner, officers who had failed the polygraph should be fired.

Alas, no one thought to check Kyrgyz law. Under their law, a person couldn't be fired from a government job based on the results of a polygraph examination. Supposedly it was against the law to even administer one to a government employee. Kyrgyzstan devolved from a Russian autonomous province to its own country. Most people were surprised that polygraphs were banned, as Russia itself was a prolific user of polygraphs.

A closer look at the polygraph results showed some people failed because of the way the examination questions were translated, and some failed because they answered truthfully about issues that, in the US, would have precluded them from work. For example, it was common practice in Kyrgyzstan for job seekers to pay someone to hire them. When asked if they had ever paid anyone for a job, the people who answered affirmatively were deemed unqualified. It was a case of at least one polygraph question not being culturally sensitive to the way life was lived in the country.

There were other issues with people because their polygraph results had shown deception. These were sorted out to everyone's satisfaction, albeit sometimes grudging satisfaction. There were more issues. The UN was constantly receiving information from people they referred to as confidential sources about corruption in the new law enforcement agency. The sources wouldn't publicly accuse individuals, and mostly the information they provided didn't include investigative leads. One constant piece of information was the accusation that a large quantity of raw opium had been stolen during the arrest of some drug dealers in southern Kyrgyzstan.

This latter issue was the most problematic for me and it was the main focus of my work. In the first place, no one had checked to see if any drugs were missing from the evidence stored at a local police station in the southern Kyrgyzstan town of Osh. The law enforcement agency was aware of the allegation of missing drugs. No police force in the country had taken any action to verify drugs were missing or if the material taken into custody was opium or any other drug. There were no facilities to test a sample of the evidence, assuming it was still stored in the evidence locker in Osh.

Although several people in the UN thought it was a fruitless effort, I eventually prevailed in taking a trip to Osh. The people at the UN reasoned if the drugs were stolen, the thieves would have replaced the stolen drugs with bunk (a harmless powder or some other material that would appear similar to the stolen drugs.) I was able to determine that not only the drugs were missing in the nearly exact amount two different confidential sources (who didn't know each other) said had been stolen, but that there had also been virtually no effort to hide the theft. Obviously the thieves thought they could act with impunity.

I had no authority to conduct an investigation on my own. All I had was some influence on an agency that seemed to have no desire to investigate the allegations. My charter was to mentor their internal affairs department and provide guidance in resolving these issues. I actually couldn't provide much guidance because the case was at least eight months old when I came on the scene, the confidential sources weren't available for me to interview, the people alleged to have stolen the drugs denied any wrongdoing, and, unless one of them decided to "come to Jesus" and puke up his guts, there were no leads. As far as a criminal case goes, this one was dead on arrival.

Since the US had financial control over the agency, I thought the best way to proceed was administratively. In an administrative investigation, only a preponderance of evidence is sufficient to prove the case. We had enough information to suggest to the head of the agency that three of his top administrators in Osh, if not actually involved in the theft of the raw opium, should have known about it and should have launched an investigation. In my mind I believed them to be culpable.

The theft happened on their watch, and they appeared unconcerned. I suggested if these men weren't terminated, the US should cease funding the agency. I was fortunate to find my suggestions were taken seriously; the internal affairs colonel and the head of the agency deemed my report fair. The president of the country terminated the three people in Osh along with the police general who headed the agency. This all happened after I left Kyrgyzstan.

During the course of these incidents, I had a great opportunity to see and learn about the country. Each week I would send reports home to family and friends. The following are some of the reports about the Kyrgyz Republic and my observations.

OSH

Osh was four hundred and fifty miles south of Bishkek. Considered the capitol of southern Kyrgyzstan, it was situated in the Fergana Valley. The valley extended through southern Kyrgyzstan and parts of Uzbekistan and Tajikistan. I heard it called the breadbasket of the area. The Valley was divided among the three states in the early twentieth century when various independent republics inhabited by tribal nations were incorporated into the Soviet Union, and Central Asia boundaries were redrawn and new republics created.

Osh was a different kind of place than Bishkek. Bishkek had a little element of sophistication. Osh was clearly a rural community populated by Kyrgyz and Uzbek people. There were fewer Russians. I saw more men wearing the traditional pointy and funny-looking hat called a *kalpak* and also the smaller informal working style hat of Uzbek origins. I saw more women in local costumes, native mostly to the Osh region and neighboring Uzbekistan. Bishkek driving was dangerous, but Osh driving I considered a weapon of mass destruction.

I had the thrill of flying to Osh on Kyrgyzstan Airlines. The airport in Bishkek didn't bode well for me as a first-time domestic traveler. As I entered the boarding area, I approached two stern-looking police officers. They checked my passport and ticket. Though I wasn't leaving the country, I needed a passport to fly. The ticket counter was only three feet past the boarding area, so a crowd had formed in the doorway.

People were squeezing toward the ticket counter. A woman checked my ticket and passport as three other women behind her all spoke loudly at the same time. They pointed to the computer screen and gestured wildly.

There was no line. The people around me pushed forward to get to the ticket counter. A couple of people reached over me and put their passports and tickets on the counter in front of me.

An old man came along and took my luggage, tagged it, and placed it behind the ticket counter. When I received my boarding pass, I walked around the counter, picked up my bag, and placed it on an X-ray machine. As my luggage went through the X-ray, I walked through the metal detector. Of course, the alarm went off. The security officer pointed to my watch and motioned for me to continue on. I walked to the other side of the x-ray and retrieved my luggage. As I did this, the x-ray screener pointed to the screen displaying the image of my luggage. He seemed to be asking me what a particular object was. I had no idea, as I couldn't make it out from the fuzzy image on the screen. In English he said, "It must be a camera."

I responded, "*Da.,*" which is Russian for yes. How quickly I picked up the language.

When it came time to board our vintage (late 1950s) Russian Yak 40 jet, everyone crowded around the tail section stairs. There was no organization. Everyone tried to give their boarding card to the lovely flight attendant whose beauty was enhanced by the upper row of gold front teeth. The flight crew boarded after everyone was seated.

The plane was smelly, dirty, and noisy and didn't appear to have much safety equipment. It put me in mind of my flight to Bosnia on the Russian charter flight. The fifty minute flight was bumpy, and the pilot flew the plane like Kyrgyz's drivers drive, with lots of twists, turns, and jerky movements. But the crew appeared sober, so I was thankful. I was most thankful when the plane landed.

I went to Osh to weigh two large seizures of drugs that had allegedly been pilfered. My colleague, an internal affairs colonel from the Drug Control Agency of the Kyrgyz Republic, would meet me the next morning at the local police station where the drugs were stored. An embassy driver met our party at the airport and delivered us to a guesthouse we had booked. We were a little anxious about the accommodations, as our colleagues from the UN, who were also in Osh working on other issues, had appropriated the only reasonably good hotel from under us. As it turned out, we had the better deal. Our accommodations were a kind of bed and breakfast place with excellent service. At twenty-five dollars a night, it was a great deal.

The next morning a translator and I went to the local police. We met the colonel, a forensic expert, and several other people. We waited for the man in charge of the evidence room. I had never seen such an evidence room. It was smelly, crowded, and unorganized. There were fifteen people standing around as the doors to the room were opened. Weighing the drugs wasn't easy. The forensic expert had a nice electronic scale. However, there weren't any electrical outlets in the evidence room. It took twenty minutes to find a working extension cord.

When the first bundle of drugs was finally located and the expert saw it, he said it was too heavy for the scale. Everyone looked at me and asked what they should do. I suggested they open the sack and weigh the individual packets of drugs inside of it, which would have fit on the scale. They were horrified. This was against Kyrgyz law. So I suggested they find a scale sturdy enough to weigh the sack.

During the next half hour while waiting for a scale, I thought maybe they would wheel in one of those scales where people could weigh themselves for a penny and get their fortune at the same time. I realized, of course, that Kyrgyz money had no coins, so we would be presented with another problem. Finally, they found a heavy-duty, old, free-weight type of scale. In short order, our suspicions were founded. The sacks were substantially lighter than the weight listed on the evidence tags.

Now, what to do? The discussion went on most of the day. The next morning they decided to open the first sack. They discovered some of the packets were missing. Having determined that drugs were missing from the first sack, I expected them to open the second one. Nothing. When I asked why they didn't open it, they were barely able to mask their surprise at my ignorance. It was, apparently, illegal for them to open the sack as it was, they told me, against Kyrgyz law. Several more hours of discussion, slowed down by the needed translations and lots of posturing by my Kyrgyz colleagues, caused my reputation for patience and understanding to wane.

They decided to call the prosecutor's office. The prosecutor arrived and went through the same procedure with the first sack. Then the prosecutor felt he had reasonable cause to open the second sack. Of course, more packets of drugs were missing. They suspected they had a crime on their hands. The prosecutor asked me what they should do. I told them they should investigate the crime with the goal of capturing the people who stole the drugs. What a plan. It took all my years of police experience to come up with that. The allegations of pilfered drugs (about ninety kilos of raw opium) had been circulating for over nine months and this was the first time anyone made an effort to determine if, in fact, drugs had been stolen.

The rest of the time in Osh was spent reviewing the progress on the new building for the Agency, which was under construction. It looked pretty good. We also had several meetings with the UN people. They were responsible for implementing the US grant that funded the Agency.

The flight back from Osh wasn't as exciting. We flew on Alyn Airline. It was a commercial airline unlike the state run Kyrgyzstan Airlines. It wasn't great but it was a bigger and somewhat newer plane, probably late 1970s. It was faster, and we arrived in Bishkek in forty minutes. It was nice to be back in what, by comparison, seemed like civilization.

Zum, Plov, and Elections

I've travelled a lot. Sometimes it was difficult to get used to foreign ways to doing things. Kyrgyzstan was no different in that regard. I usually tried not to let cultural differences and local customs bother me. There were limits, though.

I carried an embassy-issued cell phone either in my pocket or my briefcase. When my mission was about half over I thought perhaps it was time to buy a cheap carrying case for my phone. The most appropriate choice of vendors was Zum. Zum was a four-story department store, but different from a western department store.

Vendors purchased space in the building, and they established their own enterprise. It was similar to those antique malls found all over America, but more organized and in some ways more disorganized. The store was arranged by the type of merchandise being sold. Most of the vendors selling cosmetics were on the ground floor. All the large appliance vendors were on the second floor and so on. The top floor housed the souvenir dealers.

I found several cell phone vendors in among the cosmetic dealers. One was selling the same model phone I was carrying. Through witty facial expressions, intricate hand gestures, and precise pointing, I made it clear that I wanted to purchase a carrying case for my phone. I held my phone in my hand and emphatically pointed to it. No problem. My communications skills had been honed to perfection after only a short time in the country.

The saleslady had what I was looking for and handed me a phone case. To the casual observer, the case might have appeared to be leather. Upon closer inspection, I was delighted to note that it was made of a rare Chinese Yak skin with the tensile strength and appearance of cardboard. The price was right, a mere a hundred and twenty som, which amounted to three dollars. I actually bought a few extra as future Christmas gifts for some lucky friends.

I handed the young lady the a hundred and twenty som, took the case, and started to leave. "*Nyet,*" she said with a look of panic in her eyes. She motioned to a chair in front of a computer and said, "*Pazhaloosta*" (please). A true linguist and intellect, I realized the transaction wasn't over, so I sat down. Obviously she wanted to give me a receipt I thought. She completed a form, wrapped the money I had given her in the form, and handed it across the desk to another woman. The other woman, I'm sure was, at one time, a Soviet prison guard.

The former prison guard grunted something and, with meat hammer efficiency, pounded out something on an industrial strength keyboard. A nearby printer stirred and slowly produced another form. The prison guard woman handed it to the saleswoman, who filled in some blank spaces, had me sign the form, then handed it back to the other woman. The saleswoman opened a ledger book and wrote the whole transaction down and had me sign the book.

I took the case and stood, but again I heard her say, "*Nyet.*" I sat down. The other woman was banging away on her keyboard again, and the printer was spitting out two more forms. The two new forms came across the desk; the saleswoman filled them out, gave them to me for two more signatures. Okay, I was ready to go. I looked at her with an inquisitive expression as I began to rise from my seat, but she shook her head no. I realized she still hadn't given me a receipt. She obtained a receipt form from a book and completed it, asked me to sign, then handed me the receipt.

I was free to go after six pieces of paper, of which five required my signature and fifteen minutes of work by two employees for a three-dollar sale. I had taken the case from the box it came in and, as I tried to leave, the sales woman insisted I take the empty box. She placed it in a bag, which she handed to me. She wouldn't take *nyet* for an answer. Certainly all those years of Soviet rule had taken their toll.

Wanting to buy some souvenirs, I took the escalators to the top floor. At the top of each escalator sat an old woman. I wondered what they were doing. Some friends estimated these women made about seven hundred and fifty som a month ($20). Their job was to watch the escalator; why, wasn't clear. Maybe they kept kids from playing on them or kept people from getting on the wrong one (can't imagine that happening a lot). Perhaps, they were supposed to do something if there was an accident. Probably it was a job left over from the Soviet times where full employment, even useless full employment, was part of their economic plan.

I discovered another interesting local custom while I was in Osh. Our embassy translator insisted we find a place where plov was served. We joined some United Nations people who were also in Osh on related matters. Plov was an Uzbek dish similar to Spanish paella. While paella has lots of different vegetables and meats, plov consists of lamb and a few slivers of carrots in a tasty brown rice. It was served in big heaping bunches in a communal serving dish. It was surprisingly good. The only problem was we ate our plov while sitting on a bed with ten other people. Fortunately, no one had to get into his or her PJs.

The restaurant was outside and had large beds scattered around a forecourt under shade trees. There were five or six large beds. Shoes off, people sat cross-legged on the beds; it wasn't a good position for eating. There were too many of us to fit on the bed serving as our table. The waiters placed two chairs at each end of the bed. I grabbed one of the chairs. Several people had already spilled drinks on the bed forgetting they couldn't set a glass down. It was quite a sight with the local people in our group looking comfortable and us international types uncomfortable and clumsy.

I was back in Bishkek for Sunday Election Day. I volunteered to be an international election monitor through the US embassy. I worked with my partner from the Embassy. We were assigned an eight-hour, late evening shift. An embassy driver and my translator joined us. We were responsible for fifty-nine polling stations. There was no expectation we'd see all the stations during our eight-hour tour of duty. Over a thousand international election observers under the aegis of the Organization for Security and Cooperation in Europe (OSCE) were in the country and we were part of their effort to monitor the elections.

Other monitors covered the polling stations we weren't able to observe. The OSCE monitored elections in countries through out the world, and brought their expertise to this nascent democracy. This was a presidential election. The acting president of Kyrgyzstan was running against six other candidates. Going into the elections, the polls estimated he would take 80 percent of the vote.

The Bishkek population was 750,000 people. In Kyrgyzstan, as in many European countries, the voter turnout must be at least 50 percent of all registered voters or an election is null and void. They made sure to get the right turnout by the strategic placement of numerous polling stations. Many polling stations were staged next to large apartment complexes, and all were within easy walking distance for the voters who lived in the district. Each polling station represented one to two thousand plus registered voters. Each station was staffed with eight or more election workers. The staff was well trained in their duties and responsibilities.

Although definitely low-tech, the elections went off without a hitch. We had to choose a polling station to watch the ballot count after the polls closed. The one we chose finished counting forty-five minutes after closing. By the next morning, the preliminary results of the election were announced. As predicted, the acting president won handily. The voter turnout was 70 percent. The turnout demonstrated the obvious patriotism and political involvement of the Kyrgyz People.

Preventive Maintenance

For most Kyrgyz people, the concept of preventive maintenance appeared to be an alien concept. Anyone, even a casual observer would see the general state of disrepair of buildings, public grounds, vehicles, and people. Most things just looked worn out.

I've tried to get my brain around Kyrgyz thinking. Why didn't they take care of things? Stuff that doesn't work made me crazy (or maybe just crazier). My whole psyche took personal offense. Maybe, if I could have figured out why things didn't get repaired, I would have been able to deal with it without giving myself a headache.

There seemed to be some criteria involved in the Kyrgyz decision-making process relating to fixing things. I thought it went something like this: When an item broke, the first criterion was, did it affect the function? So, if a few tiles fell off one of the numerous, poorly constructed, but striking military monuments scattered throughout the city, there was a good chance the tiles wouldn't be replaced.

If bricks were missing from a pathway or the pavement was seriously uneven, well it wasn't a problem worth mentioning since people could walk around. A broken toilet seat, assuming one could be found, never demanded fixing, as the toilet would still function.

Fat Boys was a local restaurant frequented by the international crowd. They served a fairly decent Western-style breakfast, and the coffee approached drinkable. The owners were British, so they weren't all that knowledgeable about coffee matters. During my entire time in the country, the toilet seat in the restroom sat against the wall next to the toilet. I guessed if a seat were needed, the patron would set it on the toilet, sit gently, and all the planets would align eliminating the need for any repair.

The next criterion focused on how severely the damage impinged on the function. A car with a single broken headlight wouldn't necessitate repair since one functioning headlight was sufficient for night driving. One time, my driver had a minor fender bender and broke the right turn signal of his eighteen-year-old Mercedes. Surely, turn signals were necessary; therefore, this would be a required repair. Nay, nay.

There were no rules of the road. Yes, they did have vehicular laws written down some place, but the driving behavior of the Kyrgyz people demonstrated that the laws didn't matter. Some streets had lane markers, but drivers drove wherever they chose. If the street were two lanes wide, they would make three cars fit. No one ever used a turn signal, ever. My driver didn't need the right turn signal fixed, as it had nothing to do with the overall functioning of the car or his driving performance.

The final criterion was the availability of parts. Repairs would be done only if the damage affected the function and parts were available. The parts criterion prompted two questions. Was the repair part available and how much did it cost? These were important questions in a country where teachers' salaries equal about thirty dollars a month. Big, costly repairs meant having to do without.

The government itself wasn't much better in terms of what it could afford to repair. There were those who pointed to government corruption as part of the reason for the deterioration of the infrastructure. I'm sure that was true, but it was no different from other countries that had moved from a socialist system to a market economy. Government officials without experience in managing a democratic market economy with all its vagaries were often hard-pressed to effectively deal with corruption.

As a consequence, government buildings in complete disrepair were evident everywhere. They gave the appearance of having been abandoned but were not. No one mowed the lawns nor weeded in the parks that dotted most cities. The parks were completely overgrown, and park benches along walkways usually were broken. Few people swept sidewalks except for the occasional storeowner who dealt with the front of his business. Litter was everywhere, especially along the gutters and sidewalk parkways where it gathered. Rats scurried in and out of the trash.

Americans often hear, "If it ain't broke, don't fix it." That was a guiding principle of life in Kyrgyzstan. Ladas and Volgas (Russian cars) were ubiquitous on the roadways. But drivers appeared to do nothing to keep them in good order except to put gas and oil in them, but then only when the oil was dangerously low. When a car would stop running, the owner would try to fix it. The cars were fairly simple machines. They would take a car to a mechanic only as a last resort. Naturally, the cost and availability of the replacement part played into the repair decision.

The amazing thing, though, was most of the cars were old, but kept running even if held together with mismatched parts, baling wire, and a great deal of ingenuity. With little money and no access to a vibrant market place, it took hard work, patience, and considerable thinking outside the box to make life tolerable. Most Kyrgyz people had those attributes. In the worst of circumstances, they were friendly, courteous, and proud. However, they didn't do any preventive maintenance on themselves.

It was as if, like the milk we get in the market, they had an expiration date. The Kyrgyz Republic made me feel good because most Kyrgyz people in their early fifties looked old and infirmed. By comparison, I looked good. Few people exercised and not many saw a doctor except when they were terribly ill. This was understandable, as life was hard and people worked long hours for little money, so they didn't have time to exercise. The cost of a doctor wasn't too expensive, but prescribed medicines were typically outside the average citizen's financial reach. Nearly all people over forty smoked and drank. It was a hard life for most of the people and it was reflected in their appearance and their rapid physical decline as they approached middle age.

Precautionary Honking

The driving in Kyrgyzstan was difficult to understand. My amazement with Kyrgyz driving was renewed each morning during my twenty-minute ride to the Embassy and again in the afternoon riding back to the hotel. Italian driving was notorious, but in Italy, after spending a little time, you can ferret out the basic rules of the road. In Kyrgyzstan, however, it was a different story. The most basic of traffic laws and good common sense didn't win the day. Many drivers, for example, never stopped at red lights.

Riding around Bishkek was similar to a combination of the Indy 500 and a destruction derby contest. The vast majority of cars with their banged up fenders, rust, dangling parts, and smoke belching from their exhausts appeared to have been the losers in the latter race. Undeterred, they entered the race anew each day and mounted their assault on other cars and the hapless and often somewhat stupid pedestrians who competed for space in the roadway.

Occasionally there would be a street sign to guide you, but mostly they were missing or unreadable because the paint had faded. Lane lines, a truly useless guide to the Kyrgyz driver, were barely visible. Drivers never stayed in a lane, and that was probably the reason lane lines were so faint. There were many wide boulevards in Bishkek. Each driver would use the entire width of these roads maneuvering from two or three feet left of the centerline to the curb, depending on the perceived fastest way around any vehicles in front of the driver.

Each intersection presented a confused, dangerous, and adrenalin-pumping driving experience. They were usually crowded with pedestrians wanting to cross and who were not necessarily guided by the traffic lights. Then there were drivers who approached the intersections as tests of their driving skills and who believed that getting through the intersection without having to slow was a manly feat. Numerous *marshrutkas* (minivans) would dart across lanes to pick up passengers and add to the crowded intersections. Pensioners and disable war veterans solicited money from the centerline of the road. They had government credentials and would ask drivers for money. This was considered a legal way to supplement their government pensions, which amounted to around twenty dollars a month.

Marshrutkas were minivans loosely organized and privately operated. They supplemented the aging government-run bus system left over from Soviet times. The condition of these minivans ranged from deplorable to "not too bad considering." There were hundreds of them. They were crowded but considered an economical way for people to get around the city. They only cost seven som (about ten cents).

Each minivan had a number corresponding to a general route, but it would deviate from its path if someone needed to go someplace not too far off the usual route. People could get on and off wherever they chose if they could convince the driver to stop. People stood about three feet into the street and held out their arm when they wanted a *marshrutkas* to stop. Most people gathered at the intersections to hail a van. Because so many riders wanting different minivans were in the same spot, there were often four or five *marshrutkas* jostling for the same space at the intersection. They double- and triple-parked to reach their customers, and this added to the excitement pervading the intersections in central Bishkek.

Along the streets were old electric wires to power the Soviet Ikarus buses. The buses were in miserable condition. Windows were broken, metal parts were rusted through, some parts were missing, the electrical connections on the top the buses were covered in rust and dirt and the whole bus was, more likely than not, filthy. I mean scummy dirty. These, too, were crowded, and there were lots of them adding to the general state of daring-do on the roadways.

But the days in traffic seemed to be saved, to a certain extent, by precautionary honking. It was the saving grace. While there were many traffic deaths, most drivers seemed to have a sixth sense in divining what other drivers were going to do. If a person drifted into a space already occupied, a couple of toots on the horn and the offending car moved over. If a driver wanted to pass on the right, he would honk and proceed. No one appeared to get angry with other drivers. Honking was almost a courtesy. "Honk! Honk! Here I come, thank you very much." The honking was incessant and added to the din of the driving experience.

Where were the cops in all of this? They were at the intersections as well. I never saw a cop stop a car for a traffic violation, although I'm sure they probably did. I saw drivers make serious traffic violations in front of them, and those violations didn't generate even a second look. I did note they often stopped cars from outside the city. Cars registered in Bishkek had license plates starting with *B*. Most of the cars I saw stopped by the police were from other towns. Sometimes they would mount a crackdown on certain violations such as tinted windows, obviously a major cause of traffic deaths.

Once, my driver was taking several of us to the Dordoi marketplace just on the edge of the city. It was a giant open-air market. As we entered the street leading to the market, we saw six traffic police officers. They stopped our car. My driver had a letter from the embassy that identified him as an official driver of embassy personnel, so we weren't too worry.

The effort by the police was to tell drivers about a new ban on tinted windows, threaten a citation, and hope a small bribe would be offered by the driver to avoid the traffic citation. Our driver's rear passenger windows were tinted. It was an embassy security requirement. Of course, they let our driver go when they realized we were in the car.

In another instance, I was pleased to see two traffic officers were assigned to watch over several road workers making repairs in two different locations within twenty feet of each other. There was one cop for each of the repair sites on the longest and busiest street in Bishkek. But things weren't as they appeared. I assumed they would be watching oncoming traffic to ensure the safety of the road crew.

As we drew closer, I saw that both officers were smoking cigarettes and, not only watching, but fully engrossed in the work being performed. Their backs were to the oncoming traffic. I supposed in such circumstances they'd still serve as an early warning system for the road workers because if they were struck by a rogue driver, their bodies being hurled into the air would probably give due warning to the others.

Fortunately my driver obeyed the traffic laws. At least he did when I was in the car. I'm sure it was a boring experience for him. Traffic signals, like some European countries, flash green before turning yellow, then red. My driver actually slowed when he saw the green flashing light. This was a good policy as I had frequently seen cross traffic blast out into the intersection many seconds before they had the green light. Most of time my driver drove at a reasonable speed, and while he, too, ranged from one side of the road to the other, he managed to do so without whiplash-causing jerky motions. I'm not a snob, but I sat in the backseat, thinking it was safer. Thankfully, his seat belts functioned.

The thing about the ride to work was that the driving experience always had me buzzed and ready for work by the time we reached the embassy.

Dordoi Market

I've heard the expression, "Walk a mile in my shoes," but I had never walked a mile among shoes. I walked nearly a mile with all the cheap shoes I'd ever seen on both sides of a four-foot wide pathway. This happened one Sunday at Dordoi (pronounced in sort of singsong way as DOR DOY) marketplace. Tagging along with a couple from the embassy, my translator and driver, I soon discovered the ultimate in flea markets.

Dordoi covered many acres of land on the outskirts of Bishkek. It was easily three times larger than the average American flea market. It was open every day, and Sundays were the busiest. There were no buildings just shipping containers. The containers were stacked two high. The bottom served as the store showroom with the double doors opened wide jutting out into the small aisle. The doors served as extra space for the store. Some of the items on offer hung from the doors. The top containers were used for storage. There were holes cut through the roof of the bottom containers and the floors of the top container. Vendors used ladders for access to the upper storage containers.

The market was arranged with containers facing each other. Shoppers would stroll down the aisle viewing goods in stores on both sides. It was further arranged with like products found in the same area. Chinese shoes were to be found in one area, European shoes in another, clothing somewhere else, cloth and fabric close by the clothing, and so on over a large area.

Parking was random and at a premium. There was a charge for parking, but few people knew it. It wasn't clear whether the parking fee was a legitimate charge collected on behalf of a licensed vendor or the work of young opportunistic con men (boys really).

There were no signs, but as we left the car, an eight- or nine-year-old boy came by and requested the parking fee, about fifty cents. No one complained and I saw other people paying the boy when they parked. A different boy patrolled each section of parking. They would wash your car with dirty water for an additional fifty cents. There was no running water. The car washing was done with buckets filled at a nearby drainage ditch.

We found a parking spot near Shoe World where imported Chinese shoes were sold. There were men and women's shoes. There were no men's shoes larger than nine and a half. Women's shoes were similarly small so small-footed people in the market for cheap, poorly made, and often incredibly ugly shoes could have a great shopping experience. Nevertheless, shoes were virtually flying out the container doors. The local people were in a buying frenzy. Shoe World was close to being one mile long, and it was crowded and noisy.

There were men running up and down the aisles pushing and pulling handcarts loaded with merchandize yelling, "*Jol! Jol!*" It was a Kyrgyz word, meaning road. I figured it translated to something like "watch out" or "I have the roadway." I learned this after a near collision with one of the handcarts. The carts completely filled the aisle and barely missed the opened doors of the containers. To avoid a collision I had to dart into one of the containers.

Food and drink vendors also traveled the aisle, but at a slower pace. Food was sold from a piece of plywood laid on top of old baby carriages. Luke warm drinks were sold from cardboard boxes carried around by dirty street urchins. Old women sold hot tea, the favorite drink of local people, even when temperatures reach one hundred degrees or more. There were Kyrgyz sanitary standards to be met so the few communal teacups were thoroughly washed with hot water and dirty hands after each use.

So if a small-footed person were in need of cheap, poorly made ugly shoes it would be worth the airfare to Kyrgyzstan. There were no shoes over twenty dollars. Most sold in the twelve-dollar range. Many of the shoes almost looked like the brands they were trying to copy. The best selling shoes had long, pointy toes that turned upward. And they weren't just for women.

They were made in a variety styles for men, usually a loafer and always in white or beige. Foppish Kyrgyz men wore these shoes for all occasions, but they were most frequently seen when a man wanted to look particularly stylish. Businessmen wore the shoes all the time, and they could be spotted at social events on the feet of Kyrgyz men of fashion.

It was hot the day I was at Dordoi, and I was fairly exhausted after the long trek through Shoe World. But there was more to see, so we wandered over to the area selling clothes. There were many women's clothing stores (containers) selling a wide range of clothing that was generally cheap. Cheap in the sense of quality and how it looked when worn. I was impressed with the men's suits selling for under a hundred dollars. Top quality, fashionable, and "gotta have" weren't terms I would use to describe these suits. I saw one of the suits on an embassy employee (his name withheld to protect him from ridicule) and it looked, as you might expect, cheap.

One section was devoted to the containers selling fur coats and hats. I didn't know much about fur except it makes people want to throw red paint on it when worn by anything other than the animal born with it. The strange thing was that sales people couldn't provide a straight answer about the type of fur on a coat. Generally the rule of thumb was, the rattier looking the fur, the cheaper the coat. The nicer-looking fur coats had price tags of five hundred dollars, but all prices in Dordoi were negotiable. It was over a hundred degrees. My energy waned, and I lost interest in fur coats and negotiations.

We left Dordoi three hours later, feeling completely drained by the heat, noise, and the stimulation and frustration of having so many delightful, albeit cheap, shoe choices. To be clear, the shoes I bought were beige and I was the envy of every American at the embassy. I knew this because I often caught them pointing at my smart-looking pointy shoes. They were only two sizes too small.

Three Things Not Found in Kyrgyzstan

Just three things? Some people said more. There was probably a larger list depending on the number of people asked and how long they'd been there. When I first arrived, my colleague at the Embassy said there were two things I wouldn't find in Kyrgyzstan. I added a third.

Hot tea was the drink of choice. Iced tea was an abomination to Kyrgyz people. There was iced tea in hotels and restaurants catering to an international crowd, but no self-respecting local person would drink it. During the hottest days, local people drank hot tea. Tea was plentiful. Green tea and black tea were the prominent types available. One, green tea I think, was good for digestion. Black tea, I was told, had a soothing effect. Since both contained caffeine, I wondered about the medicinal claims of either. I drank both types and they were quite tasty.

Good coffee was a different matter entirely. My colleague was right when he told me I wouldn't find a cup of Starbucks coffee in Kyrgyzstan. In fact, I never heard of a Starbucks anywhere in Central Asia. Americans weren't known for making the best coffee in the world. Europeans often ridicule our weak, watered-down coffee. But since Starbucks and other coffee specialty shops have come along, we have become more international and sophisticated in our coffee drinking.

The British couple who ran the local restaurant I frequented on the weekends served weak English coffee. But I made do with it while I would kibbitz with the internationals (mostly Americans) who gathered at the end of each workweek to pass the time. I stayed in a great hotel for the duration of my assignment, but it didn't serve great coffee. I received a free European-style breakfast in the Regency Club of the hotel on the concierge-level floor where I was housed. The coffee there came from a self-serve machine. It was drinkable, but a far cry from a four-dollar Starbucks latte. The upside was, of course, that during my two-month stay, I saved enough money on coffee to pay for both grandsons' college education. Well, I may be a little short.

Another thing I didn't find in Kyrgyzstan was soft toilet paper. How right my colleague was, I thought, as I gingerly sat typing my reports. What the hell were these people thinking? Wouldn't Kyrgyz people be irritable all the time given the texture of their toilet paper? Instead, they were a smiley, friendly bunch. I suspected there was a secret cream they used copiously, but it wasn't available to foreigners. If I could have discovered what it was, I could have invested in the company, made a fortune, and had been less, lets just say, sensitive. Too, the return on my investment would also have paid for the two grandsons' college.

The third thing I couldn't find was a willingness to change on the part of the police. I think they liked the old Soviet way of doing things. Whenever local police practices differed from international standards, there was an argument. It took a lot of energy to rise to the daily confrontations this caused.

If I disagreed with the way they were doing something, the argument was that I didn't understand. Disagreeing with someone's point of view, I'd reply, wasn't the same as not understanding the basis for the point they were advancing. Well then, I didn't understand because it wasn't the same as it was in my own country. When I pointed out that what I was attempting to have them to do was based on international and not American standards, their retort centered on the way things were done in Central Asia. So we would come full circle. I knew it was the way things were done in

Central Asia; I needed to show them how to do it in a manner consistent with the way police in developed countries did things.

Change was frustratingly slow. But still the police and the general public were amazingly adaptive. The local police, for example, attended a five-year, college-level training program where the trainees earned a law degree and joined the police as junior-grade lieutenants.

During their training, they were given three hundred and fifty hours of firearms instruction. But since they couldn't afford to purchase sufficient ammunition, they only fired their weapons, using a total of nine bullets, during the entire training course. It was similar for the patrol officers who attend a five-month to two-year course depending on what job in police work they would be entering. They practiced long hours on aiming and perfecting their trigger pulls. They didn't actually shoot their weapons. When there were no other options, this was the best they could do.

Handcuffs were at a premium, and most of the local officers didn't have any. When they arrested a suspect, they either didn't handcuff them or they tied them up with rope. This wasn't state-of-the-art in police procedures but it worked. I didn't ask if they had a course in knot tying.

They were willing to learn new things, adapt to shortages as best they could, but never willingly change procedures. In a drug case, for example, two officers, two citizen witnesses, and the drug dealer suspect were required to sign the evidence tags. When it was pointed out that such a procedure didn't ensure the chain of evidence or guard against the drugs being pilfered, they vehemently argued it did. When I reminded them about several of their cases where drugs had gone missing despite lots of signatures on the evidence tags, they remained reluctant to change.

Five signatures on an evidence tag spread the responsibility for the evidence among the signatories. Why be responsible by yourself when you can share responsibility with others? Speaking about the need for clarity in the chain of evidence and the need to have the lines of responsibility well defined was an exercise that led nowhere.

Using the polygraph for periodic vetting of officers in sensitive positions was a concept one police agency accepted only grudgingly because grant monies were conditioned on it. But most local law enforcement denied the scientific principles upon which the polygraph was founded and failed to recognize it as a valuable investigative tool. People failed the polygraph, according to local officers, because they weren't familiar with it. They said using this strange machine in an area of the world where it had never been used before caused deceptive answers.

Russia used the polygraph extensively. I was surprised Kyrgyzstan, as a former Soviet Republic and a country where 40 percent of the population was Russian, rejected the use of the polygraph. Rumors of corruption in the country abounded, and outside observers suspected that maybe the origin of their polygraph concerns rested in the fear of exposure.

Many times the arguments about affecting change centered on what Kyrgyz law would allow. It didn't, they emphatically stated, allow them to open an internal investigation based on deceptive answers given in a polygraph examination.

The interesting thing was that, unlike US law, what wasn't prohibited was allowed. Kyrgyz law was the opposite. If the law didn't say you could do something, then it was prohibited. This was a difficult concept for Westerners. When I thought they might have a valid point, I'd witness them terminate an employee without any due process and for the flimsiest of reasons. On one hand, they would defend their laws and procedures, and on the other hand, they would flagrantly violate them without an inkling of concern.

In sum, I can't recommend Kyrgyzstan to those who can't live without Starbucks, don't have a tough butt, or who think they could make immediate and drastic procedural changes in the way the police perform their duties.

On Being Done

I never thought my summer assignment in Central Asia would go by as quickly as it did. I left Kyrgyzstan with mixed emotions. Of course, I was anxious to get home and to be in a country where I didn't have to avoid idiomatic language and where I didn't have to speak sooo slowly. I was looking forward to having conversations with people who pretty much knew what I was saying with all the appropriate nuances I intended. Sometimes I needed only to look into the eyes of a Kyrgyz person to know they didn't understand what I was saying to them.

About five weeks before I left the country, for example, I had dropped off a manila envelope at the front desk of the hotel for mailing. It was Sunday, and the clerk said someone would take it to the post office on Monday to determine the cost. Great. The cost would be added to my hotel account. Off I went, happily knowing that in a few weeks my grandchildren would have a pretty nice book about Kyrgyzstan containing some neat pictures.

But just before my tour of duty ended, disappointment struck. As I entered the Regency Club where they serve appetizers (of the heavy type and which usually served as my dinner), the hostess asked if the manila envelope she was holding belonged to me. It was the envelope I had left at the desk five weeks earlier. Yes, of course, it was mine. My name was in the return address section. She asked what I wanted her to do it with it. Calmly, I said I would take it. The package would arrive in the US faster if I mailed it from London, which was my next stop.

Most of the work I did involved the use of a translator for my interactions with the various officers in the Drug Control Agency. Having used translators before, I kept my sentences short and waited for her to translate. But this translator wanted to summarize the points I made. Her way was faster, so I would acquiesce. If I hadn't the meetings would have dragged on for hours.

The principal player in the Drug Control Agency was a colonel who ran the Internal Affairs unit. We didn't have a warm and fuzzy relationship. I made the mistake of pointing at him with my finger—apparently not a polite thing to do according to local culture. The appropriate and accepted gesture was to use an open hand for emphasis and not the Kennedy-like jabbing finger. I didn't learn that little tidbit until long after I had pissed him off.

Our relationship remained professional despite the fact that, in my opinion, he was a communist and was probably covering up instances of corruption. He held a similarly bad opinion of me as a know-it-all American who didn't trust him (I didn't) and only saw one way, the American way, of doing things. In the latter case, he was wrong since I was espousing methods by which his agency could reach international, not American, police standards. Of course, the nuances of a relationship were lost in the translation. It was difficult to conduct business with a partner when there was no common language or culture. Those difficulties were confounded by what I interpreted as the Agency's unwillingness to embrace international standards and aggressively root out corruption.

On a more mundane level, there were aspects of Kyrgyzstan that were both good and bad. I was a fairly rich person from the standpoint of the local people. That's an opportunity a person doesn't often experience. As a middle-class American, I had experienced two occasions where I was perceived as being wealthy. One was while I was in Bosnia for eighteen months and during the time I spent in Kyrgyzstan.

Economists estimated that 40 to 60 percent of people in Kyrgyzstan lived below the poverty line. Unemployment was over 25 percent. The hotel where I stayed during my time in the country employed a staff of a hundred and eighty people. The hotel was considered to pay good wages. Most of their employees earned the equivalent of a hundred dollars per month. People working outside of international organizations made about fifty dollars per month. My per diem pay was significantly more than what the average Kyrgyz wage earner made in a month. Local people saw the international crowd, especially Americans, as rich.

This was evident when you wanted to purchase an unmarked (priced) article from a local vendor. Souvenirs, like in most countries, were negotiable but I always left sensing that I didn't get the best price. This was often confirmed when I would speak to my local assistant at the embassy.

When I went to purchase a carpet, I felt as if I had "Westerner" tattooed across my forehead. The owner of one carpet store actually said the price he was asking for the carpet I was negotiating over was a fair price "for an American." What the hell did that mean? It was an old, Persian carpet, so there wasn't a lot of money on the table and I made the purchase despite my misgivings. Interestingly the old carpets sold for less money, which was different than in the US where older Persian carpets could cost considerably more than newer ones.

Most Americans in the country while I was there were working for the US government, government contractors, or some non-governmental organization such as Mercy Corp and the like. They all received a per diem far exceeding their needs given the local economy. In other words, most of the Americans were making good money and were certainly not spending all of their per diem. Haircuts, for example, were four dollars and lunch at the embassy was under two dollars. Eating out on the economy (which means at local restaurants) was also inexpensive. A good dinner with drinks costs no more than five dollars in most cases.

Yet while they were earning a good wage in addition to their per diem, it was amazing how cheaply a few of the international people acted when it came to doing business with locals merchants and workers. Once I spoke with a group of people who had spent the weekend in Isy Kul, a lake about a three-hour drive east of Bishkek. It was a locally famous vacation spot. The group was put off by the fact that a local three-star hotel wanted seventy-five dollars a night for a room. They would have been hard-pressed to find a room in the States at a popular resort for that price, especially since the price had included a full breakfast and dinner. It surprised me to see some of my countrymen acting as if they were living below the poverty line.

Although some beautiful places had become less beautiful because of neglect, I was taken by the sheer grandeur of the mountains that lay to the south and east of Bishkek. Some of them serve as a boundary between Kyrgyzstan and China. If I squinted my eyes while looking at the Opera House next to my hotel, I could see what a great looking building it once was. It could be again with serious refurbishing. There was a long street in the middle of Bishkek with a large park in the center running the full length of the street. It was green, leafy, and cool, even during the hottest days. There were grand old apartment buildings on each side of the road.

But the park was unkempt, benches were broken, and most of the buildings were in dire need of paint and general repair. It must have been an upscale place to live at one time.

The country was all faded glory, strange but sometimes endearing local customs, dangerous driving, and inexpensive good food. More than anything else, I left with the undeniable impression that it was a former Soviet Republic, and the behavior and mind-set of the people were formed by a socialist philosophy. The younger people ascribed to change, but unfortunately, the bureaucrats in power only professed a desire for change. More often than not, they rejected change when the opportunity was presented.

Mr. TydeBowl

For the past several years, since my Central Asia gig, I had the good fortune to work primarily for one contractor. It was a great job with great bosses and colleagues. But even in the best of times, things can go wrong. The work I did for this company took place in a small, Midwestern, private college. Most of the buildings were built prior to 1900.

I couldn't expect much from the buildings' infrastructure. Heating and cooling systems were marginal; electric was best described as dim, yet surprisingly, they did have wireless Internet that connected to a server within an hour or two. The plumbing, however, wasn't good. During its first seventy years, the college was an all-girls school focusing on nursing and teaching. As such, there weren't many urinals for the male students who now regularly attend the school.

I was a regular kind of guy throughout my life. Traveling never changed my daily constitution. While working diligently on the computer one day, my grumbling stomach alerted me to the fact I had been ignoring my daily routine.

I had reached an appropriate point in my work where I could head off to the three antiquated toilets in the formerly women's restroom. It had a bathtub but no urinals. The last stall was wide (apparently a former handicapped toilet) and inviting, so I plopped myself down and did my business; happy times, indeed. Occasionally in life, unfortunately, things go from so good to so bad so fast. I stood, adjusted my trousers, and noticed the top of the toilet tank was off and lying on the floor next to the toilet. The tank was full of water, so I knew the toilet would flush, being the home repair expert I think I am. With the bravado of a man assured of a successful flush, I pushed down on the lever.

My next thought was, *Why am I wet, and what is that roaring, God-awful noise?* It was, in fact, the toilet acting badly. The toilet had successfully flushed (thank God!), but a stream of water was shooting straight up from the back of the toilet with such force that it was hitting the ten-foot-high ceiling. In my heart of hearts, I knew I should have run away and acted surprised when the flooding toilet waters reached our work area. But I was made of sterner and, as it turned out, stupider stuff. I would fix it.

Braving the cold water, which had knocked my glasses off and soaked my sweater and trousers, I reached for the water turn-off valve. Naturally it wouldn't turn. Before I could begin to cry or run around in a circle and turn myself into butter, two others who had abandoned their calls of nature because of rising water came to the rescue. One found a bucket to cover the high-pressure stream of water so people in the stall would get less wet. The rescuers repeatedly hit the turn-off valve with the stick end of a plunger one of them found until it could be turned manually.

The emergency was over. Two inches of water on the floor of a large restroom in a building more than a hundred years old shouldn't have been a problem. The toilet emergency was abated and the school plumber was called. Before the plumber arrived, however, we were alerted to a problem on the floor below us. I walked down the back stairs to check it out. Before I was halfway down the stairs, I could hear water running, not dripping, onto something in a room at the bottom of the stairwell.

And a beautiful room it was, a lounge area really for students to come, study, and relax. Who wouldn't be able to relax in such a beautiful room filled with a leather couch, antique furnishings, and a treasure trove of books on a fluffy snowy day? Well, no one, since a ceiling tile had broken because of the toilet water from the bathroom directly above. The noise I had heard was the water flowing, yes flowing, onto the leather couch. I went into the room and thought maybe I should just leave.

Too late. The president of the college had arrived. She was a formidable woman who had snuck in behind me and asked me what happened. I told her "someone" had broken a toilet in the men's room above. Putting myself in the best possible light, I explained how I had saved the day by turning off the water to the offending toilet.

She was unperturbed and, with great efficiency, quickly organized a clean up of the room. She put in another call to the plumber and probably told him to move his ass. When I mentioned to her that "we" (well, I watched) had a difficult time getting the water shut-off valve closed, she said, "Well, it probably hasn't been turned since Christ was a student."

To which I responded, "Well, he should have reported the problem."

EPILOGUE

✯ ✯ ✯

On balance, my thirty-five-year career in law enforcement, as a corrections officer, deputy sheriff, international police monitor, and police consultant was a rewarding and fulfilling life. I'm proud to have had the opportunity to work with my police colleagues and to be part of the international police fraternity. When I look at the scale of burdens and benefits in my life's work, there is a clear and dramatic weight on the side of benefits. Every day was a new adventure, and while some days weren't as good as others, they were all good days except for the time when accusations of harassment were leveled at me.

Nevertheless, taking a macro view of my life in law enforcement, the humiliation of my forced retirement diminishes over time. I loved being a cop. I miss it tremendously.

Time places things in perspective. My old force went through turmoil when the sheriff I had worked for chose not to run for re-election. The winning candidate appeared to bring with him a breath of fresh air. There were new ways of doing things and a new paradigm for the management of the department. Unfortunately, the new sheriff and two of his assistant sheriffs were later convicted of federal crimes. Several others in the command staff were fired, two for lying to the grand jury about the death of a prisoner. Several others were terminated shortly after an interim sheriff was appointed.

The interim sheriff, appointed to complete the term of the convicted sheriff won election in her own right a few years ago. Since her appointment and subsequent election, the department has steadily improved. She has managed to bring a sense of pride back to the force. She terminated members of the command staff who had been promoted to positions beyond their capabilities under the former sheriff's deleterious selection process.

The International Police Task Force no longer exists. Its responsibilities devolved to a European Union force that focused on training middle managers and senior leaders in the local police forces of Bosnia. In Kosovo, there is only a small fragment of the UN Mission in Kosovo police. Policing duties there have been effectively taken over by the Kosovo Police Service. Most of the government contractors I worked for are still in business, although their work and focus change with the times.

For over three years, I trudged off to the heartland of America to work as an independent contractor one week each month. Now I'm always looking at the various employment opportunities on the international market, although I know in my heart of hearts that I'm not interested in any long-term assignment overseas. I'm more like a dog that chases cars. Of course, if the dog ever caught a car, he'd be in for a big surprise at the amount of damage it would inflict on him. I sit in my den and have this desire sometimes to chase nearly every international job on offer without fully considering the consequences. Eventually, maybe, one will be exactly right.

I started in police work as a missionary. I wanted to right wrongs and be, in a sense, a uniformed crime fighter. While never losing any enthusiasm for police work, I recognized that working many overtime shifts would bring me all the playthings middle-class Americans strive for in their lives. Often I thought more about the amount of money I would make by working overtime or getting promoted than the job itself. The more I took this mercenary view of work the greater the chances were that I would (and did) turn into a misfit like many cops. Clearly my decision to go to Bosnia was based, not just on wanting to get away from the turmoil of my forced retirement, but also to make money. There was no missionary component to my decision to join a peacekeeping mission; I was just a misfit who signed up as a mercenary.

Of course, I still haven't camped since my adventures at the Fall River Boys Club camp. Nor did I ever sit on a three-wheel police motorcycle like Mr. Barth's since I left Newport. I'm sure I'm the poorer for it.

END

www.ingramcontent.com/pod-product-compliance
Lightning Source LLC
Chambersburg PA
CBHW061502180526
45171CB00001B/12